The Gospel of Matthew in its Roman Imperial Context

Edited by
John Riches
David C. Sim

T & T CLARK INTERNATIONAL
A Continuum imprint
LONDON • NEW YORK

Copyright © 2005 T&T Clark International
A Continuum imprint

Published by T&T Clark International
The Tower Building, 11 York Road, London SE1 7NX
15 East 26th Street, Suite 1703, New York, NY 10010

www.tandtclark.com

British Library Cataloguing-in-Publication Data
A catalogue record for this book is available from the British Library

ISBN 0567084485   (hardback)
     0567084582   (paperback)

Typeset by Data Standards Ltd, Frome, Somerset, BA11 1RE
Printed on acid-free paper in Great Britain by CPI Bath Ltd.

CONTENTS

CONTRIBUTORS

Warren Carter – St Paul School of Theology, Kansas City, Missouri
Dennis C. Duling – Canisius College, Buffalo, New York
Philip Esler – St Mary's College, University of St Andrews
James S. McLaren – Australian Catholic University, Melbourne
Peter Oakes – University of Manchester
John Riches – University of Glasgow
David C. Sim – Australian Catholic University, Melbourne
Dorothy Jean Weaver – Eastern Mennonite Seminary, Harrisonburg,
    Virginia

ABBREVIATIONS

AB	Anchor Bible
ANRW	Hildegard Temporini and Wolfgang Haase (eds.), *Aufstieg und Niedergang der römischen Welt: Geschichte und Kultur Roms im Spiegel der neueren Forschung* (Berlin: W. de Gruyter, 1972–)
ABR	*Australian Biblical Review*
BTB	*Biblical Theology Bulletin*
CBQ	*Catholic Biblical Quarterly*
CIL	*Corpus inscriptionum latinarum*
FRLANT	Forschungen zur Religion und Literatur des Alten und Neuen Testaments
HeyJ	*Heythrop Journal*
HTR	*Harvard Theological Review*
HTS	*Hervormde Teologiese Studies*
ICC	International Critical Commentary
JAAR	*Journal of the American Academy of Religion*
JBL	*Journal of Biblical Literature*
JJS	*Journal of Jewish Studies*
JSJ	*Journal for the Study of Judaism*
JSNT	*Journal for the Study of the New Testament*
JSNTSS	Journal for the Study of the New Testament Supplement Series
JSOT	*Journal for the Study of the Old Testament*
JTS	*Journal of Theological Studies*
LCL	Loeb Classical Library
NIGTC	New International Greek Testament Commentary
NRSV	New Revised Standard Version
NTAbh	Neutestamentliche Abhandlungen
NTS	*New Testament Studies*
SBEC	Studies in the Bible and Early Christianity
SCI	*Scripta Classica Israelica*
SNTSMS	Society for New Testament Studies Monograph Series
SNTW	Studies of the New Testament and its World
ThLZ	*Theologische Literaturzeitung*
TPINTC	Trinity Press International New Testament Commentary

WUNT   Wissenschaftliche Untersuchungen zum Neuen
              Testament
ZTK   *Zeitschrift für Theologie und Kirche*

INTRODUCTION

John Riches

The massive shock of the destruction of Jerusalem and the Temple by Roman forces in 70 CE, coupled with the public humiliation to which Jews were subsequently subjected, will have presented the various Jewish groupings of the Second Temple period with an urgent need to strengthen and support their community's sense of identity. This was not something wholly new, but an acute crisis was clearly precipitated by the loss of one of the key markers of Jewish identity: the Temple and its cult.

It is *prima facie* deeply unlikely that in the traumatic aftermath of the events of 70 CE Jewish groups, already deeply divided and in conflict, would have easily found an agreed new form of communal religion. What we can say is that by the end of the second century forms of Judaism and Christianity were beginning to emerge – rabbinic Judaism, Catholic Christianity, Jewish Christianity – which (with the obvious exception of Jewish Christianity) would remain in competition/conflict with each other over the subsequent centuries: even so, we should be careful not to project later forms of conflict and separation back onto the period up to the formation of various forms of Christian orthodoxy in the late fourth and fifth centuries.[1]

Recent work in Matthaean studies in Europe, North America and Australia has concentrated heavily on the relationship of the Matthaean community to emergent new forms of Judaism in the period immediately post destruction[2] and has sought to define the relation of Matthew's community to (what such studies see as) the dominant, Pharisaic, scribal form of Judaism as sectarian.[3] Matthew's Christian Jews were locked in a

---

1. D.C. Sim, *The Gospel of Matthew and Christian Judaism: The History and Social Setting of the Matthean Community* (SNTW; Edinburgh: T&T Clark, 1998).

2. See particularly the work of J. Andrew Overman, Anthony J. Saldarini, David Sim and Graham Stanton.

3. See esp. J.A. Overman, *Matthew's Gospel and Formative Judaism: The Social World of the Matthean Community* (Minneapolis, MN: Fortress, 1990) and, for a considerably more nuanced view, Anthony J. Saldarini, *Matthew's Christian–Jewish Community* (Chicago IL: University of Chicago Press, 1994). These arguments are taken up and developed by David C. Sim, *Christian Judaism*, 109–63.

struggle with this more dominant form of Judaism, whose members (as is acknowledged in Matt. 23.2) claimed to be the guardians of the Mosaic legal tradition. But equally Matthew's community, though marginalized, had claims of its own and disputed fiercely the correctness of the Pharisees' interpretation. It sought to legitimate[4] its own claims and also to consolidate its own community, however threatened it may have felt by more dominant forms.

Matthaean scholars owe a very considerable debt to the late Anthony Saldarini[5] for the way in which he led them to think about the kinds of inner-group processes which may have been at work during this period of the regrouping and re-formation of senses of group identity. His overriding concern was to show that the Matthaean community, though regarded as deviant[6] by dominant forms of Judaism at the time, should nevertheless be seen as an integral part of first-century Jewish society. Deviant groups are necessary to the healthy functioning of a society, even though they may be regarded as evil by the dominant group. Evidence of conflict and fierce polemic between formative Judaism and Matthew's community should not therefore be taken as *eo ipso* evidence of a complete separation between the two groupings. Rather there is evidence that Matthew's community engaged in activities which are typical of deviant groups: 'Typically, they challenge the conventional standards by which community members are measured, seeking to delegitimate the societal leaders who control the definitions of deviance and ultimately to change the social order.'[7] Specifically, Matthew's community 'recruits members, develops a coherent world view and belief system, articulates an ideology and rhetoric to sustain its behavior, and attacks competing social institutions and groups'.[8]

The language of sectarianism is notoriously blunt and the more sophisticated one becomes about its use, the greater the danger in one way of being beguiled into thinking that such observations drawn from the observation of modern societal groupings and behaviours will give us the kind of hard evidence which we may otherwise lack. Saldarini makes much of deviance theory to assist him in the description of the relations between Matthew's community and the dominant Jewish group(s?). But he actually cites no evidence of the labelling of Matthew's community as

---

4. Saldarini, *Matthew's Christian–Jewish Community*, 46–7.
5. See, as well as his *Matthew's Christian–Jewish Community*, Saldarini, 'The Gospel of Matthew and Jewish–Christian Conflict' in D.L. Balch (ed.), *Social History of the Matthean Community* (Minneapolis, MN: Fortress Press, 1991), 38–61 and Saldarini, 'The Gospel of Matthew and Jewish–Christian Conflict in the Galilee' in L.I. Levine (ed.), *The Galilee in Late Antiquity* (Cambridge, MA: Harvard University Press, 1992), 23–38.
6. Cf. esp. Saldarini, *Matthew's Christian–Jewish Community*, 107–16.
7. Saldarini, *Matthew's Christian–Jewish Community*, 111.
8. Saldarini, *Matthew's Christian–Jewish Community*, 112.

deviant by other Jews (Matt. 5.11 might be thought to indicate that such stigmatization had occurred, but it is not specific about who was doing the labelling). It is true that in Matthew's Gospel (23!) there is evidence of a fierce polemic on the part of Matthew's community against the scribes and the Pharisees. This *may* be evidence that Matthew was responding to similar forms of negative labelling by the dominant Jewish group, but direct evidence is lacking.

It is also true that there are commonalities which we can observe, e.g. between the group structures and the inner-group polemics of the Qumran community against other dominant forms of Judaism pre-70 and the structures and language of the Gospel of Matthew,[9] but it is less clear what sort of inferences we should draw from these comparisons. The overall social and political situations of the Qumran community and of Matthew are after all very different indeed.

Qumran had lived a (culturally and geographically) marginalized existence, always overshadowed by the power, wealth and influence (however weakened by Rome) of the Temple priesthood. There is ample evidence for its hopes and aspirations of repossessing the Temple (*Temple Scroll*) and returning to the centre of Jewish life. Its separate existence, that is to say, was one that still encompassed a lively hope for it to become the dominant force in Jewish life, once its enemies had been overcome.

Matthew's community, perhaps located in Antioch, was living in the aftermath of the destruction of the Temple and the consequent loss of power of the dominant priesthood. At the same time the whole position of the Jewish people in the Mediterranean world had been seriously weakened by a sustained programme of public humiliation by the Roman authorities.[10] Matthew's community may have well been in conflict with a well-organized group of Antiochene Jews inspired by/ respectful of the Pharisees and their heirs. Within Antioch the Jewish

---

9.   G.N. Stanton, *A Gospel for a New People* (Edinburgh: T&T Clark, 1992). He argues (85–107) that what the similarlities between the two groups (intense intra-group conflict; social conflict, boundaries and dissent; group cohesion and centralized control) show is that they were both groups which were establishing themselves over against mainstream Judaism. Yet this is interestingly not a point that would unduly trouble scholars like Saldarini (who does not discuss it). The fact that Matthew's community, like Qumran, was in sharp conflict with (other) major groups within Judaism is of itself no argument for saying that they had separated themselves from their parent bodies, in such a way that both the Damascus Document and Matthew's Gospel 'explain and sustain the separate identity' of the two communities. (106). Such behaviour can *also* be typical of sectarian groups in conflict with their parent body for control of the community, before any such rift has occurred. The point is more that evidence of such behaviour is insufficient to sway the argument either way.

10.   See e.g. Philip Esler's fine essay below.

community would have had its own structures, built up over the years,[11] though there may well have been tensions between different sections of the community. In the aftermath of the war, there may equally have been significant differences within the Jewish community over what were the most appropriate policies for it to adopt towards the Romans, the city authorities and their Syrian neighbours. In that case the voice of Matthew's group will have been one among many.

But it is also perfectly possible that there was indeed a united front which adopted a broadly quietist position, avoiding conflict with the authorities where possible, setting tight boundaries between themselves and the rest of the community and avoiding any suggestions of aggressive intentions towards their neighbours. In this case the Jewish community in Antioch would have been at odds with other Jewish groups in the Syrian province (embracing, that is, Antioch, Galilee and Judaea/Jerusalem) which still dreamed of (and planned for) military action, or of some divine intervention which would sweep away all forces hostile to the Jews. Such a strategy of separation would also have been out of sorts with those more accommodating Jews who for reasons of (political, cultural or even commercial) expediency sought to emphasize the common ground between Jews and Romans and other Hellenized groups in the Mediterranean world (such as Philo did earlier and, in this period, Josephus).

Where strongly held alternative views became the preferred option of a more or less organized group within, let us suppose, a largely united, quietist Jewish community in Antioch, as would have been the case if Matthew's community was situated there, such a group would presumably have attracted suspicion and enmity; the more organized, the greater such opposition would have been. Matthew's community was explicitly committed to establishing relations with its non-Jewish neighbours and indeed to 'making disciples of them'. It had close links with other groups of 'disciples' who had adopted itinerant, mendicant lifestyles in order to

---

11. See J.M.G. Barclay, *Jews in the Mediterranean Diaspora: From Alexander to Trajan (323 BCE to 117 CE)* (Edinburgh: T&T Clark, 1996), 242–58 for a sketch of the relations between Jews, Syrians and Romans in Syria at this period. Jews had very mixed relations with their Syrian neighbours and there was fierce antagonism between the two sides in the period running up to the First Jewish War. On the other hand, Herod had been responsible for large public works in Antioch, and relations between Jews and Syrians/Romans among the wealthier sections of the population may have been quite equable. After the destruction of Jerusalem, the spoils of the Temple were displayed on the city gates by Titus (Malalas, 260, 21–261,14), though Josephus (*Bell.* 7.100–11) reports that Titus intervened to stop the Jews being deported. This story, even if it requires to be read with some caution, nevertheless indicates ways in which some Jews, in their new political environment, may have come to see the Romans as in a measure their protectors.

attract new members to the group. It had its own initiation rites and even its own written texts.

How is one to describe, in this admittedly hypothetical scenario, Matthew's community's relations to the wider community in which it lived? How long could a group with its own initiation rites, its own scriptures and links with other itinerant groups which included Gentiles and, indeed, a history of open relationships with Gentiles in Antioch (Gal. 2), have continued to nurture the hope that they would be accepted by such a separatist, quietist Jewish community? Such questions are of course entirely legitimate, though clearly not without their difficulties, given the hypothetical nature of any reconstruction of the precise nature of Matthew's group's relations with its local Jewish community. The vigorous pursuit of answers of such questions has indeed shed much light on the nature of Matthew's Gospel, but while they will continue to engage scholars there are other questions which also deserve attention, and it is the intention of this volume to address at least some of these.

For there are aspects of any reconstruction of the situation in Antioch post 70 CE which are more certain than others. One thing above all is quite clear, and that is that both Matthew's group and the wider Jewish community in Antioch were living in the aftermath of the Jewish war and of the Roman humiliation of the Jews. If any group had been stigmatized, it was the Jews by the Romans. If part of the definition of a sect is that it is marginal to the dominant group/s within its society, then clearly Jews were marginal within the Roman principate. Of course it is also part of the definition of a sect that it sees itself as having a rightful place within the wider society in which it is set, even though it is stigmatized by that society. In this latter respect, it would be odd to describe most Jews as *Roman* sectarians. Deviants they might be, but they hardly had aspirations to occupy positions of power in Rome. Can the same be said of Matthew's community, whose Jesus lays claim to all authority on heaven and earth? Attention to such questions may not necessarily shed light on the vexed question of whether Matthew's community had already parted with the Jewish community as a whole, or indeed of how far Matthew's group still saw itself as Jewish, but it may well contribute to a better understanding of the history of early Christianity and the process whereby it emerged as the dominant religious force in the Mediterranean.

One of the interesting features of Saldarini's treatment of Matthew's community as a deviant sect is that he focuses almost exclusively on the relationship between Matthew's group and its relationship to 'Judaism and the Jewish community'.[12] But while there is at best only indirect evidence of Jewish labelling of Matthew's group as deviant, there is ample evidence of Roman stigmatization and humiliation of Jews. There is

12. Saldarini, *Matthew's Christian–Jewish Community*, 107.

moreover not a little evidence that Matthew was defining the ethos of his group not only against the Jews, as argued by Saldarini, who cites Matthew 6.2, 5, 16 and 5.20–48,[13] but also against the Gentiles, as in Matthew 5.47. In this respect, Gerd Theissen has argued powerfully that the ethos of the early Christian community is forged in a process of interaction with the dominant values of the pagan world, where values such as love of enemies are taken over and transformed by the Christian communities. Moreover, he claims this is a process that goes back to Jesus himself.[14] All this suggests that attending to Matthew's relations to the wider world of the Roman Empire may open up new insights both into Matthew's Gospel and the community out of which it came and also into the progress of early Christianity towards its ultimate acceptance by the empire itself.

Such enquiries in New Testament studies are not altogether new, as is noted elsewhere in this volume. Richard Horsley has considered such questions, in relation to Jesus, Paul and Mark. Peter Oakes has examined these issues in more detail in relation to Colossians and, more generally, in a book of essays on *Rome in the Bible and the Early Church*.[15] In the field of Matthaean studies, Warren Carter has published a monograph on *Matthew and Empire*.[16] Both of the last two contribute generously to this volume.

In setting out to examine Matthew's relationship to his wider imperial context in this collection of essays, we have sought to advance three main areas of enquiry: first, into the nature of empire and of colonialism, how such political realities are structured and controlled and how the subject peoples attempt to resist the powerful; second, into the ways in which other groups and individuals responded during this period to the power of Rome; and third into the ways in which Matthew's Gospel itself reflects his and his community's attitudes and beliefs about secular power and authority in general and Rome in particular.

The book is divided into two sections, the first picking up the first two topics above and the second offering more detailed considerations of Matthew's text and its setting. Both Dennis Duling and Philip Esler offer an introduction to theories of empire and colonialism, considering both the economic and political structures which hold large conglomerates of people together, as well as the methods of control and equally of resistance. The huge difference in terms of numbers between those who

---

13.   Saldarini, *Matthew's Christian–Jewish Community*, 92–3.

14.   G. Theissen, *A Theory of Christian Religion* (London: SCM Press, 1999), esp. 81–117, and G. Theissen, 'Jesusbewegung als charismatische Wertrevolution', *NTS* 35 (1989), 343–60.

15.   P. Oakes (ed.), *Rome in the Bible and the Early Church* (Carlisle: Paternoster, 2002).

16.   W. Carter, *Matthew and Empire: Initial Explorations* (Harrisburg, IL: Trinity Press International, 2001).

principally benefit and hold power on the one hand and those who are primarily contributors to the wealth and power of the few on the other draws attention to the importance within any such system of mechanisms of control other than the simple use of coercive force, which is a matter of last resort, even if it was wielded relentlessly by Rome when required. Ideological control, exercised most impressively through the imperial cult but also through the many cultic and civic associations of the cities, will have contributed greatly to a sense of belonging to a wider whole on the part of people of very different ethnic origins and with very different religious traditions and cults. Respect for other peoples' traditional mores and deities will equally have served to create an atmosphere of reasonable tolerance within the Graeco-Roman cities, which were key components in the distribution of power. Such political and civic deities and their cults clearly helped to remind people of the very considerable benefits which they owed to the Principate with its 'peace and security', and will have accounted for the quite ambiguous attitudes which subject peoples, even those who had felt the force of Rome's military might, harboured towards the imperial power. Equally, awareness of the sheer weight of Rome's power when fully applied would have seriously discouraged active resistance in all but in the most extreme of circumstances when people's resentment and desperation reached boiling-point. Some religious rhetoric may indeed have had the effect of raising passions to such heights that active revolt ensued; other rhetoric may have had the effect of sublimating such feelings and of projecting the desire for revenge onto some future state. Other forms of resistance, as James Scott has shown,[17] will have served more as ways of softening the worst effects of the political and economic regime under which people laboured in the world of the first-century Mediterranean.

The first section also looks at some of the different responses to Rome, outside those embedded in the Gospel of Matthew. James McLaren looks at Josephus's complicated relationship to Rome. To what extent was his *Jewish War* a work of Flavian apologetic? How far, for all its public acceptability does it represent an – albeit muted – critique of Roman administration and conduct of the war? What hints does Josephus give of his own beliefs about the ultimate destiny of Israel and Rome?

Philip Esler looks at Rome in apocalyptic and rabbinic literature. How are Rome and its allies portrayed in this diverse literature? What kinds of codes are used within literature such as 2 Baruch and 4 Ezra for referring to Rome and its actions and hoped-for fate? How does the experience of defeat by Rome and the subsequent humiliations inflicted on Jews

---

17. J.C. Scott, *Weapons of the Weak: Everyday Forms of Peasant Resistance* (New Haven, CT: Yale University Press, 1985) and J.C. Scott, *Domination and the Arts of Resistance: Hidden Transcripts* (New Haven, CT: Yale University Press, 1992).

influence Jewish attitudes to military resistance and shape their hopes for the restoration of Jewish sovereignty? What visions of the subsequent course of history do we find in such works?

Finally in this section, Peter Oakes looks at the way Rome is presented in New Testament writings outside Matthew, examining attitudes to Rome and the ways in which they portray the Roman authorities and assist their readers in living under its rule. Here we have an opportunity to see both the extent to which concern over Rome was present in other New Testament writings and also the sheer span of opinions which is to be found, and this assists in placing Matthew within early Christianity.

The second section turns to the Gospel of Matthew itself. David Sim asks to what extent Matthew's eschatology (his account of the ultimate conflicts between good and evil in the world and its ultimate resolution), is coloured by the conflict between the Jews and Rome, between imperial power elites and their subalterns. Dorothy Jean Weaver offers a literary analysis of the role in Matthew's story of identifiably Roman characters: the centurion in Chapter 8; Pilate; the centurion and the soldiers at the cross and tomb. To what extent do such characters offer an account of Roman imperial views of power and of Jesus? How far do they subvert such views and suggest that they are reformable/alterable? What kind of development is there in the narrative? John Riches examines Jesus's commission to the disciples to go and make disciples of all nations. To what extent is Matthew mirroring Roman claims and attitudes to imperial expansion and control over the known world? How far does Matthew's language borrow from Roman usage? To what extent is he formulating alternative notions of power and authority? What kind of rhetoric of resistance is to be discerned in the Matthaean text? Finally, Warren Carter looks at Matthew's Christology as it is reflected in the opening of the gospel. Matthew's titles for Jesus include some which have distinctly royal connotations: Son of David, Son of God, Christ. Others have associations with judgement and power, such as 'Son of Man'. But the latter title is also closely associated with Jesus's defencelessness and suffering. How, at the outset of the gospel, are notions of authority and power being formulated of Jesus as he sets out on the road to his death and resurrection?

Clearly a volume like this will raise many questions that it will not answer and some that may well never find an answer. I hope that raising good questions is one of its strengths; but I also hope that these essays may serve to stimulate a fruitful discussion and to shed light on the fascinating tensions which are to be found in early Christianity's attitudes towards imperial Rome, specifically as these are seen through Matthew's Gospel. One thing is quite certain: Rome was the dominant force in the lives of people living in the eastern Mediterranean. Equally clear is that Jews had been severely dealt with and humiliated by Rome. In what way is this reflected in Matthew's Gospel?

Rome in Apocalyptic and Rabbinic Literature

Philip F. Esler

1.1 *Colonial and Post-colonial Perspectives*

In contemporary discourse 'colonialism' refers mainly to the conquest and direct control of other lands and peoples in the Americas, Africa, Asia and Oceania begun by European powers in the sixteenth century and continued on into the twentieth. The nations that engaged in this process derived from it immense economic wealth and political power. Yet colonialism in this sense was a form of imperialism intimately associated with the globalization of the capitalist mode of production. Colonies were acquired to secure new markets for manufactured goods and to obtain sources of cheap raw materials, as well as to deny these economic advantages to other European powers. Capitalism thus penetrated into areas of the world that had been characterized by pre- or non-capitalist forms of social organization.[1]

From 1947 onwards the colonies began to achieve independence, either through largely peaceful processes (India) or through violent revolution (Vietnam, Algeria, Kenya). These events allow use of the term 'post-colonialism' for the situation that has resulted, and there is a large body of scholarship devoted to exploring its implications.[2] Having said this, it is worth noting that the persistence of neo-colonialism or imperialism under guises other than direct colonial rule has always made the term somewhat problematic. At one level 'post-colonial' conveys a chronological meaning

---

1. P. Williams and L. Chrisman, 'Colonial Discourse and Post-Colonial Theory: An Introduction' in P. Williams and L. Chrisman (eds), *Colonial Discourse and Post-Colonial Theory: A Reader* (New York: Harvester Wheatsheaf, 1993), 1–20, at 2.

2. On post-colonialism, see I. Adam and H. Tiffin (eds), *Past the Last Post: Theorizing Post-Colonialism and Post-Modernism* (Hemel Hempstead: Harvester Wheatsheaf, 1991), H.K. Bhabha, *The Location of Culture* (London: Routledge, 1994); P. Childs and R.J.P. Williams, *An Introduction to Post-Colonial Theory* (London: Prentice Hall and Harvester Wheatsheaf, 1997); P. Williams and L. Chrisman (eds), *Colonial Discourse and Post-Colonial Theory: A Reader* (New York: Harvester Wheatsheaf, 1993).

– the historical period that began when once-colonized nations obtain independence. But the word also carries a rather different reference, namely, to an attitude taken by representatives of colonized peoples to the experience of colonization, often beginning before independence is achieved and continuing afterwards. The Canadian critic Stephen Slemon helpfully categorizes this aspect of post-colonialism as

> a specifically anti- or *post*-colonial *discursive* purchase in culture, one which begins in the moment that colonial power inscribes itself into the body and space of its Others and which continues as an often occulted tradition into the modern theatre of neo-colonialist international relations.[3]

Given the ample role that Bible-bearing Christian missionaries played in the processes of European colonization, it is not surprising that contemporary post-colonial writing includes discussion of the complex status of the Bible in the experience of many colonized peoples. Biblical texts were used by the colonizers to legitimate their control, as well as by the colonized to articulate discourses of survival or even resistance in response to the patterns of domination to which they were subjected. Biblical insights are also being used now among the independent peoples to help them understand the colonial experience and develop strategies against its insidious perpetuation under forms other than direct political control.[4]

This expansion of the meaning of 'post-colonialism' beyond a chronological reference to the period of independence beginning in the late 1940s so as to include an attitude taken to rule by a foreign and imperial power allows its application to traditions among subaltern peoples in the ancient world. Although ancient modes of imperial rule in this period were not driven or accompanied by capitalist forces, and their aristocratic dimensions must be taken very seriously,[5] they exhibited three essential characteristics of European colonialism that highlight marked similarities between these ancient and modern forms. These were: first, political control over subject peoples backed up by overwhelming military force; second, the voracious extraction of economic resources; and third, an ideology legitimating these processes conveyed by discourses of various kinds. Jon Berquist has well described the Persian occupation of Judah in

---

3. S. Slemon, 'Modernism's Last Post', in Adam and Tiffin (eds), *Past the Last Post*, 1–11, at 3.

4. See the essays in L.E. Donaldson (ed.), *Semeia 75. Postcolonialism and Scriptural Reading* (Atlanta, GA: Scholars Press, 1996).

5. See J.H. Kautsky, *The Politics of Aristocratic Empires* (Chapel Hill, NC: University of North Carolina Press, 1982).

these terms.[6] In the present essay, however, our interest lies specifically with the Judaean *ethnos* in its exposure to Roman rule from 63 BCE onwards. It will be necessary first to offer a broad outline of the history and character of Roman imperial rule over the Judaeans and then, in the bulk of the essay, to consider Judaean responses.[7] We will briefly consider the many ill-fated uprisings before focusing on literary responses, mainly in apocalyptic and rabbinic texts.

Since Rome maintained its control over Judea (which it called 'Palestina' from the second century CE onwards) until the fifth century CE, we do not have a 'post-colonial' moment in the chronological sense during the period we are considering. Nevertheless, there is a clear 'post-colonial' dimension to this literature in the way that its authors sought to find space for Judaean identities in spite of Roman control over their land and people. Given that many strategies of survival or resistance among subject peoples take the form of the small-scale and largely invisible acts described by James Scott in his *Weapons of the Weak: Everyday Forms of Peasant Resistance* or the oral phenomena of the 'little tradition' first explored by Robert Redfield in his *Peasant Society and Culture*,[8] the fact that so much literary material survives from the Israelites under Roman rule is a cause for wonder.

1.2 *Roman Imperialism*

Debate rages over whether Rome acquired its empire accidentally, reluctantly, defensively or, surely most plausibly, deliberately and aggressively – imperial expansion being driven by the need of a small and highly competitive elite to acquire power, honour, riches and clients.[9] Whatever the reasons motivating the growth of the empire, the pattern of

6. See J.L. Berquist, *Judaism in Persia's Shadow: A Social and Historical Approach* (Minneapolis, MN: Fortress, 1995) and his essay 'Postcolonialism and Imperial Motives for Canonization' in Donaldson (ed.), *Semeia* 75, 15–35.

7. For the detailed reasons for my view that 'Judaean' is far preferable to 'Jew' or 'Jewish' until the third century CE (at the earliest), see P.F. Esler, *Conflict and Identity in Romans: The Social Setting of Paul's Letter* (Minneapolis, MN: Fortress, 2003), 40–76.

8. See J.C. Scott, *Weapons of the Weak: Everyday Forms of Peasant Resistance* (New Haven, CT.: Yale University Press, 1985), and R. Redfield, *Peasant Society and Culture* (Chicago, IL: University of Chicago Press, 1956), both of whom consider the experience of peasantry under all forms of rule, not just imperial.

9. See P.D.A. Garnsey and, C.R. Whittaker, 'Introduction' in P.D.A. Garnsey and C.R. Whittaker (eds), *Imperialism in the Roman World* (Cambridge: Cambridge University Press, 1978), 1–6; see also W.V. Harris, *War and Imperialism in Republican Rome* (Oxford: Clarendon Press, 1979) (strongly critical of defensive imperialism notions) and J. Rich, 'Fear, Greed and Glory: The Causes of Roman War-Making in the Middle Republic' in J. Rich and G. Shipley (eds), *War and Society in the Roman World* (London and New York: Routledge, 1993), 38–68 (suggesting the picture was more variegated than Harris allows).

its operation was well established under the Republic by the second century BCE, when Rome and Judea first encountered one another, and continued in a similar form after the establishment of the Principate by Augustus and the development of rule by emperors.

The foundation of Roman imperial success was the extreme effectiveness of its military machine. War came naturally to the Romans, and in the Republican period their legions marched out every spring for the next campaign. Their Greek contemporaries observed that the Romans waged war with more determination and ferocity than other peoples of their time, characteristically using violent force wherever necessary.[10] This approach continued under the emperors. Roman martial savagery reached its acme in the sacking of cities. Where a city was taken by force, the Romans first killed all male adults. They then plundered the city, the word *direptio* being used of this process. Plundering meant the legionaries being given (or sometimes simply taking) free rein to rape all available women and children and to pillage the property of the inhabitants. Sometimes the Romans killed the entire population, and their animals as well.[11] If there were survivors, they were regularly enslaved. In many cases, but not all, the city was burnt.[12] Even when a city surrendered, the Romans often killed all adult males and unleashed *direptio* on the rest of the population.

A Roman general, and later an emperor who won a major victory against an opponent who put up stout resistance, earned a triumphal procession through Rome, preceded by captive representatives of the enemy and his own victorious troops bearing samples of the booty. A triumph represented a status elevation ritual for the Roman general or emperor, his city and his gods, and a status degradation ritual for his vanquished opponents and their gods.[13]

Rome exercised imperial control over the Mediterranean lands either through client kings (individually referred to as *rex sociusque et amicus,* 'king and ally and friend') or directly through provinces run first by senatorial legates and later by a mixture of legates despatched by the Senate or the emperor.[14] Client kings were not required to pay regular taxes to Rome, but many showered gifts of various sorts on Rome to

---

10. Harris, *War*, 50–3; also see P.F. Esler, 'God's Honour and Rome's Triumph: Responses to the Fall of Jerusalem in 70 CE in Three Jewish Apocalypses', in P.F. Esler (ed.), *Modelling Early Christianity: Social-Scientific Studies of the New Testament in Its Context* (London and New York: Routledge, 1995), 239–58, at 239–40.

11. See A. Ziolkowski, '*Urbs direpta,* or How the Romans Sacked Cities', in Rich and Shipley (eds), *War*, 69–91.

12. Ziolkowski, '*Urbs Direpta*', 72.

13. See Esler, 'God's Honour', 242–4.

14. For the client kings, see D.C. Braund, *Rome and the Friendly King: The Character of Client Kingship* (London: Croom Helm, 1984).

cement what was, like all patron–client relationships, an unequal although mutually beneficial arrangement. Direct taxes were collected in all provinces and indirect taxes were farmed out to *publicani*. Sometimes when client kings died, or were performing poorly, their territory was turned into a province under direct Roman rule.

There were some positive aspects to Roman imperial rule. The chief of these was occasional protracted periods of peace. Particularly significant was the period that began with the victory of Octavian at Actium in 31 BCE, thus ending a long period of civil war, and continuing until 67 CE, when Nero died and a period of conflict ensued, with four emperors emerging in quick succession (Galba, Otho, Vitellius and Vespasian). The achievement of Octavian (who received the title 'Augustus' from the Senate in 27 BCE) in inaugurating a long period of peace was commemorated in Rome with the erection of the *Ara Pacis* (completed in 9 BCE) and was a cause for celebration across the Mediterranean world.

Michel Foucault has powerfully demonstrated the ineluctable connection between power and discourse.[15] Roman domination expressed itself in various forms of discourse that legitimated its imperial ideology (with 'ideology' here meaning a pattern of discourse imposed by a dominant power). This ideology finds unashamed expression in the Augustan poet Virgil's description of the Roman mission as *parcere subiectis et debellare superbos* (*Aeneid* 6.853) which literally means 'to spare the vanquished and to subdue the arrogant' but which I paraphrase as 'Grovel and live; resist and die.' It also features on the legends of numerous Roman coins. Yet the phenomenon of post-colonialism in the non-chronological sense reminds us that sometimes peoples subjected to imperial rule not only actively revolt against it but also develop a counter-discourse to that propagated by their rulers. This represents one aspect of a phenomenon well articulated by Foucault. Having noted that humanity installs its various violences 'in a system of rules that proceeds from domination to domination', he goes on to say:

> Rules are empty in themselves, violent and unfinalized; they are impersonal and can be bent to any purpose. The successes of history belong to those who are capable of seizing these rules, to replace those who had used them, to disguise themselves so as to pervert them, invert their meaning, and redirect them against those who had initially imposed them; controlling this complex mechanism, they will make it function so as to overcome the rulers through their own rules.[16]

---

15. See the collection of his works in P. Rabinow (ed.), *The Foucault Reader: An Introduction to his Thought* (London: Penguin, 1986).
16. See Rabinow, *The Foucault Reader*, 85–6.

In some parts of the world the discursive response of colonized peoples to their subjugation took the form of millennarian mythopoiesis. Here myths were generated that looked forward to the transformation of the present situation, the destruction of the invader and the restoration of traditional lands, culture and power.[17] All of these features figure in the history of Rome's interaction with the Judaean *ethnos*, to which I now turn.

1.3 *The History of Rome and the Judaeans*

The history of active interaction between the Judaeans and Rome begins with the attempt of Antiochus IV Epiphanes, the Seleucid ruler of the country, to suppress the Judaeans and their religion, beginning in 167 BCE. This prompted a rebellion led by one Mattathias and his sons, prominent among whom was Judas Maccabaeus. Success came fairly quickly, but around 160 BCE (by which time Mattathias had died) Judas Maccabaeus and his brothers, seeking to consolidate their position, despatched embassies to Rome to conclude a Judaean–Roman treaty of friendship and alliance.[18] During the second century BCE the Judaeans regarded Rome as 'a great and friendly giant'.[19]

In the first century BCE, however, the relationship changed irrevocably. In 63 BCE Pompey, seizing an opportunity offered by the feuding between the last two Hasmonean claimants to the throne, led his legions into Jerusalem. In due course he entered the Temple.

From 63 BCE onwards Rome ruled Judea and its surrounding areas. For the first century of its control it did so through a mixture of client high priests or kings and its own provincial legates. The most notable client king was the Idumean Herod the Great, Roman-appointed king of Judea and later also of many other surrounding territories from 37–34 BCE. There were serious disturbances in Judea and Galilee on his death. These included an uprising led by one Judas, son of the bandit Ezechias in Galilee (whose men stormed the royal palace in Sepphoris), the actions of Simon, a slave of Herod who claimed the kingship and plundered the

---

17. In general, see S. Thrupp (ed.), *Millennial Dreams in Action: Essays in Comparative Study* (The Hague: Mouton, 1972); K. Burridge, *New Heaven, New Earth: A Study of Millennarian Activities* (Oxford: Basil Blackwell, 1969) and P. Worsley, *The Trumpet Shall Sound: A Study of 'Cargo' Cults in Melanesia* (London: Paladin, 1970 [1957]). For examples of millennarian mythopoiesis in the Bible and other Judaean literature, see P.F. Esler, 'Political Oppression in Jewish Apocalyptic Literature: Social-Scientific Approach', *Listening: Journal of Religion and Culture* 28 (1993), 181–99, at 183–4.

18. See 1 Maccabees 8; 12.1–4; 14.24; Josephus, *Judean Antiquities* 13.259–66.

19. G. Vermes, 'Ancient Rome in Post-Biblical Jewish Literature' in G. Vermes, *Post-Biblical Jewish Studies* (Leiden: E.J. Brill, 1975), 215–24, at 216.

royal palace in Jericho, and attacks on Romans led by a certain Athronges.[20] This situation prompted Roman intervention.

The Romans divided Herod the Great's large territory between his three sons, Herod Antipas (tetrarch of Galilee and Peraea), Archelaus (ethnarch of Judea, Samaria and Idumea) and Philip (tetrarch of the largely non-Judaean regions of Batanea, Trachonitis, Auranitis and Gaulanitis). Herod Antipas ruled until 39 CE, when Caligula replaced him with his nephew. This is the Herod mentioned in the Gospels as having John the Baptist beheaded. Philip ruled successfully until his death in 34 CE, whereupon his territory was put under direct Roman rule. Archelaus, however, did not prove a success and in 6 CE Augustus decided to replace him with direct Roman rule.

So Augustus sent P. Sulpicius Quirinius as governor of Syria, with orders to conduct a property census, in a region that included Judea. This action was a prelude to the exaction of taxation. At about the same time, Augustus despatched Coponius as the first Roman procurator of the new province of Judea (a position he held from 6–9 CE). During this period a man known as Judas the Galilean (who may or may not be the same man that caused trouble in Galilee in 4 BCE) incited the Judaeans to revolt instead of consenting to pay tribute to the Romans and tolerating them as masters, when they had previously had God for their lord.[21] Luke briefly recounts this uprising and its result in Acts 5.37: 'After him Judas the Galilean arose in the days of the census and drew away some of the people after him; but he was slain and all who followed him were scattered.'[22]

The most serious uprising was the First Revolt, which began in 66 CE.[23] This was finally ended for all practical purposes with the capture of Jerusalem by the legions of Titus in 70 CE, the destruction of the Temple by fire, the slaughter and enslavement of the population in the manner characteristic of *direptio* and the levelling of much of the city. Some of the horror of these events is captured by the Flavian client, the Judaean Josephus, in Book 7 of his *Judean War*. Titus returned to Rome in 71 CE and he and his father Vespasian (who had led the campaign in Judea for a while but had returned to Rome in 69 CE to claim the throne) celebrated a triumph at which were paraded precious items taken from Jerusalem, including the Temple vessels – a scene still visible on the carvings on the triumphal arch of Titus at the top of the Forum.[24] Also included in the

---

20. See the graphic accounts in Josephus, *Judean War* 2.56–65 and *Judean Antiquities* 17.188–298.

21. See Josephus, *Judean War* 2.118 and *Judean Antiquities* 18.1–10.

22. The initial 'him' referred to was Theudas.

23. For a recent account of the causes of the revolt, see M. Goodman, *The Ruling Class of Judaea: The Origins of the Jewish Revolt against Rome AD 66–70* (Cambridge: Cambridge University Press, 1987).

24. For an account of the triumph, see Josephus, *Judean War* 7.123–57.

procession were 700 Judaeans, probably young men, 'remarkable for their height and beauty'.[25] But according to Josephus, nothing excited so much astonishment as the moving stages, or scaffolds, many of them three or four storeys high, on which were depicted representations of episodes in the war ('Here a prosperous country was displayed devastated, there whole formations of the enemy slaughtered ...').[26] To the Flavians, the defeat of Judea was as significant as had been Octavian's victory at Actium one hundred years earlier. They used it to legitimate their rule and to present themselves as bringing peace after a period of major disruption. They memorialized the event in various ways, especially by minting a series of *Iudaea capta* coins in some fourteen distinctive styles.[27] Some of these refer to their having saved the citizens.[28] Perhaps the most remarkable of all these coins is an *aureus* minted at Lugdunum which contains an image depicting both Vespasian in his triumphal chariot (*quadriga*) and a bound Judaean captive. In the one image we have the two intertwined rituals – of Roman status elevation and Judaean status degradation. The captive may well be Simon bar Gioras, a Judaean leader of the revolt who was captured in Jerusalem, brought back to Rome for the triumph and executed at its conclusion in the Mamertine prison on the side of the Capitoline hill.[29] The 700 Judaeans who were also displayed in the triumph were probably enslaved. Why waste good slave-flesh?

H. St J. Hart described the legends on the *Iudaea capta* coins (that also appear on some other Flavian artefacts, such as statues) as 'the official commentary'. He accurately observed that this use of the ubiquitous 'coinage, with its legends and pictures, gave emperors, and the city mints that echoed Roman policy, a most potent instrument in the ancient world for fashioning opinion and influencing men's views'.[30] In Foucauldian terms, coins enunciated the discourse of imperial power and reinforced the rules by which the emperors held sway over subject and client peoples.

The second and final revolt by the Judaeans against Roman rule seems to have begun in the spring of 132 CE. It was led by someone known to Church writers as bar Kochba (literally 'son of a star', a messianic nickname based on Num. 24.17), but now known (from papyri found in the Judaean desert) to have been called Simon bar Kosiba. The rebels had some initial successes. They recaptured Jerusalem, which Hadrian had

---

25.　Josephus, *Judean War* 7.118.

26.　Josephus, *Judean War* 7.139–47.

27.　See the drawings of one representative of each of the fourteen styles, done from the originals in the British Museum by Tess Rickards, in Esler, 'God's Honour', 249–54.

28.　See Esler, 'God's Honour', 254 (Illustration 13, which has on the shield depicted on the coin, 'Ob cives ser[vandos]').

29.　Josephus, *Judean War* 7.154.

30.　H. St J., Hart, 'Judaea and Rome: The Official Commentary', *JTS* n.s. 3 (1952), 172–98 (plus six plates), at 175.

indicated he intended to refound as a Graeco-Roman city named Aelia Capitolina, and many other strongholds throughout the country. They also minted their own coins (which they provocatively restruck on Roman originals). In due course, however, the Romans once more captured Jerusalem and destroyed the city. They also destroyed hundreds of villages. The revolt was finally suppressed in the summer of 135, some of the last survivors being starved to death or slaughtered in the caves of Nahal Hever and at Muraba'at. Jerusalem was indeed now converted into the Graeco-Roman city of Aelia Capitolina, and temples to pagan gods were erected in it, including temples of Jupiter and Hadrian himself on the site of the Temple of Yahweh. Judaeans were excluded from the city, except for one day a year when they could enter to lament the city's plight at the Wailing Wall. The province of Judea was renamed as Syria

Palaestina. There is evidence for a Hadrianic persecution of Judaeans, extending to his prohibiting circumcision.[31]

With the accession of the emperor Antoninus Pius in 138 CE, who ruled until 161 CE, the situation of the Judaeans improved. Early in his reign he relaxed Hadrian's Judaean policy. Judaeans were still forbidden entry to Aelia Capitolina, but the ban on circumcision was partially lifted.

1.4 *Rome in Judaean Literature: Early Examples*

There is not a single reference to Rome or to Italy in the Hebrew Bible. In Daniel 11.30, however, it is said that 'Ships of Kittim shall come against him and he shall be disheartened.' This is an allusion to the events at Alexandria in 168 BCE when Popilius Laeanas, commanding a Roman fleet, delivered to Antiochus IV Epiphanes the Senate's veto on the continuation of his military campaign in Egypt. The reference is clearer in the Septuagint of this verse, with Kittim translated as *Rômaioi*.[32] In 1 Maccabees Rome is depicted as friendly toward the Judaeans, entering into treaties with them at the request of the Hasmoneans, as noted above.

Pompey's entry into Jerusalem in 63 BCE did, however, provoke an eloquent literary response in three of the Psalms of Solomon, a collection of eighteen psalms probably written in Jerusalem around 50 BCE. Here we find ample recognition of the negative side of Rome and Romans:

> Arrogantly, the sinner [sc. Pompey] broke down the strong walls with a
> battering ram and you did not interfere.
> Gentile foreigners went up to your place of sacrifice;
> They arrogantly trampled (it) with their sandals. (Ps Sol. 2.1–2).[33]

The author depicts the Judaean inhabitants of Jerusalem as mired in sinfulness. Pompey is God's agent of punishment. In Psalms of Solomon 8.15–21 it is stated that God brought someone (clearly Pompey) from the end of the earth who attacked the city, was let into it by its leaders (a historical fact) and captured its fortified towers (held by another faction), whereupon he killed many of its inhabitants and led others away. There is further reference to Pompey's lawless and violent actions in Jerusalem in

---

31. On the Second Revolt, see E.M. Smallwood, *The Jews under Roman Rule: From Pompey to Diocletian* (Leiden: E.J. Brill, 1976), 429–66, the source for the material in this paragraph.

32. See Vermes, 'Ancient Rome', 215.

33. Translation in R.B. Wright, 'Psalms of Solomon (First Century BC)' in J.H. Charlesworth (ed.), *The Old Testament Pseudepigrapha. Volume 2. Expansions of the 'Old Testament' and Legends, Wisdom and Philosophical Literature, Prayers, Psalms and Odes, Fragments of Lost Judeo-Hellenistic Works* (London: Darton, Longman & Todd, 1985), 639–70, at 651–2.

Psalms of Solomon 17.11–18. The author of the Psalms of Solomon made sense of these events by interpreting Pompey's desecration of the Temple as a result of Israel's sin, which God justly punished. This was an idea, with a long history in Israel, that would reverberate for centuries afterwards.[34]

A similarly cautious, if not downright negative, picture of Rome appears in the Qumran Commentary on Habakkuk. This text refers to the Romans as 'Kittim' on several occasions. Here is a sample passage:

> Its interpretation concerns the Kittim, who are swift and powerful, to slay many [with the edge of the sword] in the kingdom of the Kittim; they will vanquish [many countries] and will not believe in the precepts of [God].[35]

The author of this text was well aware of the Romans' capacity to take and sack cities:

> The interpretation of this concerns the leaders of the Kittim, who despise the fortresses of the peoples and with disdain laugh at them, they surround them with a huge army to capture them. And through dread and fear they surrender to their hands, and they demolish them because of the wickedness of their occupants.[36]

On the other hand, Column 1 of the War Scroll looks to the day when the Kittim fall at the time of the great battle between the Sons of Light and the Sons of Darkness.

John Collins has noted that the worldview of the Qumran community has considerable similarities to the conceptual framework of Judaean apocalyptic literature. For this reason it is appropriate to refer to Qumran as an apocalyptic community even if revelation, the core of the apocalyptic genre, takes on very distinctive forms in this group.[37]

Finally, there are a number of references to Rome in Book 3 of the Sibylline Oracles: a text which emerged in Judaean circles in Egypt in the mid-second century BCE and was added to as time went on.[38] Rome is referred to in a number of places.[39] These passages speak either of Roman power or of the inevitable fall of Rome. Here is a sample:

34. See M.E. Stone, *Fourth Ezra: A Commentary on the Book of Fourth Ezra* (Hermeneia; Minneapolis, MN: Fortress Press, 1990), 196–7.

35. 1QpHab 2.12–15; translation in F.G. Martínez, *The Dead Sea Scrolls Translated: The Dead Sea Scrolls in English*, translated from the Spanish by Wilfred G. E. Watson (Leiden: E.J. Brill, 1994),

36. 1 QpHab 4.5–8; translation Martínez, *The Dead Sea Scrolls*, 199.

37. J.J. Collins, *The Apocalyptic Imagination: An Introduction to the Jewish Matrix of Christianity* (New York: Crossroad, 1987), 140–1.

38. See J.J. Collins, 'Sibylline Oracles (Seventh Century BC – Seventh Century AD)' in Charlesworth (ed.), *Pseudepigrapha. Volume 1*, 317–472, at 354–61.

39. Verses 46–62, 175–95, 350–66, 464–9, 470–3 and 520–35 (see G. Stemberger, 'Die Beurteilung Roms in der rabbinischen Literatur', *ANRW* II.19.2 338–96, at 342).

But when Rome will also rule over Egypt
guiding it toward a single goal, then indeed the most great kingdom
of the immortal king will become manifest over men.
For a holy prince will come to gain sway over the scepters of the earth
forever, as time presses on.
Then also implacable wrath will fall upon Latin men.
Three will destroy Rome with piteous fate.
All men will perish in their own dwellings
when the fiery cataract flows from heaven.[40]

1.5 *Rome in Judaean Apocalyptic Literature*

The capture and destruction of Jerusalem and the Temple by Titus in 70 CE
was a catastrophe for the Judaean people, especially since it deprived them
of their central cult place where they worshipped God who was considered
to be in some sense present. The only event to match this in Israelite
history had been the destruction of the First Temple by the Babylonians in
587 BCE. Any hope for a restoration after 70 CE was extinguished by the
failure of the revolt led by Simon bar Kosiba in 132–5 CE.

Not surprisingly, therefore, the fate of Jerusalem and its Temple in 70
CE produced a variety of literary responses. In particular, there are three
texts extant in the apocalyptic genre: that is, in texts that take the form of
apocalypses (revelations) to Judaean seers. These are 4 Ezra (which
contains the most extensive material on Rome), 2 Baruch, and the
Apocalypse of Abraham, all of them probably composed around 100 CE
and all of them having survived, oddly enough, by processes of Christian
rather than Judaean/Jewish transmission.[41] A central concern is, as
Michael Stone has noted, that of theodicy – the need to justify the fact of
God's permitting the destruction of his own centre of worship.[42] Tied
inevitably to this are questions of Judaean identity; where does the
destruction and God's acquiescence in it leave the Judaeans? What sort of
people are they or should they be, living as they do in the shadow and the
aftermath of the horrors of 70 CE? It is in such a context that Rome
sometimes appears in this literature. How is Rome, the agent of the
destruction, to be understood? How should Judaeans respond to this
imperial giant which deprived them of their opportunity to sacrifice to
their God? Such questions can only be answered by examining these texts.

---

40. Sib. Or. 3.46–54; translation in Collins, 'Sibylline Oracles', 363. The 'holy prince' in
line 49 is probably a reference to the Messiah. Collins suggests that the 'three men' in line 52
refer to the First Triumvirate of Antony, Lepidus and Octavian.

41. James Davila, of the University of St Andrews, is currently writing a monograph on
this puzzling but important phenomenon.

42. See M.E. Stone, 'Reactions to Destruction of the Second Temple: Theology,
Perception and Conversion', *JSJ* 12 (1981), 195–204.

1.5.1 *Rome in 4 Ezra*

The text of 4 Ezra consists of a (possibly Christian) introductory section (1–2) followed by an apocalypse consisting of seven angelic revelations, and attributable to the Judaean author (3–5.20; 5.21–6.34; 6.35–9.25; 9.26–10.59; 11.1–12.51; 13.1–58; 14.1–48) and an appendix (15.1–16.78). The author writes under the guise of the prophet Ezra who was a captive in Babylon following the destruction of the First Temple in 587 BCE (3.1–3). He uses Babylon in reference to Rome (possibly, in part, a strategy to disguise the character of the text from the Romans should it fall into their hands): 'In the thirtieth year after the destruction of our city, I, Salathiel, who am also called Ezra, was in Babylon. I was troubled as I lay on my bed, and my thoughts welled up in my heart, because I saw the desolation and the wealth of those who lived in Babylon.' Throughout the text, the author struggles with why God has let his people suffer. Yet the character and immensity of this suffering and Rome's role in it have a prominent place. Here is how the author describes Jerusalem's end in 70 CE, citing phenomena all too familiar within the general context of Roman practices of city-conquest and *direptio* and the specific features of the Flavian triumph of 71 CE, with the captive Judaeans and Temple vessels paraded through the streets of Rome:

> For you see that our sanctuary has been laid waste, our altar thrown down, our temple destroyed; our harp has been laid low, our song has been silenced, and our rejoicing has been ended; the light of our lampstand has been put out, the ark of our covenant has been plundered, our holy things have been polluted, and the name by which we are called has been profaned; our free men have suffered abuse, our priests have been burned to death, our Levites have gone into captivity, our virgins have been defiled, and our wives have been ravished; our righteous men have been carried off, our little ones have been cast out, our young men have been enslaved and our strong men made powerless. And, what is more than all, the seal of Zion – for she has now lost the seal of her glory, and has been given over into the hands of those who hate us.[43]

That God could have permitted Jerusalem to be destroyed by a nation so sinful as Rome produces agonized puzzlement on the part of the author. He dares to question the very premise of God's justice:

> Then I said in my heart, Are the deeds of those who inhabit Babylon [here = Rome] any better? Is that why she has gained dominion over Zion? For when I came here I saw ungodly deeds without number, and

---

43. 4 Ezra 10.21–23; translation in B.M. Metzger, 'The Fourth Book of Ezra (Late First Century AD): With the Four Additional Chapters' in Charlesworth (ed.), *Pseudepigrapha. Volume 1*, 517–59, at 546–7.

my soul has seen many sinners during these thirty years. And my heart failed me, for I have seen how you endure those who sin, and have spared those who act wickedly, and have destroyed your people, and have preserved your enemies, and have not shown to anyone how your way may be comprehended.[44]

The trigger for Ezra's finding of a satisfactory explanation for Israel's misfortune comes in his vision of the mourning woman in the fourth vision (9.26–10.59). Whereas in the previous three sections he has been conducting an orderly and rational, if passionate, discussion with God's angel, now he has an experience of supernatural dimensions. Ezra has a vision of a woman mourning the death of her son. He tries to console her by insisting that her sorrow is not to be compared with the humiliation and the desolation of Zion, and it is here that we have the description of Jerusalem captured quoted above. He adopts to her something like the reassuring role that the angel had previously adopted to him. Yet it is not by what he says to her that a resolution is achieved. Instead, this is brought about by an extraordinary vision of the woman transformed into a city resting on huge foundations. This may refer to the heavenly Jerusalem which will be revealed at the end[45] and affords comfort to the seer in his grief for the loss of the earthly city. After the rational discussions hitherto, this is the first numinous phenomenon in the text and paves the way for further visions to come. The text makes clear that the new reaches of human experience into which Ezra wins access by this vision involve the privation of his rational faculties: 'I lay there like a corpse', he says, 'and I was deprived of my understanding.'[46] A little further on he adds: 'For I have seen what I did not know and I have heard what I did not understand.'[47] In other words: 'Truth which was difficult for Ezra to accept in the to-and-fro of rational debate becomes accessible when the mode of instruction shifts from the cognitive to the visionary.'[48]

The seventh and last vision in the text relates how God directed Ezra to be his agent in the pre-inscription and propagation of the law. God inspired Ezra to proclaim the law and it was taken down by five scribes

44. 4 Ezra 3.28–32; translation in Metzger, 'The Fourth Book of Ezra', 529.

45. Stone observes on this point: 'Questions as to whether the city is the heavenly Jerusalem or an eschatological one should probably be answered with an ambiguous "Yes!"' (*Fourth Ezra*, 335).

46. 4 Ezra 10.30; translation Metzger, 'The Fourth Book of Ezra', 547.

47. 4 Ezra 10.36; translation Metzger, 'The Fourth Book of Ezra', 547.

48. P.F. Esler, 'The Social Function of 4 Ezra', in *The First Christians in their Social Worlds: Social-Scientific Approaches to New Testament Interpretation* (London and New York: Routledge, 1994), 110–30, at 120 (which essay contains a fuller account of my interpretation of 4 Ezra which I am relying upon here).

and recorded in 24 books that were to be made public and another 70 that were kept secret.[49] In this part of 4 Ezra the scribe emerges as virtually a second Moses. Israel obtains a second chance to observe the law in spite of its earlier transgressions that led to the obliteration of Jerusalem.

Critics like Michael Stone have suggested that 4 Ezra has some points of contact with rabbinic thought.[50] Although this is very likely, the apocalyptic genre is more central to the character and meaning of the work. In this regard, the text mediates between a past where apocalyptic discourse played a fairly ample role (as in the Book of Daniel) and a future in which the people, denied access to Jerusalem and the opportunity there to perform sacrificial worship of God, would rely increasingly on the law as the central focus of their ethnic identity. The old dream of repelling Roman imperial rule by force, led by men like Judas the Galilean, Simon bar Giora and Simon bar Kosiba, would disappear entirely, to be replaced by an identity focused on the quiet fulfilment of ethical obligations. The Mosaic law, and the oral traditions of its interpretation that would come to be inscribed in Mishnah and Talmud, would provide a mode of behaviour to ensure the continued existence of Judaean/Jewish life and identity.

Yet in 4 Ezra the Judaean imagination, even though it provides a convincing modality for the continued existence of the people, is not content to let Rome off the hook. It looks to God to settle an old score. This perspective appears in the eagle vision, the fifth in the text (11.1–12.51). The Book of Daniel had described four beasts that came out of the sea, apparently representing earthly empires, the fourth being particularly savage (7.3–12). These hold sway for a time but are eventually replaced or destroyed. Apocalyptic imagery was used to represent the succession of political power held by one empire after another. This became an influential model in subsequent apocalypses (and even in rabbinic literature later on). The eagles which formed so prominent a feature of legionary standards make it impossible not to associate Rome with the eagle described in the fifth vision of 4 Ezra. In the vision a lion rises from a forest to rebuke the eagle, after which it is consumed in fire. The author clearly sees the imperial reference in his allusion to Daniel 7.3–12. The lion says to the eagle: 'Are you not one that remains of the four beasts which I had made to reign in my world, so that the end of my times might come through them?'[51] The author also celebrates the fact that eagle will eventually be destroyed:

49. 4 Ezra 14.37–48.
50. Stone, *Fourth Ezra*, 38–9.
51. 4 Ezra 11.39; translation Metzger, 'The Fourth Book of Ezra', 549.

And so your insolence has come up before the Most High, and your pride to the Mighty One. And the Most High has looked upon his times, and behold, they are ended, and his ages are completed! Therefore you will surely disappear, you eagle, and your terrifying wings, and your most evil little wings, and your malicious heads, and your most evil talons, and your whole worthless body, so that the whole earth, freed from your violence, may be refreshed and relieved, and may hope for the judgment and mercy of him who made it.[52]

In the interpretation of this vision the lion is the Messiah, who will denounce the eagle and then destroy it, and deliver in mercy a remnant of the people.[53] It is important to note that the text leaves the destruction of the eagle/Rome entirely in the hands of the Messiah; there is no suggestion that Israel will be involved.

Thus, in 4 Ezra the counter-discourse generated to the triumphant ideology of Roman imperialism takes the form of a future myth, not dissimiliar to those of other oppressed peoples in modern times, as a way of giving voice to a destiny in which the evident wrongs of the present will be righted. This, then, is an important feature of the 'post-colonial' movement of this text. Nevertheless, it is difficult to avoid the conclusion that while in the Judaean imagination Rome would one day get its come-uppance, the real weight of the work rests on the seventh and final vision, with its potent presentation of re-inscription of the law of Israel. And so it was that the future of the people would ultimately lie in the fulfilment of Mosaic law and not in the overthrow of imperial rule. Hopes in military resistance and for the restoration of Jewish sovereignty would fade away, but allegiance to Moses would grow and grow.

1.5.2 *Rome in 2 Baruch*

The dramatic setting of 2 Baruch is also the time of the destruction of the First Temple, when the word of the Lord comes to Baruch to warn him of this coming event.[54] Yet a most surprising feature of this text in comparison to 4 Ezra is that the violence and brutality that accompanied the Roman capture of Jerusalem in 70 CE hardly figure.[55] Thus, when Baruch responds to the prospect of the city being destroyed, he expresses concern not so much for the death and suffering and exile that this would entail as for the honour of Israel and God that will be trampled in the process:

---

52. 4 Ezra 11.43–46; translation Metzger, 'The Fourth Book of Ezra', 549.
53. 4 Ezra 12.31–39.
54. 2 Baruch 1–2.
55. For a fuller account of this dimension of the text, see Esler, 'God's Honour', 255–6.

But one thing I shall say in your presence, O Lord: Now, what will happen after these things? For if you destroy your city and deliver up your country to those who hate us, how will the name of Israel be remembered again? Or how shall we speak again about your glorious deeds? Or to whom again will that which is in your glorious law be explained? Or will the universe return to its nature and the world go back to its original silence?[56]

God answers that the city will be spared for a time, but that the real Jerusalem is the heavenly one, seen by Adam, Abraham and Moses: 'Behold, now it is preserved with me – as also Paradise.'[57] This prospect of a heavenly Jerusalem one day to be revealed possibly also featured in 4 Ezra, as noted above.

When Baruch replies to this, we observe explicit concern for the honour of God that would be besmirched by the capture of the city, rather than any real interest in the human tragedy attending this event:

So then I shall be guilty in Zion,
that your haters will come to this place and pollute your sanctuary,
and carry off your heritage into captivity,
and rule over them whom you love.
And then they will go away again to the land of their idols,
and boast before them.
And what have you done to your great name?[58]

It is this question of his 'name', or honour, that attracts God's reply:

My name and my glory shall last unto eternity.
My judgment, however, shall assert its rights in its own time.[59]

In fact, God does take active steps to preserve his name. First, we are told that God's angels actually break down the walls so as to facilitate the entry of the 'Babylonians', for the express reason that 'the enemies do not boast and say, "We have overthrown the wall of Zion and we have burnt down the place of the mighty God."'[60] Second, the Temple vessels are not captured by the 'Babylonians', but are hidden in the earth.[61] Presumably by making this claim the author was reassuring his readers that the vessels the Romans had carried off to Rome and that had been displayed during the triumph of Vespasian and Titus in 71 CE were not the real vessels at

---

56. 2 Baruch 3.4–7; translation in A.F.J. Klijn, '2 (Syriac Apocalypse of) Baruch (early Second Century AD)' in Charlesworth (ed.), *Pseudepigrapha. Volume 1*, 615–52, 621.
57. 2 Baruch 4.6; translation Klijn, '2 (Syriac Apocalypse of) Baruch', 622.
58. 2 Baruch 5.1; translation Klijn, '2 (Syriac Apocalypse of) Baruch', 622.
59. 2 Baruch 5.2; translation Klijn, '2 (Syriac Apocalypse of) Baruch', 622.
60. 2 Baruch 7.1; translation Klijn, '2 (Syriac Apocalypse of) Baruch', 623.
61. 2 Baruch 6.8–9.

all. The real vessels, safely hidden in the earth, would reappear 'when Jerusalem will be restored for ever'.[62] These two aspects of the text represent a counter-discourse to that of the dominant Roman one, that was emblazoned on coins which its readers must have quite often seen or held.

Yet the counter-discourse and the post-colonial dimension of 2 Baruch goes much further than this. Frederick Murphy has argued that the author of 2 Baruch deliberately urged pacifism on his Judaean contemporaries. Writing after 70 CE but before 132 CE this author, so Murphy reasonably suggests, took his side with those who opposed active vengeance against the Romans and resistance to their rule.[63] He finds the clearest expression of this sentiment in 52.6–7: 'Enjoy yourselves in the suffering which you suffer now. For why do you look for the decline of your enemies? Prepare your souls for that which is kept for you, and make ready your souls for the reward which is preserved for you.'[64]

Murphy also correctly points out, however, that the author does insist that Rome will be punished – only by God, not by Israel. God promises that the enemies of Israel will eventually be punished in 2 Baruch 13. Moreover, as with 4 Ezra, 2 Baruch contains a vision of the future detailing such destruction. In Chapter 35 Baruch has a vision of a forest, a vine, a fountain and a cedar. The details of the vision and its interpretation in Chapter 39 make clear that this is a version of the succession of empires originally set forth in the apocalypse in Daniel 7.3–12, mentioned above. The fourth kingdom, alluding to Rome, will have a power which is 'harsher and more evil than those which were before it . . . and the truth will hide itself in this and all who are polluted with unrighteousness will flee to it like the evil beasts flee and creep into the forest'.[65] But at the time of its fulfilment 'my Anointed One' (that is, the messiah) will be revealed and he will uproot the multitude of its host.

Then, in a quite remarkable manner, the text continues as follows:

> The last ruler who is left alive at that time will be bound, whereas the entire host will be destroyed. And they will carry him on Mount Zion, and my Anointed One will convict him of all his wicked deeds and will assemble and set before him all the works of his hosts. And after these things he will kill him and protect the rest of my people who will be found in the place that I have chosen.

62. 2 Baruch 6.9; translation Klijn, '2 (Syriac Apocalypse of) Baruch', 623; on this dimension of the text, see Esler, 'God's Honour', 256–7.

63. See F.J. Murphy, '2 Baruch and the Romans', *JBL* 104 (1985), 663–9.

64. 2 Baruch 52.6–7; translation Klijn, '2 (Syriac Apocalypse of) Baruch', 639.

65. 2 Baruch 39.5–6; translation Klijn, '2 (Syriac Apocalypse of) Baruch', 633.

As I have suggested elsewhere, this scene constitutes a parody of a Roman triumph, probably that of Vespasian and Titus in 71 CE discussed above. The fate of the last ruler here parallels that of Simon bar Gioras in Rome in 71 CE. Just as Simon, his army destroyed, was led in the procession, probably bound (as in the passage above), so too the last ruler, with his host destroyed, will be led bound. Just as the Romans carried scenes of the war, so too will the Anointed set before the last ruler all the works of his hosts. Just as Simon was taken up the side of the Capitol and executed in the Mamertine prison, so too will the Anointed kill the leader. Just as the Flavians celebrated their victory over the Judaeans as the legitimation of their rule and the salvation of the citizenry, so too will the Anointed protect his people. In other words, what the Romans did to the Judaeans will be done to them by the messiah. To summarize:

> In Foucault's terms, we have here an inversion of the Roman processes of violence and their re-direction against those who had originally imposed them. The rulers will be overcome with their own rules. The Messiah will visit the Roman ideology of *debellare superbos* upon Rome itself. Rome's triumph will become God's.[66]

Yet this will indisputably be the doing of the Lord and his Anointed. It is not for Israel to wreak such vengeance on Rome. As in 4 Ezra, the role of Israel is to gather itself around, to rediscover its identity in the Mosaic law. As Baruch says in the letter to the nine-and-a-half tribes of the dispersion that appears at the end of the text:

> Also we have left our land, and Zion has been taken away from us, and we have nothing now apart from the Mighty One and his Law. Therefore, if we direct and dispose our hearts, we shall receive everything which we lost again by many times. For that which we lost was subject to corruption, that which we receive will not be corruptible.[67]

1.5.3 *Rome in the Apocalypse of Abraham*
The Apocalypse of Abraham is the third apocalypse written after 70 CE that attributes the destruction of Jerusalem to the infidelity of Israel toward its covenant with God and the 'opportunistic politics of some of its leaders'.[68] Issues of true and false worship figure prominently in this text. The first part (Chapters 1–8) describe Abraham's conversion from idolatry. The second (Chapters 9–32) is an apocalypse that details his

---

66. Esler, 'God's Honour', 257–8.
67. 2 Baruch 85.3–5; translation Klijn, '2 (Syriac Apocalypse of) Baruch', 651.
68. R. Rubinkiewicz, 'Apocalypse of Abraham (First to Second Century AD)', in Charlesworth (ed.), *Pseudepigrapha. Volume 1*, 681–705, 685.

dealings with an angel and his ascent into heaven where he has a vision of the enthroned city and receives revelations concerning the cosmos and the future. One of these revelations covers the destruction of the Temple in terms that reflect its sack by the Romans in 70 CE:

> ... behold the picture swayed. And from its left side a crowd of heathens ran out and they captured the men, women, and children who were on its right side. And some they slaughtered and others they kept with them. Behold, I saw (them) running to them by way of four ascents and they burned the Temple with fire, and they plundered the holy things that were in it.[69]

God promises that the time of justice will come upon them.[70] But the author is not very interested in Rome in this text and there is no reference to the honour of God being desecrated by the destruction of his Temple. Rather, the emphasis falls on the major theme of right and wrong cultic activity.

1.5.4 *Rome in the Apocalypse*
Finally, it is worth mentioning briefly that there is a very negative picture of Rome in the Apocalypse. Although it is wrong to seek to 'decode' the rich imagery of this text on any one-to-one basis, that Rome is referred to cannot be doubted. The text presents a cycle of myth in which Rome features as a beast in league with Satan, with a murderous enmity towards Christ-followers. One feature of the text is that it castigates the demonic dimensions of Rome in the manner of a witchcraft accusation (cf. 18.23) known to us from anthropological research.[71]

1.6 *Rome in Rabbinic Literature*

The expression 'rabbinic literature' covers a huge corpus of extant literature, encompassing most notably Mishnah, Talmud and Midrash.[72] There is, moreover, such a great quantity and variety of references to Rome within this corpus that all that is possible within the scope of this essay is to outline some of the main themes, such as Rome as an imperial power, Rome as an agent of civilization (yes or no?) and Rome's relations

---

69. Apocalypse of Abraham 27.3–5; translation Rubinkiewicz, 'Apocalypse of Abraham', 702.

70. Apocalypse of Abraham 27.10.

71. P.F. Esler, 'Sorcery Accusations and the Apocalypse', in *First Christians*, 131–46.

72. For a good introduction, see H.L. Strack and G. Stemberger, *Introduction to the Talmud and the Midrash*, translation by Markus Bockmuehl (Edinburgh: T&T Clark, 1991).

with Israel.[73] A number of more expansive treatments are available for consultation.[74]

The history of rabbinic literature has its roots in the disaster of 70 CE. Yohanan ben Zakkai, an influential Pharisee opposed to the rebellion being undertaken by the Zealots, managed to leave Jerusalem before the end and to survive the rebellion in good grace with the Romans. He became the head of the Judaeans of Palestine.[75] This may have occurred in Yavneh/Jamnia, on the reasonable assumption that there is a core of truth behind a tradition embellished with legend.[76] Among rabbis like ben Zakkai, the view obtained that the guilt for the destruction of Jerusalem rested with Israel not the Romans; for them Vespasian (and his son Titus) were executing God's will by punishing Israelite sinfulness.[77]

One of the most remarkable pieces of evidence for the view that the success of Rome was divinely sanctioned and, in part at least, a response to Israelite sinfulness came in the rabbinical reworking of that part of the myth of Rome's foundation involving Romulus and Remus. The rabbis applied the saying in Psalm 10.9, 'You have been the helper of the fatherless', to the legend of Romulus and Remus who were suckled by a wolf, and thus saved for their future careers as kings and founders of the city of Rome.[78] In addition, the foundation of Rome was linked to the sins of Israelite kings:

> The day that Solomon married the daughter of Pharoah Nekho, Michael the Great Prince came down from heaven and planted a great pole in the sea. A sandbank grew on this spot, and it became a bed of reeds. This was the future site of Rome. The day that Jeroboam made the two calves of gold, Romulus and Remus came to the reed-bed and

73. See I. Herzog, 'Rome in the Talmud and in the Midrash' in I. Herzog, *Judaism: Law and Ethics: Essays by the Late Chief Rabbi Dr Isaac Herzog* (London, Jerusalem and New York: Soncino Press, 1974), 83–91, at 83–4.

74. See R. Loewe, '*Render Unto Caesar': Religious and Political Loyalty in Palestine* (Cambridge: Cambridge University Press, 1940); P. Kieval, 'The Talmudic View of the Hasmonean and Early Herodian Periods in Jewish History' (Brandis University dissertation, 1970); Herzog, 'Rome in the Talmud', 83–91; Vermes, 'Ancient Rome'; N.R.M. de Lange, 'Jewish Attitudes to the Roman Empire' in Garnsey and Whittaker (eds), *Imperialism*, 255–81, 354–7; Stemberger, 'Die Beurteilung Roms'; L.H. Feldman, 'Rabbinic Insights on the Decline and Forthcoming Fall of the Roman Empire', *JSJ* 31 (2000), 275–97.

75. De Lange, 'Jewish Attitudes', 264–5.

76. See Stemberger, 'Die Beurteilung Roms', 382, and the literature he cites, and P.F. Esler, 'Palestinian Judaism', in D. Cohn-Sherbok and J.M. Court (eds), *Religious Diversity in the Greco-Roman World* (Sheffield: Sheffield Academic Press, 2001), 21–46, at 45–6.

77. See Stemberger, 'Die Beurteilung Roms', 382.

78. See Herzog, 'Rome in the Talmud', 85–6.

built two quarters of Rome. The day that Elijah ascended, a king was proclaimed in Rome.[79]

Yet the currents among the Judaean *ethnos* that ben Zakkai represented were opposed by those who longed for direct and violent challenge to Roman rule, such as burst out under Simon bar Kosiba in 132 CE. At that time the leading rabbi, Akiva, supported the revolt.[80] Other rabbis did not. A rabbinical dispute as to the benefits brought by Rome (that has a strong resonance with a famous scene in the film *Monty Python's Life of Brian* on the theme of 'What did Rome ever do for us?) brings out the flavour of the deep-seated disagreement over the Romans and their imperial power:

> Rabbi Judah (bar Ilai), Rabbi Yose (ben Halafta) and Rabbi Simeon (bar Yohai) were sitting talking ...
>   Rabbi Judah began: 'How splendid are the works of this people! They have built market-places, baths and bridges.'
>   Rabbi Yose said nothing.
>   Rabbi Simeon bar Yohai answered him: 'Everything they have made they have made only for themselves: market-places, for whores; baths, to wallow in; bridges, to levy tolls.'[81]

Division such as this continued for centuries, with the actions of Hadrian against Judaean religion in areas as central as circumcision, noted above, doing much to fuel the negative view.

From Hadrian's time onwards Rome came to be identified in rabbinical literature with the biblical figures of Esau or Edom, long interpreted as types of the non-Israelites opposed to Israelites. The use of such names also perhaps represents an example of the occulted language that Stephen Slemon has suggested is typical of post-colonial discourse. In addition, the story of the relationship between Jacob and Esau allowed a resource from the collective memory of Israel to be deployed in order to speak of the relationship between Rome and Israel.[82]

Yet even this motif could be used to make positive or negative statements about Rome. While the rabbis frequently offered a prophetic interpretation of Genesis 25.23, 'Two nations are in thy womb', as referring to Israel and Rome, they differed as to what this actually meant. Many insisted that the irreconcilable hostility between Jacob and Esau

---

79. J. Levi, 'Abodah Zarah 39c; cf. B Shabbath 56b; Sanhedrin 21b; Song of Songs Rabba 1.6.4; translation and citations from Lange, 'Jewish Attitudes', 273.

80. Lange, 'Jewish Attitudes', 267.

81. See B Shabbath 33b; cf. Abodah Zarah 2b; translation in Lange, 'Jewish Attitudes', 268.

82. Lange, 'Jewish Attitudes', 269–70.

was replicated in the relationship of Israel and Rome, but others said that they were still brothers, with complementary roles to fulfil in the world.[83]

There continued to be a rich appreciation in rabbinic circles of the tremendous military and extractive powers of Rome. The apocalyptic view of a progression of empires under the guise of four beasts found in Daniel 7, and the particular identification of Rome with the fourth beast in the post-70 Judaean apocalypses discussed above, was widely accepted among the rabbis.[84] Rabbi Johanan ben Nappaha (*c.* 180–279 CE), for example, was the outstanding Judaean scholar in Palestine. Asked how important were the Romans, he quoted Daniel 7, in particular verse 23, asserting that it referred to Rome, whose power is known throughout all the world: 'And he shall devour the whole earth and shall tread it down and break it into pieces.'[85] Another eminent third-century CE rabbi, Shimon ben Laqish (better known as Resh Laqish), who had been a gladiator before becoming a rabbi, both acknowledged Roman power and complimented the Roman system of justice, while nevertheless insisting that Rome was wicked.[86]

Rabbi Ulla, a student of Rabbi Johanan ben Nappaha, who lived in Palestine during the second half of the third century CE, was much taken with the sheer size, economic power and impregnability of Rome, and this prompted a pronounced degree of exaggeration in his description of the city:

> The great city of Rome covers an area of 300 parasangs [approximately 1200 miles] by 300. It has 300 markets corresponding to the number of days in the solar year. The smallest of them is that of the poultry sellers, which is sixteen mil [approximately sixteen miles] by sixteen. The king dines in one every day. Everyone who resides in the city, even if he was not born there, receives a regular portion of food from the king's household ... There are 3000 baths in it, and 500 windows the smoke from which goes outside the wall. One side of it is bounded by sea, one by hills and mountains, one side by a barrier of iron.[87]

The reference here to the portions of food that were distributed has its basis in the regular daily distribution, the *frumentum publicum*, that was a feature of life in Rome for centuries.[88] The wheat for these distributions came largely from Egypt. This fact led one rabbi, the third-century

---

83. Genesis Rabba 75.4; cf. Leviticus Rabba 15.9; see Lange, 'Jewish Attitudes', 271.
84. Lange, 'Jewish Attitudes', 271.
85. Abodah Zarah 2b; cited in Feldman, 'Rabbinic Insights', 281.
86. Midrash Leviticus Rabbah 13.5 (Roman power), Genesis Rabbah 9.13 (Roman justice) and 65.21 (Roman wickedness); see the discussion in Feldman, 'Rabbinic Insights', 282.
87. Megillah 6b; translation in Feldman, 'Rabbinic Insights', 283.
88. See G. Rickman, *The Corn Supply of Ancient Rome* (Oxford: Clarendon Press, 1980).

Babylonian Rabbi Judah, to declare in the name of his teacher Shmuel that the biblical Joseph was able to obtain all the wealth of the world while he was administrator of Egypt, and that after his death it passed on from nation to nation, finally ending up in the hands of the Romans, who still control it.[89]

Among the rabbis there was a clear-eyed understanding of the rapacious taxation and conscription of personnel that lay at the foundation of Rome's wealth. An appreciation of the economic dimensions of imperial power predates modern colonial theory. Here, for example, is a passage from Pesikta Rabbati (10.1):

> Just as a bramble snatches at a man's clothing, so that even if he detaches it on one side it sticks to the other, so the empire of Esau annually appropriates Israel's crops and herds. Even before that, it pricks them with its poll tax. And even as this is being exacted, Esau's men come to the people of Israel to levy conscripts.[90]

In spite of all this, however, the rabbis did consider that Rome would eventually meet its end. Many, if not most, of them (especially after 135 CE) were opposed to Israel doing anything to actually bring this about,[91] but happen it would, at the hands of the Messiah. On one view, the Messiah would even lead a clandestine existence in Rome before he did so, like Moses among the Egyptians![92] By the middle of the second century CE rabbis were predicting the overthrow of Rome. Thus, at this time (and possibly reflecting Hadrian-inspired bitterness toward Rome) the Palestinian rabbi Shimon bar Yohai stated in the name of Rabbi Meir that God showed Jacob the dominion of Edom that had ascended and would also descend. This statement was repeated during the late third and early fourth centuries.[93] There are many rabbinic statements to similar effect.[94] They constitute a powerful counter-discourse to the Roman discourse of domination, however it might be dressed up.

This pattern of a life characterized by a quietist observation of the law, coupled with a hope that one day Rome would fall, continued the approach that we have already observed in 4 Ezra and 2 Baruch. In the circumstances, it was clearly the most viable option for Israel and was accompanied by a rich understanding of Roman imperial rule and a variegated response to it.

89. Pesahim 119a; cited in Feldman, 'Rabbinic Insights', 284.
90. Translation in Lange, 'Jewish Attitudes', 274.
91. See the material cited by Lange, 'Jewish Attitudes', 278–81.
92. B Sanhedrin 98a; Vermes, 'Ancient Rome', 223.
93. Feldman, 'Rabbinic Insights', 284.
94. These are well discussed by Feldman, 'Rabbinic Insights', 284–8.

1.7 *Conclusion*

For nearly five centuries Israel fell under the sway of Roman imperial rule, and on two occasions, in 66–70 and 132–5 CE, it experienced the full and devastating force of Roman military power. The aristocratic empire that was Rome controlled this subject people with an iron grip, subjected it to heavy taxation and legitimated these processes in numerous ways, not least by the legends on many coins that jangled in people's purses. Yet one of the marvels of the Israelites is that they produced such a vibrant array of discourse, much of it reliant on the myth of the four beasts in Daniel 7, to counter that of Rome. There is a rich stream of post-colonial reflection (in the sense we have pursued in relation to the ancient world) in this literature. As we now look back on all this, it is difficult not to note that Rome is long destroyed, but the rabbis and rabbinic traditions are with us still. In the long run, then, the Israelites became post-colonial in relation to Rome in the chronological sense as well.

A RELUCTANT PROVINCIAL: JOSEPHUS AND THE ROMAN EMPIRE IN *JEWISH WAR*

James S. McLaren

It is common to view Josephus as a ready recipient of Roman protection. He appears to celebrate his change of circumstances, making no effort to hide his receipt of benefaction from the Flavian household, through the famous story of his capture and the reference to subsequent privileges granted when in Rome (*War* 3.383–408; *Life* 414–29). This change in circumstances has, in turn, often resulted in Josephus being roundly condemned for betraying his fellow Judaeans. He is a quisling, an unrepentant traitor. However, any discussion of Jewish attitudes regarding Rome in the late first century CE without some reference to Josephus would be incomplete, no matter what judgement is offered about the decisions he made during his lifetime. Josephus provides a tangible and immediate link between Judea and imperial Rome.

His curriculum vitae is beyond dispute. He grew up in Judea, and was well versed with the machinations of life in Jerusalem. He fought against the Romans, even if only briefly. He also lived almost 30 years in Rome. Furthermore, he chose to write about a number of these experiences. There are, therefore, many avenues by which we could profitably explore Jewish–Roman interaction through a study of Josephus. They include his presentation of Roman administrators, especially of various provincial officials; his views on the city of Rome; his views on the Roman way of life; and his views on the Roman political 'system'.[1] Understandably,

---

1. Discussion of the Roman administrators is a prominent feature of scholarship on the political situation in Judaea prior to the revolt. What little comment there is offered in existing scholarship regarding the city of Rome universally presumes that Josephus was profoundly impressed by its grandeur. For example, see M. Hadas-Lebel, *Flavius Josephus: Eyewitness to Rome's First Century Conquest of Judea*, trans. R. Millar (New York: Macmillan, 1993), 63–5. S. Mason, 'Flavius Josephus in Flavian Rome: Reading on and between the Lines' in A.J. Boyle and W.J. Dominik (eds), *Flavian Rome* (Leiden: Brill, 2003), 559–89 provides a fruitful explanation of how Josephus's *Jewish Antiquities – Life* can be

where most attention has been paid to date is the emotive topic of Josephus's attitude toward Roman rule. Such enquiry is particularly focused on whether or not there was room for a believer in the God of the Judaeans also to accept Roman hegemony, and if so, on what terms and to what extent this acceptance might translate into a tangible relationship. It is this fundamental issue that will be the focus of the following discussion.

Throughout Josephus's lifetime Roman rule was an explicit reality of everyday life. A response of some nature was unavoidable.[2] There were two stark, extreme alternatives. One was total acceptance of Roman rule to the point of renouncing the Jewish cultural heritage. The best-known example of this approach is Tiberius Julius Alexander. At the other extreme were people who steadfastly chose to reject Roman rule, even to the point of preferring death, like some of the *sicarii* depicted by Josephus (*War* 7.410–19).[3] Between these two extremes stood the vast majority of Jews, seeking a compromise position, negotiating a means of living with Roman rule. Within this spectrum lies Josephus. According to his own account he had the opportunity to behave in the same manner as the *sicarii* did in Egypt, but declined. It seems likely that he also had several opportunities to adopt Tiberius Julius Alexander's approach of renouncing his heritage, but never did so. Instead Josephus lived as a Jew within the Roman Empire. The key question being addressed here is exactly where on the spectrum we should place him. Two broad schools of thought have tended to dominate discussion of this issue over the past century. In the first section both approaches will be reviewed. The bulk of attention, however, will be devoted to outlining the case for a third position on the topic: that Josephus was never a supporter of Roman rule. Instead, he was consistently resentful of Roman rule and any claims to superiority made by its rulers and their representatives. In accord with this ideological stance Josephus openly opposed Rome at the outbreak of the revolt but was compelled to modify radically how he expressed this stance because of a choice he made at Jotapata.

---

read as a comment on life in Rome under Domitian. Discussion of Roman military matters is also a major area of study, but this is not so much undertaken for insight regarding how an outsider viewed the Roman army as to find information describing the Roman army system in a supposedly apolitical manner.

2. The outbreak of the revolt drew a line in the sand, especially from a Roman perspective, between those Jews supporting the revolt and those Jews supporting Rome. See J.S. McLaren, 'Christians and the Jewish Revolt: AD 66–70', in A.M. Nobbs, C.E.V. Nixon, R.A. Kearsley and T.W. Hillard (eds), *Ancient History in a Modern University, Vol. 2* (Grand Rapids MI: Eerdmans, 1997), 53–60 for discussion of the different Jewish responses to the conflict.

3. Josephus also acclaims the Essenes as being willing to suffer torture and death rather than compromise their way of life (*War* 2.152–3).

2.1 *Josephus and Roman Rule in Scholarship*

2.1.1 *In paid employment: Josephus and the Flavians*

The early part of the twentieth century was dominated by an approach to Josephus that cast him as a spokesperson for the Flavian family.[4] It was proposed that Josephus drew directly from Vespasian's own account of the war to construct a pro-Flavian text. He was commissioned to record the war in an effort to reinforce the position of the new imperial family. He did so willingly, constructing an account that heaps praise on Vespasian and his eldest son and levelling all responsibility for the loss of the Temple on rogue Jews. After strong criticism of *Jewish War* from his compatriots, Josephus's later writings reflected a less pro-Flavian perspective on what had happened in Judea.

Coinciding with the upsurge in Josephan studies in the 1970s this approach to the reading of Josephus received a significant boost from S.J.D. Cohen. He forcefully argued that *Jewish War* was a propaganda text for the Flavians. A more 'Jewish' flavour evident in *Jewish Antiquities* was to be explained as a calculated attempt by Josephus to win over the confidence of the emerging rabbinic movement.[5]

The mud has stuck rather solidly in some circles, with Josephus being given the mantle of being no more than a 'lackey' of Flavian propaganda. The level of criticism of Josephus is such that cautionary comments are almost always attached to the mention of his name in terms of the need to allow for his overt and overbearing bias toward the Flavians.[6] While never going as far as Tiberius Julius Alexander, Josephus stood toward the end of the spectrum that found compromise with Rome a sensible, easy option.

---

4. For example, see R. Laqueur, *Der jüdische Historiker Flavius Josephus: ein biographischer Versuch auf neuer quellenkritischer Grundlage* (Darmstadt: Wissenschaftliche Buchgesellschaft, 1920) and H. St J. Thackeray, *Josephus: The Man and the Historian* (New York: Ktav, 1929).

5. See S.J.D. Cohen, *Josephus in Galilee and Rome: His Vita and Development as a Historian* (Leiden: Brill, 1979). What makes Cohen's criticism of Josephus particularly intriguing is his support for the view that Josephus was an active rebel at the beginning of the war.

6. For recent examples of this view see M. Beard, 'The Triumph of Flavius Josephus' in A.J. Boyle and W.J. Dominik (eds), *Flavian Rome* (Leiden: Brill, 2003), 543–58; W. Carter, *Pontius Pilate. Portraits of a Roman Governor* (Collegeville: Liturgical Press, 2003), 50–52 and J.A. Overman, 'The First Revolt and Flavian Politics' in A. Berlin and J.A. Overman (eds), *The First Jewish Revolt* (London: Routledge, 2001), 213–21. Beard is particularly noteworthy because she argues that it is Josephus's bias that makes him so invaluable: he provides a direct link to the official Flavian view.

2.1.2 *Just friends: Josephus's common-sense approach to Roman rule*
The increased interest in the works of Josephus since the 1970s has witnessed the emergence of a second school of thought regarding his relationship with Roman rule. It begins from the premise that Josephus accepted Roman rule as a reality of life. However, rather than view this as the work of a paid employee, Josephus's favourable disposition toward Rome was acquired from his family and social circumstances.[7] As an aristocrat educated in Jerusalem, Josephus learnt to see Roman rule as a fact of life. Yes, he was complimentary about Titus and he advocated living with Roman rule, but this was not at the cost of his cultural heritage.

Fundamental to this school of thought is the notion that Josephus articulates a Jewish understanding of the revolt and the current Roman domination. Drawing on such biblical figures as Jeremiah and Daniel, Josephus explained his own actions.[8] On the broader level of explaining the disastrous revolt, Josephus placed the loss of the Temple and the defeat of the Jews under the umbrella of God's control. Rome's standing as the ruler of the world was the result of divine choice. God was punishing the Jews for sins committed by certain rogue elements of the community. Here Josephus thought and spoke as a Jew.

The shift to place emphasis on Josephus's dependence on his cultural heritage indicates a degree of complexity to understanding his relationship with Rome. Although Josephus accepted Roman dominance here and now, it would eventually end. The clues for this outlook are derived primarily from his rewriting of the biblical narratives in *Jewish Antiquities* 1–11.[9] Working within the framework of the rise and fall of earthly kingdoms, Josephus appears to have aligned Rome with the fourth kingdom in the predictions of Daniel 2.34–35 (*Ant.* 10.207). The current situation, however, is not the end of the story. In the retelling of Numbers

---

7. Among the key initial contributors in this approach see T. Rajak, *Josephus: The Historian and his Society* (London: Duckworth, 1983) and P. Bilde, *Flavius Josephus between Jerusalem and Rome: His Life, his Works and their Importance* (Sheffield: JSOT, 1988).

8. See H. Lindner, *Die Geschichtsauffassung des Flavius Josephus im Bellum Judaicum* (Leiden: Brill, 1972).

9. See M. de Jonge, 'Josephus und die Zukunftserwartungen seines Volkes' in O. Betz, K. Haacker and M. Hengel (eds), *Josephus-Studien: Untersuchungen zu Josephus, dem antiken Judentum und dem Neuen Testament. Otto Michel zum 70. Geburtstag gewidmet* (Göttingen: Vandenhoeck & Ruprecht, 1974), 205–19; S. Mason, 'Josephus, Daniel, and the Flavian House' in F. Parente and J. Sievers (eds), *Josephus and the History of the Greco-Roman Period. Essays in Memory of Morton Smith* (Leiden: Brill, 1994), 161–91; P. Bilde, 'Josephus and Jewish Apocalypticism' in S. Mason (ed.), *Understanding Josephus: Seven Perspectives* (Sheffield: Sheffield Academic Press, 1998), 35–61. P. Spilsbury, 'Flavius Josephus on the Rise and Fall of the Roman Empire', *JTS* 54 (2003), 1–24, clearly establishes the case for Josephus envisaging the demise of the Roman Empire in *Jewish Antiquities* and *Against Apion*.

22–24 Josephus has Balaam predict the future restoration of Israel (*Ant.* 4.112–17, 126–30, esp. 126–7). In *Apion* 2.41 Josephus indicates the temporary nature of the situation, speaking of the Romans as being 'now lords of the universe'. For Josephus, the future would involve the downfall of Rome and the restoration of Israel.[10] At no stage, however, has it been suggested that Josephus was advocating any action by humans that would usher in this change. If anything the exact opposite argument is proposed: Josephus was a pacifist and saw Daniel's prediction about the various kingdoms as a message that prompted non-resistance to foreign rule. Everything was under God's control. The task of the believer was to be law-abiding and patient. In turn, Josephus saw the revolt and the actions of those he casts in the role of the rebels as foolish. Opposing Rome was wrong. Now was the time of Rome and it would be God who would decide when it was over. Above and beyond any practical arguments against going to war, this pacifist ideology provides the fundamental explanation of Josephus's claimed opposition to the revolt.[11]

The nuance advocated in this second school of thought provides a tonic to the rather simplistic notion that Josephus was on the payroll of the Flavian emperors as one of their propaganda agents. Furthermore, it encourages the modern reader to view Josephus as an author of his own text, working to his own agendas, shaping the content and direction of the texts accordingly.

In turn, the recognition of Josephus's literary activity has resulted in an increased level of attention being paid to positioning him within the context of life in imperial Rome. Two aspects of this context have attracted the most interest. One is the prevailing attitude of the Flavian family toward public speech. Blatant criticism was not an option for anyone who desired to remain alive and well. Although the need for due caution was particularly evident during the reign of Domitian, we have no reason to suggest that Vespasian or Titus were open to the idea of entertaining explicit mockery or criticism on a large scale. To write about contemporary events required caution, especially if there was any

---

10. See T. Rajak, 'The *Against Apion* and the Continuities in Josephus's Political Thought' in S. Mason (ed.), *Understanding Josephus: Seven perspectives* (Sheffield: Sheffield Academic Press, 1998), 222–46, who argues that the description of theocracy as the ideal constitution in *Against Apion* reflected a willingness on the part of Josephus to share with his readers his political manifesto late in life. D.R. Schwartz, 'Rome and the Jews: Josephus on "Freedom" and "Autonomy"' in A.K. Bowman, H.M. Cotton, M. Goodman and S. Price (eds), *Representations of Empire. Rome and the Mediterranean World* (Oxford: Oxford University Press, 2002), 65–81 depicts Josephus as preferring independence from foreign rule.

11. Mason, 'Josephus, Daniel', provides the most thorough articulation of this line of argument.

suggestion of criticism of the new regime in the text.[12] The other significant aspect of the context was the manner in which the Flavian rulers had used the suppression of the revolt to enhance their public image. Numerous issues of coinage, a new tax, public buildings and a shared triumph all point to an active campaign to gain as much mileage as possible out of the revolt. Although Judaism was at no stage outlawed, it was certainly not a good time to boast about being a Judaean Jew in Rome.[13]

All of these significant developments in the interpretation of Josephus associated with the second school of thought have resulted in shifting his positioning on the spectrum. He stands in the middle between the two extremes.[14] His ideal political realm may not have included foreigners. Yet Josephus was a realist and he accepted that coexistence with Rome was possible and permissible. Proof of this outlook is derived from his social circumstances and his own hand. As a provincial aristocrat Josephus had much to gain from cooperating with the Romans. To oppose Rome would be to oppose the source from which he stood to prosper.[15] Even more telling, the content of *Jewish War* displayed his astute assessment of the situation. The depiction of various people, especially in terms of the speeches associated with several characters and the details provided regarding events, are seen as pointing toward the view that Roman rule was acceptable.

A persistent thorn in the side to the view that Josephus was a realist regarding the dominance of Rome is his involvement in the revolt. On face value, Josephus was on the side of the rebel cause at the beginning of the war. He accepted a commission that took him to Galilee, where he fought against the Romans until his capture at the siege of Jotapata.[16] Why would Josephus go to war against the Romans if, as an aristocrat, he knew

12. See H. Fearnley, 'Reading the Imperial Revolution: Martial *Epigrams* 10' in A.J. Boyle and W.J. Dominik (eds), *Flavian Rome* (Leiden: Brill, 2003), 613–35 and Mason, 'Flavius Josephus in Flavian Rome', 561–65.

13. See Spilsbury, 'Flavius Josephus', 1–3. The public dislike for Titus's association with Berenice is also suggestive of the Roman suspicion of the Jews from the East.

14. For example, see the approach taken by F.W. Walbank, '"Treason" and Roman Domination: Two Case-Studies, Polybius and Josephus' in F.W. Walbank, *Polybius, Rome and the Hellenistic World: Essays and Reflections* (Cambridge: Cambridge University Press, 2002), 258–76 and T. Rajak, 'Friends, Romans, Subjects: Agrippa II's Speech in Josephus' *Jewish War*' in T. Rajak, *The Jewish Dialogue with Greece and Rome. Studies in Cultural and Social Interaction* (Leiden: Brill, 2001), 147–58.

15. See P.A. Brunt, 'The Romanization of the Local Ruling Class in the Roman Empire' in P.A. Brunt, *Roman Imperial Themes* (Oxford: Clarendon Press, 1990), 267–81.

16. The account in *Life* (esp. 17–23, 27–8) is often cited as helping explain the narrative in *Jewish War*. See S. Mason, *Flavius Josephus. Translation and Commentary. Volume 9. Life of Josephus* (Leiden: Brill, 2001), xliv–vi, 29–33, who seeks to understand the way Josephus portrays his actions as mirroring the advice on statecraft offered by Plutarch.

the revolt was doomed and he believed that the Romans had been divinely sanctioned to rule the world now? Much effort has been devoted to providing a solution to this problem. It has even resulted in a level of altruism being attached to his course of action. He, and other aristocrats, advocated a 'moderate' path. Once war began they saw their role as leaders of the community as requiring that they remain in Jerusalem and seek to bring the conflict to a peaceful resolution as soon as was possible. As realists they knew Rome would win and that it was crucial the victory did not exact a heavy toll on the Jews.

2.2 *Mocking Rome in* Jewish War: *Treading with Care*

There is a further solution to why Josephus was involved in the revolt and yet also able later to write of living with Rome as a viable option for dealing with the reality of the defeat. This third approach to understanding Josephus's attitude regarding Rome builds upon the increasing attention paid to the way he presents Rome's dominance as a temporary situation. The key component of this approach is the positioning of Josephus at the outbreak of the war as an active supporter of the decision to break away from Roman rule.[17] What underpinned this course of action was a belief that God would help to ensure the establishment of an independent state. Josephus, however, soon found himself faced with the stark choice between either capture and probable death in some public display, or finding a way of coming to terms with Roman rule and, hopefully, securing his own fate in the process. For Josephus this was achieved by a radical shift in his thinking about whom God favoured. Divine support now resided with Rome. This view was a legitimate way for him to explain what had happened and yet retain some sense of credence for the principles of his faith tradition. It was his sudden exposure to the threat of death at Jotapata that forced Josephus to reassess what was happening. Choosing to live for another day, he began the process of adjusting his articulation of the principle that God was all-powerful. The accommodation that resulted, however, should not be regarded as a radical change of mind. Josephus retained the same outlook regarding God's control of world events throughout his life. What did change, in a very radical way, was his understanding of how God went about controlling what happened. In 66 CE Josephus believed God would help the rebels break free from Roman rule. By early 67 CE he probably began to realize that all was not going according to plan. By late 70 CE he

---

17. See J.S. McLaren, 'The Coinage of the First Year as a Point of Reference for the Jewish Revolt (66–70 CE)', *SCI* 22 (2003) 135–52. For Josephus as a rebel, see H. Drexler, 'Untersuchungen zu Josephus und zur Geschichte des jüdischen Aufstandes', *Klio* 19 (1925), 277–312.

knew that God had decided to act in an entirely different manner to that
he had hoped for back in 66 CE. At the moment of his capture Josephus
took the first explicit step to respond to this new understanding of what
was happening. His literary output while residing in Rome under imperial
patronage exhibited a further extension of this reorientation. However, at
no stage did this reorientation amount to a willing acceptance of Rome as
the dominant world power. Josephus's realism was learnt through hard
experience; he was never predisposed to such a line of thinking.

This reading of Josephus necessitates an alternative explanation of the
two assumptions underpinning the existing schools of thought: the
aristocracy favoured Rome because of the material benefits; and the way
the content of *Jewish War* should be read. We commence with the claim
that Josephus's aristocratic origins provide a natural leaning toward
accepting Roman rule, which is associated primarily with the second
school of thought. It is safe to state that aristocrats stood to gain the most
of any local group within a province from the imposition of Roman rule.
Local leaders were regularly sought to act in the interests of Rome, and
Judea was no exception to this approach. Wealthy members of the
priesthood, generally identified by the label 'chief priests', and members of
the Herodian family are mentioned by Josephus as intermediaries between
the Roman officials and the local population. In a conflict between Rome
and a given province the aristocracy would appear to have much to lose
by siding with any armed opposition to Roman rule. The onus was on the
aristocrats favoured by Rome to help keep the peace.

However, the dynamic of the relationship between members of a local
aristocracy and the Roman rulers is not so straightforward. The study by
S. Dyson of several native revolts from the late republican and early
imperial period suggests that we should avoid trying to cast the situation
in such black-and-white terms.[18] Dyson shows that at least some members
of the native aristocracy were willing to reject Roman rule. Although
heavily edited, the narrative of Josephus regarding the events of 66 CE also
depicts a similar situation: some aristocrats opposed war while others
were at the forefront of instigating the move to independence.[19] Whatever
the exact timing of such people as Ananus, Jesus and Josephus becoming
involved in the conflict, Eleazar bar Ananias, the son of an ex-high priest,
took a leading part in starting the revolt, although his father and uncle
actively argued against such a move. When an outsider, Menahem, tried

18. S.L. Dyson, 'Native Revolts in the Roman Empire', *Historia* 20 (1971), 239–74.
19. See M.D. Goodman, *The Ruling Class of Judaea. The Origins of the Jewish Revolt
against Rome AD 66–70* (Cambridge: Cambridge University Press, 1987), 152–75; J.J. Price,
Jerusalem under Siege: the Collapse of the Jewish State, 66–70 CE (Leiden: Brill, 1992), 1–59
and J.S. McLaren, *Power and Politics in Palestine. The Jews and the Governing of their Land,
100 BC–AD 70* (Sheffield: Sheffield Academic Press, 1991), 172–84.

to seize control of the revolt he was quickly disposed of and his followers dispersed. Pedigree appears to have been among the criteria for leadership, according to Josephus. It is not a case of trying to claim that all aristocrats favoured taking up arms against Rome. Rather, in line with what has been argued by Dyson regarding a number of major revolts in other parts of the empire, it was possible for some aristocrats in Judea to opt for rebellion and to take a leading role in armed opposition to Rome. It is not simply the case that because Josephus was an aristocrat he automatically favoured a policy of accepting Roman rule, no matter what the particular circumstances of Judea in the early 60s CE.

We turn to the other main argument: the nature of the actual content of *Jewish War*. Here the context in which the text was written is all important. Although there are no other extant contemporary Jewish accounts, we know Josephus was not the only Jewish person to write about the conflict. If we can place any credence in the claims he makes in the preface to *Jewish War*, other non-Jewish accounts were also in existence.[20] The context we need to bear in mind is the city of Rome, where Flavian claims of a great military success were being readily asserted and where explicit criticism of the regime was not a viable option.[21]

Space does not allow a detailed discussion of the entire text. Instead, the focus will be on the four major components of *Jewish War* that regularly feature as the supposed indicators of Josephus's ready acceptance of Roman rule (if not his open support of the Flavians). Although interconnected, each one will be addressed in turn and it will be shown how they can all be read as a slight on claims being made by the new rulers of Rome rather than as an attempt to display acceptance and/or compliance. The first is the lengthy speeches of Agrippa II (*War* 2.345–401), Titus (*War* 6.33–53, 327–50), Josephus (*War* 5.362–419; 6.96–110) and Eleazar bar Jairus (*War* 7.323–36, 341–88).

It is universally agreed that Agrippa II's long speech gives voice to Josephus's own views about the futility of the revolt. The might of Rome is displayed by the long list of peoples conquered by the Romans. At the heart of Agrippa II's explanation for why the revolt will fail is the claim

---

20. The prime known example is that of Justus of Tiberias (*Life*, 336–7).

21. Of particular significance is the dedication on the original arch of Titus in the Circus Maximus (*CIL* VI.944). The key part of the inscription reads: 'with the guidance of his father and under his auspices, he [Titus] subdued the Jewish people and destroyed the city of Jerusalem, which all generals and kings of other people before him had either attacked without success or left entirely untried'. Note also the allusions to the victory in the contemporary poets Valerius Flaccus, *Arg.* 1.10–12 and Silius Italicus, *Punica* 3.599–606. Clearly, grand claims were being made about the nature of the military success achieved against the Jews.

that God's favour lies with the Romans.[22] This theme also underpins the other major speeches delivered in *Jewish War*. The revolt will fail because God has decreed that Rome will triumph. According to Josephus, it is not because of anything positive the Romans have done to win God's approval. Rather, God is punishing the Jews for their own iniquities. The Romans are agents of divine retribution. Editorial comments made throughout the narrative help reinforce this explanation of the disaster that befell the Jews (*War* 5.11–20).

There is no doubt that this theme of divine favour now residing with Rome could help Josephus and his fellow Jews learn to cope with the reality of life. However, it is equally important that this theme is understood in the context of Flavian claims regarding the war. As Titus boasts of how he was the first to subdue the Jews, Josephus makes the victory a rather hollow one. It was faction, famine and the Romans, under divine control, that brought about the destruction of Jerusalem. Josephus could not afford openly to dispute any claims to success. He could, however, provide those who took the time to read the detail of the account an explanation for what happened that reduced the Romans to the role of a divine instrument. Choice lay with the Jews in terms of how they behaved in their relationship with God, never with the Romans. The central role allocated to the theme indicates that it constitutes a rather barbed compliment to the Flavian claims to success.

The second prominent component is the digression on the Roman army (*War* 3.70–109). Josephus justifies the length of this account in part as an attempt to console those conquered by the Romans and to deter others from rebelling (*War* 3.108). Here he appears to recognize the foolishness of opposing Rome. Again, caution is more than warranted. The core theme of the account is the extent of Roman order and strict discipline. It pervades training, marching and the positioning of the camps and the division of labour within the camps. Such is the extent of order that by the time the battlefield has been reached the result of the engagement is a foregone conclusion.[23]

Taken in isolation, this reads as praise of Roman military might. The main problem, and it is quite a substantial one, is that the description of the fighting in Galilee and Jerusalem casts the Roman troops in a very different light. Nowhere is this more evident than at the very moment when Roman order and discipline should be on full view: during the

---

22. M. Stern, 'Josephus and the Roman Empire as Reflected in *The Jewish War*' in L.H. Feldman and G. Hata (eds), *Josephus, Judaism, and Christianity* (Detroit, MI: Wayne State University, 1987), 71–80 and Rajak, 'Friends, Romans', 152–7 argue that the speech is far from glowing in its comments about Roman rule.

23. This concern to highlight Roman order is also flagged in the preface (*War* 1.21) and is noted as a characteristic of the Roman soldiers in battle (*War* 4.45–6). See B.D. Shaw, 'Josephus: Roman Power and Responses to it', *Athenaeum* 83 (1995), 372–7.

assault on the Temple. Josephus goes so far as to provide a detailed account of the background to the order that the Temple was not to be destroyed. However, his description of what follows completely contradicts the claims of Roman order. The troops disobey the orders and set fire to the Temple. They act in direct defiance of Titus's personally issued orders, even as he apparently stands among them on the Temple mount (*War* 6.254–66).[24] A further slight on the claim that Roman discipline and order was all-important is a key theme embedded in all the main speeches: it was God who decided what would happen. This undermines the relevance of Roman discipline in deciding the outcome of the conflict. As such, the praise offered about Roman order is directly contradicted by the description of the conflict and the explanation of its resolution.

The third component is the portrait of Titus. There is much overlap here with the discussion of Roman discipline, or lack of it, in the fighting. There is an overwhelming consensus that Josephus has provided a very complimentary picture of Titus. Indeed, he is the subject of far more discussion than his father. His courage and bravery in battle and his clemency, especially in regard to the Temple, are often cited as evidence of Josephus's desire to enhance the image of Titus.[25] However, we should not be so eager to view all this as a compliment. As noted above regarding the Temple, Titus was presented as not able to control his troops. In a similar vein, his personal intervention to save the Tenth Legion from assault at the beginning of the siege would not have been necessary if due caution had been taken regarding their initial deployment (*War* 5.70–97). It is also questionable as to whether it was appropriate for the commander-in-chief to engage in battle. Writing some twenty years before Josephus, Onasander stated that the commander needed to be in a position where he could oversee the battle, but should never be entangled in the fighting (*Strat.* 33.6).[26] Furthermore, however much Josephus has Titus declare his alleged desire to save the Temple, it does not happen. The apparent concern to display clemency is also contradicted by Titus's willingness to allow the city to be destroyed (*War* 6.353–4; 7.1–4). Yes, Titus is prominent in the text, but he is not held in high esteem.

The fourth component to consider is the nature of the connection between Josephus's version of the war and the Flavian family. Josephus claims that Vespasian and Titus gave their approval for the account.

---

24. The reference to the troops being overwhelmed by a supernatural force can also be read as an allusion to God being in charge of the situation.

25. B.W. Jones, 'The Reckless Titus', in C. Deroux (ed.), *Studies in Latin Literature and Roman History VI* (Brussels: Latomus, 1992), 408–20 presumes that Josephus was trying to present a positive portrait of Titus but that he was struggling to make the young military figure look good from what took place in Judea.

26. See A. Goldsworthy, *The Roman Army at War, 100 BC–AD 200* (Oxford: Oxford University Press, 1996) for a detailed discussion of the role of the commander in battle.

There are, however, several problems with this supposed imprimatur. In *Apion* 1.50 and *Life* 361 Josephus states that he willingly presented a copy of the text to Vespasian and Titus after it had been written, apparently in order to vouch for the accuracy of the account. Further on, in *Life* 363, Josephus then says Titus declared that the account should be accepted as the official one and had commanded its publication. The proof Josephus then provides that he had openly shared his account with others comes in the form of quoting several letters from Agrippa II (*Life* 365–6). This is not a simple case of Josephus writing a commissioned work, or of either Vespasian or Titus reading the entire text. If anything, it is possible Josephus showed selections to Vespasian and/or Titus, as was his implied practice with Agrippa II from the letters quoted.

On an even more fundamental level, caution is warranted regarding the accuracy of the claims about imperial approval. Josephus makes no mention of such approval in the preface to *Jewish War* where he attacks the lack of accuracy of other accounts. It is only in texts which post-date the lives of Vespasian and Titus that such claims of approval are made. Given what Josephus has to say about Justus choosing not to publish his work at an earlier date (*Life* 359), it is rather contradictory of him not to mention the alleged imperial stamp of approval in *Jewish War*. The location of the reference to the imperial viewing in *Apion* and *Life* is also cause for concern. Josephus's focus is an assault on other writers in order to defend his integrity. He attacks their accuracy and/or unwillingness to write while the key figures in the conflict were still alive (*Apion* 1.44–6; *Life* 357–60). There is no reason to see Josephus as being beyond reproach when it came to the idea of adding, deleting and altering material in order to defend himself. As it stands, the claim of imperial approval made by Josephus can be seen as no more than an attempt, long after the event, to defend his credibility. It is possible that he submitted selected passages for Vespasian and/or Titus to sample. More likely, however, Josephus added the reference to imperial readership having never submitted his text for approval.[27]

All of the key elements of *Jewish War* that are proposed as evidence that the text was an apology for Roman rule can be read as a criticism of Rome, while the claim of imperial approval is extremely dubious. Broadening the scope, it is apparent that two further aspects of *Jewish War* help to reinforce the argument that Josephus deliberately set out to counter claims of Roman greatness and that he actually held the Romans in disdain. One is the lengthy summary of the Roman governors in *Jewish*

---

27. Josephus's motivation for claiming imperial approval is probably best explained in terms of the nature of Justus', criticism and as part of a counter-claim that he, not Justus, was the well-connected author. Most of Josephus's focus lies on trying to place himself in close proximity with Agrippa II while distancing Justus from him (*Life*, 354–6, 358–67).

War 2. The other is the choice of subject matter at the beginning and the end of the narrative.

It has often been noted that Josephus cites the actions, and/or lack of action, by some governors as a factor in the build-up to the outbreak of war. At no stage does Josephus openly criticize the system of provincial administration as such in his account. There are even examples of what appear to be good administrators, like the legate Petronius. However, given that the focus of *Jewish War* was on the actual revolt and the capture of Jerusalem, there is no obvious explanation as to why so much attention is given to describing the years of direct Roman rule. In fact, by allocating blame to the poor standard of administration by some governors Josephus detracts attention from the supposed unrepresentative Jewish rebels and tyrants who are intended to act as the prime stimulus for God to punish the Jews. A possible explanation for Josephus's allowing attention to be drawn away from this theme of divine punishment lies in his apparent distaste for the provincial system. A brief statement about provincial administration is put into the mouth of Tiberius (*Ant.* 18.174–6). In explaining why he allowed governors to remain in office for so long, Tiberius compared them with parasites feeding off the blood of a wounded person. Removing the old parasites who had taken their fill would only expose the wounded person to yet more parasites hungry for blood.[28] Such a negative depiction of provincial rule is softened by having the emperor make the proclamation. Josephus could never make this sort of statement himself. However, it could easily reflect his underlying opinion of what life had been like in Judea under Roman rule.

The other indication of Josephus's antagonism toward Rome is the choice he makes for the beginning and the ending of the narrative. The first event described in *Jewish War* is the assault on Jerusalem by Antiochus IV, and his desecration of the Temple. The account, therefore, commences with an outrage against the Jews and immediately moves on to how retribution was exacted. At the end of *Jewish War* Josephus describes the destruction of the Temple at Leontopolis (*War* 7.420–36). Among the background information about the origin of the Temple Josephus makes reference to how Ptolemy willingly supported its construction (*War* 7.426–30). In stark contrast, the unnamed emperor (*War* 7.421) was suspicious of the Jews and ordered its closure. Josephus then concludes the text with an account of what happened to Catullus, the governor of Libya. Apparently eager to gain renown by attacking the Jews (*War* 7.443) he became embroiled in making accusations against many Jews, including Josephus (*War* 7.447–50). Josephus and the others falsely accused are saved by Vespasian and Titus (*War* 7.450). Catullus then

---

28. On the long term of office for some governors see also Tacitus, *Annals* 1.80 and Suetonius, *Tiberius* 41.

receives a reprimand from the emperors. However, their authority is superseded by what follows. Josephus claims Catullus suffered a terminal illness as a punishment inflicted by God. Although Vespasian and Titus intervene to help Josephus, their manner of resolving the incident is far from satisfactory in the light of what Josephus goes on to say. Ultimately it is God who has control and will ensure that the wicked are punished. By noting that Catullus received his just punishment, it is possible Josephus is leaving open the idea that those who took action against the Temple would also be punished in due course, just as Antiochus IV suffered when he abused the Temple.[29]

2.3 *Conclusion*

The primary focus of *Jewish War* is Josephus seeking to make sense of what had happened in 66–70 CE, on a personal and communal level. The text defends his actions and those of his colleagues. In the process of fulfilling these goals Josephus outlines a view that accepts the reality of Roman rule. Clearly, it is not a text calling for open rebellion, nor overtly attacking the Romans. Such a project would be senseless. The revolt had been quashed and he would have become a target for punishment if he explicitly portrayed the Flavians as criminals. However, Josephus's acceptance of Roman rule was neither unconditional nor necessarily his preferred option.

In 66 CE Josephus stood alongside Eleazar bar Ananias and all the other priests who boldly declared their independence from Rome. He went to Galilee, to the front-line, as an active rebel leader. At Jotapata he came face to face with the military power of Rome. All of a sudden God was not there. Josephus was faced with a crucial choice: fight to the death or surrender and risk the humiliation of probable execution in subsequent victory celebrations. At that moment Josephus began the process of compromise. Exactly how he managed to save himself is not clear. Providing logistical information about Jerusalem and its defences is possibly part of the explanation. The key point is how he was about to justify the shift from outright rejection of Rome to acceptance of the ongoing reality of Roman rule. Here his cultural heritage was all-important. His acceptance of defeat and the need to live with Rome was possible because of his continued belief in the omnipotence of God.[30] At the outset of the revolt victory was deemed possible because of a belief

---

29. A subsidiary theme in these two connected stories is the destructive role played by certain Jews who draw on foreign aid to help resolve intra-Jewish issues. In this context Onias and Jonathan are the subject of Josephus's criticism.

30. It is likely that at least a degree of self-preservation was involved in the practical decisions Josephus made.

that he and other rebels were acting as agents of God. Defeat was now to be tolerated because the same God had decided to punish the Jews. Any notion of pacifism, at least in terms of accepting defeat, was something Josephus acquired through experience.[31] Rome was never a friend. It held dominion now but it too would one day lose that power. Any claims to greatness being proclaimed by the Flavians drew a veiled criticism from Josephus that was to run through all his texts.

Such a reading of *Jewish War* and Josephus's circumstances leaves open the notion of a person not entirely happy with the way things had worked out. It has been observed that the presentation of Eleazar bar Jairus in his efforts to convince those with him to die rather than surrender at Masada is somewhat favourable.[32] It marks an unusual end to the conflict between Jews and Romans in Judea, as it is a hollow victory for Rome. Furthermore, it is in stark contrast to the way Josephus behaves when confronted by likely capture and death at Jotapata. From the preceding discussion it is apparent that denying Rome and its rulers the honour for the victory was not a problem for Josephus: a choice made by God was the reason that Rome was victorious. What remains puzzling is the conviction of Eleazar, as depicted by Josephus, to see his chosen course of action through to the bitter end. It is just possible that Josephus decided to create a hero, a character who could do what he thought he himself should have done several years before: namely to see through his conviction of rejecting Rome even to the point of death.

31. The Josephus who lived in Rome learnt to say the words he put into the mouth of David: 'It is not a terrible thing to serve even a foreign master, if God so wills' (*Ant.* 7.373).

32. See, for example, T. Rajak, 'Dying for the Law: The Martyr's Portrait in Jewish–Greek Literature' in T. Rajak, *The Jewish Dialogue with Greece and Rome. Studies in Cultural and Social Interaction* (Leiden: Brill, 2001), 99–133 at 125 and S.J.D. Cohen, 'Masada: Literary Tradition, Archaeological Remains, and the Credibility of Josephus', JJS 33 (1982), 385–405; cf. D.J. Ladouceur, 'Josephus and Masada' in L.H. Feldman and G. Hata (eds), *Josephus, Judaism, and Christianity* (Detroit, MI: Wayne State University, 1987), 95–113.

Empire: Theories, Methods, Models

Dennis C. Duling

3.1 *Empire*

'Empire is back in fashion!' So writes political scientist Alexander J. Motyl of Rutgers University.[1] To be sure, there has been continual interest in empires on the part of historians, archaeologists, anthropologists and international relations theorists. However, with the possible exception of Michael Doyle's work,[2] empire as *political system* has been largely ignored.[3] It is hard to define, it fits research agendas awkwardly, and it has had less appeal in the wake of pressing post-colonial tasks.

The tendency to ignore empires as political systems, however, is changing. One reason is the end of the Cold War and the collapse of the Soviet Union, now often regarded as an empire. Another is '9/11' (2001), the attack on the World Trade Center, a place that for many people symbolized US imperialism. The association of the United States with empire is also found among US allies. A British journal article published in 2003 was entitled 'The Last Emperor'. Its author had in mind the US President. She described his post-'9/11' speech to the United Nations in terms of a powerful Roman emperor lecturing a relatively impotent Roman Senate.[4] Whatever one thinks about such views, it is clear that 'empire is back in fashion!'

Scholarly interest in empire is also apparent in the recent academic

---

1. *Imperial Ends. The Decay, Collapse, and Revival of Empires* (New York: Columbia University Press, 2001), 1.

2. *Empires* (Ithaca, NY: Cornell University Press, 1987).

3. For a brief empire bibliography, see Dimitris Kottaridis, 'Empires: A Comparative Study in a World Context' *http://www.whc.neu.edu/whc/gradstudy/bibliograd/themes/KottaridisD.html* (accessed 20/July/03).

4. P. Toynbee, 'The Last Emperor', *Guardian Unlimited*, 13 September 2002, in reference to President Bush's speech before the United Nations (*http://www.guardian.co.uk/Iraq/Story/0,2763,791347,00.html* (accessed 21/July/03).

study of religion. Richard Horsley has edited *Paul and Empire* (1997)[5] and written *Jesus and Empire* (2003)[6] and *Religion and Empire* (2003);[7] Peter Oakes has edited *Rome in the Bible and the Early Church* (2002);[8] and Warren Carter has published *Matthew and Empire* (2001).[9] Many articles on empire have appeared and the Matthew section of the Society of Biblical Literature held a paper/panel session on Matthew and Empire at Atlanta in 2003.[10]

In the wake of newfound interest, I focus this chapter on definitions of empires, theories of their origins, models of their social stratification, models of their imperialistic goals, models of how they affect the peasant strata, and a view of the ethnocentric and ideological perspectives of imperialists.[11] I shall do so with the hope of clarifying the Roman Empire as the context for the Gospel of Matthew and thereby of laying a general foundation for more specific studies to follow.[12]

5.   *Paul and Empire. Religion and Power in Roman Imperial Society* (Harrisburg, IL: Trinity Press International, 1997).

6.   *Jesus and Empire. The Kingdom of God and the New World Disorder* (Minneapolis, MW: Fortress, 2003).

7.   *Religion and Empire. People, Power, and the Life of the Spirit* (Minneapolis, MN: Fortress, 2003).

8.   *Rome in the Bible and the Early* Church (Carlisle: Paternoster, 2002).

9.   *Matthew and Empire: Initial Explorations* (Harrisburg, IL: Trinity Press International, 2001). See also L. Thompson, *The Book of Revelation: Apocalypse and Empire* (Oxford: Oxford University Press, 1990).

10.   Papers were by Dorothy Jean Weaver, John Riches, Warren Carter and Dennis Duling, with a response by Steve Friesen.

11.   It is acknowledged that historical critics and social-scientific critics have not always agreed on how to approach their common subject matter. This debate is documented by P. Burke, *History and Social Theory* (Ithaca, NY: Cornell University Press, 2nd edn 1993). Some Postmodernists have criticized both historical and social-scientific approaches; see for example F.W. Burnett, 'Historiography' in A.K.M. Adam (ed.), *Handbook of Postmodern Biblical Interpretation* (St Louis: Chalice Press, 2000), 106–12. My own position is found in D.C. Duling, 'Matthew 18.15–17: Conflict, Confrontation, and Conflict Resolution in a "Fictive Kin" Association', *BTB* 29 (1999), 4–6. A very illuminating discussion is G.G. Iggers, *Historiography in the Twentieth Century: From Scientific Objectivity to the Postmodern Challenge* (London: Wesleyan University Press, 1997). In general I agree with M.I. Finley, *Ancient History: Evidence and Models* (London: Pimlico, 2000), 66; T.F. Carney, *The Shape of the Past. Models and Antiquity* (Lawrence: Coronado Press, 1975); and B.J. Malina, *The New Testament World: Insights from Cultural Anthropology* (Atlanta, GA: John Knox, 3rd edn 2001) on the importance of models and the need for their clarification.

12.   I would like to thank members of the Society of Biblical Literature and the Context Group for their comments, and especially Prof. Ronald Piper of St Andrews University, who wrote an excellent critique of an earlier version of this paper.

3.2 Definitions

The *Oxford English Dictionary* traces the English term 'empire' to the Latin *imperium*, which is based on the verb *imperare*, 'to command'. During the Roman Republic the victorious Roman army acclaimed its commanding general *imperator* on the field of battle. Thus, the English term 'empire' suggests military authority. Correspondingly, the *OED* defines 'empire' as 'an extensive territory (*esp.* an aggregate of many separate states) under the sway of an emperor or supreme ruler' who 'owe(s) no allegiance to any foreign superior'.[13]

Modern empire theorists' definitions are similar.[14] Ronald Grigor Suny defines empire as a 'particular form of domination or control, between two units set apart in a hierarchical, inequitable relationship'.[15] Michael W. Doyle also emphasizes control: 'a relationship, formal or informal, in which one state controls the effective political sovereignty of another political society'.[16] So does George Lichtheim: the 'relationship of a hegemonial state to peoples or nations under its control'.[17] Geir Lendesta says that 'empire simply means a hierarchical system of political relationships with one power being much stronger than any other'.[18]

These definitions express or imply a vertical structure, a pyramid, a hierarchical system in which one absolute authority at the apex dominates and controls all other units. They also imply horizontal extension of power, that is, control of other subordinate polities.

3.3 The Emergence of Empires

3.3.1 Hydraulic societies and oriental despotism

One of the most famous classical views of empire is Sinologist Karl Wittfogel's theory that the great historical empires emerged because they were technologically superior to their neighbours.[19] For Wittfogel, the key technological innovations were large-scale waterworks developed to irrigate large dry, but potentially fruitful, tracts of land. Irrigation made

---

13. *Oxford English Dictionary* (Oxford: Clarendon Press, 2nd edn 1969), Vol. V, 187–8; see also 'emperor', 187; 'imperial', Vol. VII, 710–12.

14. See Motyl, *Imperial Ends*, 125–6, n. 27, for the following definitions and their sources.

15. 'The Empire Strikes Out: Russia, the Soviet Union, and Theories of Empire', an academic paper discussed at the conference 'Empires and Nations: The Soviet Union and the Non-Russian Peoples' (University of Chicago, 24–26 October 1997), 5.

16. *Empires*, 45.

17. *Imperialism* (New York: Praeger, 1971), 5.

18. *The American 'Empire'* (Oslo: Norwegian University Press, 1990), 37.

19. *Oriental Despotism. A Comparative Study of Total Power* (New Haven, CT: Yale University Press, 1957). See G. Taylor, 'Karl A. Wittfogel', *International Encyclopedia of the Social Sciences Volume 18* (London: Collier, 1979), 812.

possible an increased supply of food, a larger population, cities and towns, a military establishment, increased trade, specialization and commerce. Wittfogel called societies based on irrigation 'hydraulic societies'. He thought that such societies developed large, centralized, absolutist, hierarchical bureaucracies and that they exploited lower social strata. Most of Wittfogel's hydraulic societies were from the East – China, India, Mesopotamia, Egypt; and so, following Marx, who had British predecessors such as J.S. Mill, Wittfogel referred to an 'Asiatic mode of production'. Montesquieu had defined 'despotism' as rule by a single authority based on fear and brutality.[20] Wittfogel termed the combination of oppressive, fear-based rule and the Asiatic mode of production 'Oriental Despotism'. He argued that the Romans inherited Oriental Despotism from the Greeks and Egyptians: '*Hellenization means Orientalization ...*'[21] When the Roman Empire replaced the Republic, a despotic emperor and his retainers replaced the landowning aristocracy. In short, Wittfogel believed that imperial Rome should be aligned with the great hydraulic, agro-managerial, despotic absolutisms of the East.

3.3.2 *The very delicate balance*

Wittfogel had his critics, in part because Rome did not rely directly on irrigation systems. An alternative classic view is associated with S.N. Eisenstadt,[22] who showed how 'centralized historical bureaucratic empires' evolved from simpler political systems.[23] He argued that when a 'feudal system'[24] has fallen into social chaos, a strong ruler or conqueror, normally from the elite strata, surfaces to rescue it. The new ruler must check his political opponents, establish peace and order, achieve political unity, and strive for territorial expansion.[25] Most important, the emperor attempts to establish the political sphere as discrete and autonomous. To do so he must weaken political ties to, and ideologies of, traditional 'ascriptive' groups based on kinship, clan, territory and religion.[26] This task is not easy. Even if a new empire is legitimated by charismatic leadership, those who hold traditional, sacred values *expect* hereditary rule. The result is paradoxical tension. Thus,

---

20. *Spirit of the Laws* VI.
21. *Oriental Despotism*, 211–12.
22. *The Political Systems of Empires: The Rise and Fall of the Historical Bureaucratic Societies* (Glencoe: Free Press, 1963); 'Introduction' in *Decline of Empires* (Englewood Cliffs, NJ: Prentice Hall, 1967); 'Processes of Change and Institutionalization of the Political Systems of Centralized Empires' in G. Zollschan and W. Hirsch (eds), *Exploration in Social Change* (Boston, MA: Houghton Mifflin, 1964), 432–51.
23. *The Political Systems of Empires*, 11.
24. He calls the simpler forms 'patrimonial empires' and 'feudal systems'.
25. *The Political Systems of Empires*, 3, 13–18.
26. *The Political Systems of Empires*, 19.

centralized historical bureaucratic empires develop only *some* political/ administrative autonomy and *some* centralization; traditional, ascriptive political forms persist. To survive, the ruler must maintain a 'very delicate balance' between the new supportive bureaucracy and traditional oppositional groups – all in a context of political apathy on the part of the masses. 'It was only insofar as the ruler could maintain such a balance that the political system he instituted could prevail.'[27]

Eisenstadt's 'very delicate balance' offers a clue to understanding the Roman Empire. When Roman conquests put stress on the Republic, the Romans looked to their military leaders to rescue them and they brought with them a strong, centralized, bureaucratic rule. The political intrigues and assassinations of first-century CE Rome illustrate the resistance of the old aristocracy to the new imperial order and indicate accommodation to traditional ascriptive groups. Provincial administration in the gospel stories illustrates certain accommodations to traditional ascriptive groups as well.

3.3.3 *Advanced agrarian societies*

A third theory about the emergence of empires is suggested by Gerhard Lenski.[28] Influenced by Marxist theorists,[29] Lenski also stresses technological innovation, that is, that agrarian societies emerged at the time of the harnessing of wind, water and animal power, and the inventions of the wheel, the alphabet and writing, and the calendar (late fourth millennium BCE). Most important, however, was the plough, which made possible greater agricultural production, and thus agrarian societies. Lenski then argues that the *iron-tipped* plough led to more complex, '*advanced agrarian societies*' (second millennium BCE).[30] Economically there was more division of labour, expansion in business and increased commerce. Politically, urban ruling strata needed large bureaucracies and military establishments and exploited peasants. With respect to kinship the family lost some of its importance as more complex social organization developed. In religion, theocracy waned and local cults were often integrated into the ideology of the empire; magic and fatalism increased.

27. *The Decline of Empires*, 4.

28. G. Lenski, *Power and Privilege: A Theory of Social Stratification* (New York: McGraw-Hill, 1966), 49, 54–5, 81, 84, 158–9; P. Nolan and G. Lenski, *Human Societies: An Introduction to Macrosociology* (Boston, MA: McGraw Hill, 8th edn 1998), 153–95; 'Rethinking Macrosociological Theory', *American Sociological Review* 53 (1988), 163–71; 'Societal Taxonomies: Mapping the Social Universe', *Annual Review of Sociology* 20 (1994), 1–26.

29. V.G. Childe (see D.R. Harris [ed.], *The Archaeology of V. Gordon Childe: Contemporary Perspectives* [Chicago, IL: University of Chicago Press, 1994]) and Walter Goldschmidt, for whom see *http://www.mnsu.edu/emuseum/information/biography/fghij/goldschmidt_walter.html* (accessed 12/02/04).

30. *Human Societies*, 194.

3.4 *The Vertical Dimension*

Lenski's model accents sharp vertical social stratification.

This model implies that those who successfully compete for control of the growing agricultural surplus gradually grow in political and economic power, privilege and prestige. These are Lenski's three main criteria for vertical social ranking. The highest social stratum consists of rulers; beneath them are other governing strata and their 'retainers', that is, those who serve them. Still lower are merchants, peasants and artisans. At the bottom are the 'expendables', such as bandits and prostitutes. The dotted line (added) illustrates the very great gap between the upper stratum and the lower strata; the width-line at the bottom hints at the relative size of the strata.

Lenski is well aware that his macro-model oversimplifies;[31] in reality people rank each other in a variety of ways, such as family, gender, ethnicity and education. Lenski calls these various ways of ranking 'class systems'[32] and they contain more variables, for example, contexts for ranking ('weight'), social distance between the upper and the lower classes ('span'), and relation to the whole social system ('shape'). Lenski calls all the variables taken together the 'distributive system', and he constructs a hypothetical model of a Latin American society to illustrate it, which I have elsewhere revised for the Roman Empire.[33]

I would add that social ranking varies from time to time (a historical factor) and place to place (a local factor), and that variables such as self- and other-identity, that is, ranking *other* peoples ethnocentrically, must be taken into consideration. It is also the case that when an individual perceives that his or her ranking in a society is relatively high in one class system and relatively low in another – for example, in actual versus fictive kin relations – 'status dissonance' can result. This is a recurring feature in marginality.[34] To be complete an analyst would have to plot each of the 'class systems' from these different perspectives: a daunting, if not impossible, task. Hence, there is a tendency to retreat to the macro-model,

31. It is an outside observer's constructed model (an etic model), not a native person's usually implicit model (an emic model); it highlights representative parts of a structure (a 'homomorphic' model), not the whole structure in detail (an 'isomorphic' model). See J.H. Elliott, 'Social-Scientific Criticism of the New Testament: More on Methods and Models', in J.H. Elliott (ed.), *Semeia 35. Social-Scientific Criticism of the New Testament and its Social World* (Decatur: Scholars Press, 1986), 1–33; Malina, *The New Testament World*.

32. *Power and Privilege*, 75, 78. For an analytical discussion of the terms social 'class' as contrasted with social 'stratum', see R.L. Rohrbaugh, 'Methodological Considerations in the Debate over the Social Class Status of Early Christians', *JAAR* 52 (1984), 519–46.

33. Lenski, *Power and Privilege*, 82; for the Roman Empire, see D.C. Duling, 'Matthew as Marginal Scribe in an Advanced Agrarian Society', *HTS* 58 (2002), 530.

34. Duling, 'Matthew and Marginality', *HTS* 51 (1995), 1–30; 'Matthew as a Marginal Scribe'.

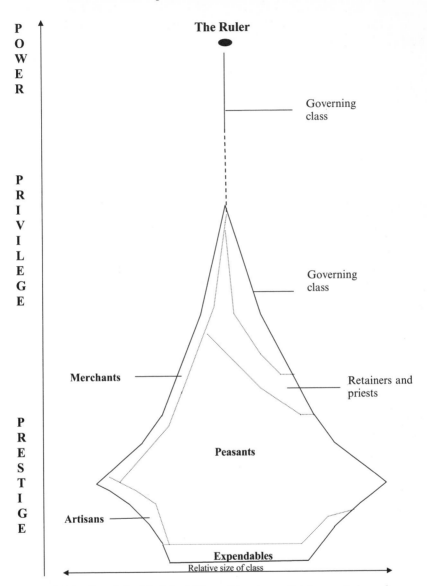

**Model 1   Lenski's Model of Class Structure of Advanced Agrarian
Societies**
Source: Nolan and Lenski, *Human Societies* and Lenski, *Power and Privilege*
(slightly altered)

as Lenski himself does, because of its simple heuristic potential and power.[35]

Here I offer two examples that can be viewed as applications of the Lenski vertical stratification model: independent analyses of ancient cities and Roman orders. I shall also offer a third, one from the Matthaean narrative, after I take up the horizontal dimension.

3.4.1 *Ancient cities*

Influenced by Weber, sociologist Gideon Sjoberg of the University of Texas (Austin) and his spouse Andrée[36] construct from cross-cultural examples three types of society: simple 'folk society', 'preindustrial civilized society', and 'industrial urban society'. Their book *The Preindustrial City* is 'a survey of the preindustrial civilized society with special emphasis upon the city, the hub of all major activity therein'.[37]

The Sjobergs offer rich descriptions of the daily life, politics, economics and religion in ancient cities. Cities were mostly small, approximately 5000–10000 people;[38] about 10 per cent of the population lived in them. They were crowded and insanitary. Autocratic kings ruled them with absolute authority, collected taxes and maintained law and order. City bureaucracies were rigidly hierarchical and family/friendship-based. Their economies were underdeveloped and corruption was rampant. Guild-organized craftspersons minimized competition and controlled pricing.[39] Elite families controlled hierarchical religion. Educated males interpreted the religious norms that justified the social and religious order.

This paragraph only hints at the Sjobergs' rich descriptions. However, Richard Rohrbaugh makes excellent use of the Sjobergs' work and his Sjoberg-influenced model of the pre-industrial city can serve as an illustration.[40]

---

35. In *Societal Stratification: A Theoretical Analysis* (New York: Columbia University Press, 1984), 61–2, Jonathan Turner, a Lenski admirer, says that Lenski sometimes allows his abstract macro-model to obscure his 'class systems' analysis.

36. *The Preindustrial City: Past and Present* (New York: Free Press, 1960). See G. Sjoberg 'The Preindustrial City', *American Journal of Sociology* (1955), 438–45, reprinted in G. Gmelch and W.P. Zenner (eds), *Urban Life: Readings in the Anthropology of the City* (Long Grove: Waveland Press, 3rd edn 2001), 20–31. Thanks to Prof. Sjoberg for sending me the latter article. Together the Sjobergs published 'The Preindustrial City: Reflections Four Decades Later', in Gmelch and Zenner, *Urban Life*, 94–103. See *http://www.la.utexas.edu/socdept/faculty/sjoberg.html* (accessed 13 November 03).

37. *Preindustrial City,* 332.

38. *Preindustrial City,* 323.

39. *Preindustrial City,* 325–6.

40. Modified from R.L. Rohrbaugh, 'The Preindustrial City in Luke–Acts' in J.H. Neyrey (ed.), *The Social World of Luke–Acts: Models for Interpretation* (Peabody: Hendrickson, 1991), 135.

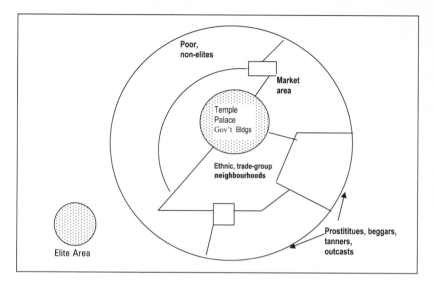

Model 2   The Pre-industrial City
Source: After Rohrbaugh, 'The Preindustrial City in Luke–Acts', in J. Neyrey
(ed.), *The Social World of Luke–Acts*, 135

In this model of a typical pre-industrial city, elites live in the central city adjacent to temple, palace and government buildings, while artisans, the poor and outcasts live on the periphery. Real, visible walls divide physical space, which replicates the social boundaries that divide social space.[41]

The Sjobergs also have their critics and they themselves say that their early work should have included more about gender and great literature.[42] Nonetheless, and most important here, their 'pre-industrial city' model offers a snapshot of social stratification in the cities of the Roman Empire.[43]

3.4.2 *Roman orders*

Lenski's most frequent example of vertical social stratification in an advanced agrarian society is the Roman Empire.[44] This focus is not surprising. Ramsay MacMullen once said that the key to Roman social relations was 'verticality',[45] and T.F. Carney argued that social relations

41.   *Preindustrial City*, 324–2.
42.   'The Preindustrial City: Reflections Four Decades Later'.
43.   They often mention the Roman Empire; see *Preindustrial City*, 44, 56–7, 69, 71–3.
44.   *Human Societies,* 166, 167, 169, 170, 173, 175, 176, 177, 180.
45.   *Roman Social Relations. 50 BC to AD 284* (New Haven, CT: Yale University Press, 1974).

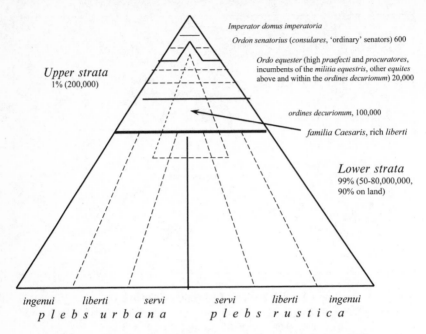

Imperator domus imperatoria

Ordon senatorius (consulares, 'ordinary' senators) 600

Ordo equester (high *praefecti* and *procuratores*, incumbents of the *militia equestris*, other *equites* above and within the *ordines decurionum*) 20,000

Upper strata
1% (200,000)

ordines decurionum, 100,000

familia Caesaris, rich *liberti*

Lower strata
99% (50-80,000,000, 90% on land)

ingenui   liberti   servi   servi   liberti   ingenui
p l e b s   u r b a n a   *p l e b s   r u s t i c a*

Model 3   The Roman Orders: Strata Structure and its Effects
Source: Alföldy, *The Social History of Rome*, 146 (Alföldy's statistics added)

in antiquity were typified by many pyramids of power.[46] An especially potent application of this sort of pyramidal social stratification is the analysis of Roman orders by social historian and epigrapher Géza Alföldy.[47]

Alföldy's pyramid does not reflect as well as Lenski's the unequal size of upper and lower strata, or the tremendous gap between them,[48] or the unequal size of urban (*plebs urbana*) and rural (*plebs rustica*) populations.[49] It is nonetheless an excellent clarifying model of the Roman social class system. By way of historical background, Alföldy says that

46. *The Shape of the Past*, 90.
47. *The Social History of Rome* (Totowa: Barnes & Noble, 1985). For publications, see *http://www.uni-heidelberg.de/institute/fak8/sag/htmls/A-BIBLneu.html* (accessed 1 November 03).
48. *The Social History of Rome*, 109. The wealthiest documented fortune in the Roman Empire was 400,000,000 sisterces. An illustration of great poverty is that 64 poor Egyptian peasant families shared a single *aroura* (2,200 square metres).
49. About 90 per cent of the population was on the land. See the urban/rural modifications of Lenski in D.A. Fiensy, *The Social History of Palestine in the Herodian Period: The Land is Mine* (SBEC 20; Lewiston: Edwin Mellen Press, 1991), 158; D.C. Duling, *The New Testament: History, Literature, and Social Context* (Belmont X: Thomson/ Wadsworth, 4th edn 2003), 17.

economically there was little difference between the Republic and the early empire; politically, however, there were indeed new developments and these radically altered the social system. Most important, the emperor and his household displaced the old patrician oligarchy at the top of the political/social pyramid. Senators, provincial legates, equestrians and client kings increasingly served an emperor who had absolute power. A client king who received the emperor's title 'friend of Caesar' with its attendant gifts and Roman citizenship received the greatest honour.[50]

Alföldy emphasizes Roman *ordo*, or 'orders',[51] a political category of the native distribution system. The emperor himself conferred *ordo*. It was based not only on recipients' political power, wealth and social prestige but also on being a freeborn male of aristocratic heritage, a full citizen, and, if from the provinces, a person of favourable ethnicity.[52] Upward social mobility between orders was rare, but advancement *within* orders was possible on the basis of merit, skill, education, experience, legal expertise and loyalty to the emperor. It was especially common in the military, the chief means of upward social mobility.

Under Augustus, the highest, or senatorial, order (*ordo senatorius*) became more uniform, restricted and separate.[53] There were only 600 senators[54] and being a senator required land-based wealth of at least 1,000,000 *sesterces*.[55] There was sharp internal stratification, yet some internal mobility.

The equestrian order (*ordo equester*) was larger, about 20,000,[56] and required assets of 400,000 *sisterces*. It was more loosely structured and had more offices. It was possible for provincials, citizens of other ethnic backgrounds, sons of freedpersons, and occasionally even a freedperson, to enter this order on the basis of individual achievement, especially in the military. The most highly placed equestrians became members of the aristocracy.

A third order, the decurions (*ordo decurionum*), consisted of elites in each city of the empire, usually magistrates and wealthy members of the town council who supported public works as patrons.[57] High birth was not an absolute requirement. There were about 1,000 cities, each with

50. For the 'friend of Caesar' type, see D. Braund, *Rome and the Friendly King: The Character of Client Kingship* (New York: St Martin's Press, 1984).
51. *The Social History of Rome*, 106. Eventually there were basically two strata, the *honestiores*, or few at the top, and *humiliores* and *tenuiores*, or the many at the bottom.
52. E.g., not Greek, Asian, Cappadocian, Syrian, Judaean and especially Egyptian.
53. *The Social History of Rome*, 106.
54. Suetonius, *Augustus*, 39.2.
55. Earlier 400,000; cf. Dio, 54.17.3; 54.26.3f (Alföldy, *The Social History of Rome*, 115). Actual wealth was much greater.
56. *The Social History of Rome*, 122.
57. *The Social History of Rome*, 126.

about one hundred or so decurions who had uniform functions: criminal law, administration, overseeing distribution of food, and public works. One could advance from vice-head of the community (*aedilis*) to head (*duumvir*). Decurions from large cities might advance to the equestrian order.

Another upper-stratum group in the cities consisted of wealthy freedpersons (*liberti*) who owned land and engaged in trade, banking and craft production. They often became benefactors. However, they did not usually move to the higher orders because of their servile origins.

The last upper-level group was the *familia Caesaris*, or the emperor's slaves and freedpersons. Despite their power – some freedmen had freeborn wives – they could not join the senatorial order and only rarely entered the equestrian order.

With respect to the lower social strata, the boundaries were more fluid. The main division, again, was between urban and rural. In the cities they included professionals, administrators, small businessmen, shopkeepers, smiths, musicians, artists, actors, secretaries, philosophers, craftspersons, freedpersons and slaves. Perhaps a third to a half of urbanites consisted of slaves, and many more had servile backgrounds. Freedpersons usually became clients of their former masters.

3.5 *The Horizontal Dimension*

The vertical dimension, social stratification in advanced agrarian societies, is useful for visualizing social ranking throughout the Roman Empire, and Roman orders provide a specific example of extension to the Roman provinces. Thus, the vertical dimension can be supplemented with a horizontal dimension, shifting the focus in the direction of imperialism.

3.5.1 *Imperial control of weaker polities*

Michael Doyle's definition of 'empire' stresses control.[58] In Doyle's language a 'metropole', defined as 'a center of great size or enormous population, spectacular wealth and resources or a large army',[59] controls both the domestic and foreign politics of other governments. It can do so because it has a strong, centralized governmental bureaucracy; a sense of community evoked by a belief among both elite and masses that its control is legitimate; and enough social differentiation to have many resources. For Doyle, a polity is weaker than a metropole not simply because of technology – well-organized armies often defeat their technological superiors – but because of less developed social organization. He

58. *Empires*, 24–30; see above under 'Definitions'.
59. *Empires*, 128.

describes several subtypes of weaker polities: (1) 'tribal' (no centralized state, little stratification, strong communal village loyalties); (2) 'patrimonial' (centralized state, some stratification, weak community loyalties); (3) 'feudal' (disaggregated state, some social differentiation, common civilization, pyramidal loyalties); (4) 'fractionated' (central state, thorough social differentiation, shared civilization, pyramidal loyalties); and (5) 'settler' (colonial government, differentiated society, community loyalty toward metropole). These can be used to analyse polities in the Roman Empire.

Another of Doyle's definitions suggests the relationship between empire (a polity) and imperialism (a policy):

> Empire ... is a relationship, formal or informal, in which one state controls the effective political sovereignty of another political society. It can be achieved by force, by political collaboration, by economic, social, or cultural dependence. Imperialism is simply the process or policy of establishing or maintaining an empire.[60]

Doyle's perspective provides a lens for viewing the horizontal dimension of the Roman Empire.

3.5.2 *Core–periphery model (a rimless wheel, hub and spokes)*

Motyl adds to and structures this kind of analysis by defining and modelling interactions between 'the core' (Doyle's 'metropole') and multiple 'peripheries' (Doyle's weaker polities); he also includes non-peripheries, those beyond empire control.[61] Motyl defines 'empire' as

> ... a hierarchically organized political system with a hublike structure – a rimless wheel – within which a core elite and state dominate peripheral elites and societies by serving as intermediaries for their significant interactions and by channeling resource flows from the periphery to the core and back to the periphery.[62]

Motyl presents his view of empire so defined with a simple etic, homomorphic model of a rimless wheel with hub-and-spokes.

For Motyl, an empire must have at least two peripheries (P); otherwise, it would have no geographical boundaries. Spokes with no rim represent the flow back and forth between core and periphery. There are no significant political and economic links between or among the peripheral

---

60. *Empires*, 45.

61. *Imperial Ends*, see note 1. Motyl builds on the theory of J. Galtung, 'A Structural Theory of Imperialism', *Journal of Peace Research* 8 (1971), 81–117 and several studies of R. Taagepera, which for the Roman Empire period are best presented in 'Size and Duration of Empires: Growth–Decline Curves, 600 BC to 600 AD', *Social Science History* 3 (1979), 115–38.

62. *Imperial Ends*, 4.

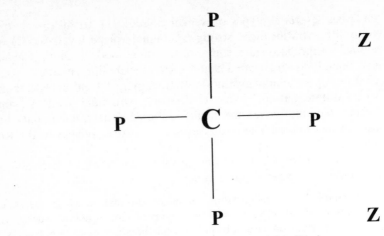

(**C** = core; **P** = peripheries; **Z** = non-imperial polities)

Model 4   The Core–Periphery Structure of Empire (Rimless Wheel, Hub and Spokes)
Source: Motyl, *Imperial Ends*, 16

polities themselves, hence no rim. Likewise, there are no significant links between the various empire polities (**P**) and polities beyond or outside the empire (**Z**).[63] It needs to be added that Motyl also thinks of the 'interaction structure' between core and periphery as *vertical* – the core not only controls but is (and considers itself) superior to peripheries – and to that extent his horizontal model can be easily correlated with the vertical models described above simply by imagining a three-dimensional figure raising the '**C**'.

Motyl also analyses several empire subtypes, which represent variations in the model. For example, the spokes and length and number of spokes can differ. There can be a few short spokes ('tightly massed' and 'territorially contiguous') called a 'continuous empire' (e.g., the Habsburg Empire, the Prussian Empire, the Napoleonic Empire, the Chinese Empire). There can be many long spokes representing distant, far-flung peripheries, called a 'discontinuous empire' (e.g., the Spanish Empire, the Portuguese Empire, the British Empire). There can be a mixture, which Motyl calls a 'hybrid empire' (e.g., the Third Reich). There can be different kinds of elite rule of peripheries which he, like Doyle, describes as *formal* (much interference in local affairs) and *informal* (substantial local rule).

For Motyl, empires are *political systems* that, as Eisenstadt put it,

---

63.   There can be economic triangular relationships such as occurred between England, the United States, and Africa in the slave trade.

require maintaining a 'very delicate balance' to survive.[64] Yet they provide 'the most massive and enduring form of government [people have ever] known prior to the modern period'.[65] Why? They are able to channel resources, provide security and promote the common defence. Yet their hub-like structure encourages furthering dominance of the elite core over non-elite peripheries. There is little chance of successful rebellion because elites in peripheral regions benefit immensely from their relationship with core elites.

3.5.3 *The horizontal dimension and the Roman Empire*

Doyle stresses the generally accepted historical fact that most Roman expansion took place under the Republic; the goal of the emperors was to preserve what the senators had accomplished.[66] He goes on to say that Roman expansion can be analysed from several perspectives. It had social and cultural roots in the core values of fidelity, honour and religion. The economic need was for more land to support a growing population. It had a military machine with appropriate means of advance. Land was confiscated by Roman farmer-soldiers and booty was lucrative for the conquerors. Whole provinces became client states of their Roman patrons. Thus, using Doyle's categories, the metropole controlled weaker polities which in the West were mainly tribal societies centred in villages and in the East mainly patrimonial monarchies and fractionated republics.

From Motyl's perspective the Roman Empire can be described as a 'discontinuous empire' because it had many long spokes, mainly to Mediterranean coastal areas. Doyle thinks that the Roman pattern was *formal*, which he defines further as 'rule by annexation and government by colonial governors supported by metropolitan troops and local collaborators'.[67] However, it should be added that rule was more *informal* in certain senatorial provinces and native-ruled polities where client kings 'collaborated'. That would be the case in Palestine under Herod the Great, where regional gubernatorial control directly responsible to Caesar was combined with local client king rule and ratified by the emperor's grant of the title 'friend of Caesar'. While for Motyl there are many peripheries that can establish boundaries, the outer boundaries under Rome remained fluid – less 'geographically fixed' than in modern nation-states.

Alföldy's analysis also offers more insight into how the Roman order was extended to the provinces.[68] Important factors included new road

---

64. *Imperial Ends*, 21.

65. *Imperial Ends*, 23.

66. *Imperial Ends*, 83.

67. *Empires*, 135.

68. See, e.g., Fergus Millar, *The Roman Empire and its Neighbours* (London: Duckworth, 2nd edn 1981).

networks, admission of provincials to the military, grants of citizenship to provincial elites, and new cities, the main location of imperial expansion.[69]

3.6 *Vertical and Horizontal Dimensions in the Gospel of Matthew*

Lenski's model of vertical stratification has been widely used in biblical scholarship.[70] With the aid of Alföldy's discussion of Roman orders, David Fiensy 'regionalized' it for Herodian Palestine.[71] It has also been very suggestive for understanding the Matthaean perspective.[72] The following outline offers an inventory of groups in the gospel that I have created in relation to Lenski's, Alföldy's and Fiensy's vertical pyramids. However, it also represents conditions that should be understood in terms of horizontal analysis – specifically ancient 'colonialism' represented by the province of Syria at the time of the composition of the gospel and the Herodian kingdom, the context for its narrative.[73]

I. Ruling strata
Caesar (22.17, 21 [x3]); **Rulers of the Gentiles** (20.25); **'Great Ones'** (20.25; cf. 5.35).
II. Provincial rulers
General Prefects/Procurators (2.6 [Mic. 5.2]; 10.18); **Pilate** (27.2, 11 [x2], 14, 15, 21, 27); **Kings and Client Kings** (10.18; 11.8; 17.25; 18.23; 22.2, 7, 11, 13; 25.34, 40); **Herod** (2.1, 2, 3, 9, etc.); **Archelaus** (2.22);

---

69.   Or, in the East, promotion of Hellenistic city-states.

70.   R.L. Rohrbaugh, *The Biblical Interpreter: An Agrarian Bible in an Industrial Age* (Philadelphia, PA: Fortress, 1978); 'The Social Location of the Markan Audience', *Interpretation* 47 (1993), 380–95; M. Chaney, 'Systemic Study of the Israelite Monarchy' in J.H. Elliott (ed.), *Semeia 35. Social-Scientific Criticism of the New Testament and its Social World* (Decatur: Scholars Press, 1986), 53–76; Elliott, 'Social-Scientific Criticism of the New Testament', 13–14; H. Waetjen, A *Reordering of Power. A Socio-Political Reading of Mark's Gospel* (Minneapolis, MN: Fortress, 1989); R.A. Horsley, *Sociology and the Jesus Movement* (New York: Crossroad, 1990); E.W. Stegemann and W. Stegemann, *The Jesus Movement: A Social History of its First Century* (St Paul: Fortress, 1999); J.D. Crossan, *The Birth of Christianity* (San Francisco, CA: Harper, 1998).

71.   Fiensy, *The Social History of Palestine*, 158; adapted in Duling, *The New Testament*, 17.

72.   For a lengthy list of Matthaean scholars who have used Lenski, see Duling, 'Matthew and Marginality', n. 37 and 'Matthew as Marginal Scribe in an Advanced Agrarian Society', n. 8. J.C. Anderson, 'Life on the Mississippi: New Currents in Matthaean Scholarship 1983–1993', *Currents in Research: Biblical Studies* 3 (1995), 169–218 stresses the importance of this approach in research on Matthew.

73.   From D.C. Duling, 'Matthew's Plurisignificant "Son of David" in Social Science Perspective: Kinship, Kingship, Magic, and Miracle', *BTB* 22 (1992), 102–3; 'Matthew and Marginality', 1–30. See further E.-J. Vledder, *Conflict in the Miracle Stories: A Socio-Exegetical Study of Matthew 8 and 9* (JSNTSS 152; Sheffield: Sheffield Academic Press, 1997); Carter, *Matthew and Empire*, Chs 1 and 2.

Philip (14.4); **Antipas** (14.1, 9); [**ancient kings** (1.2–17; 12.3)]; [**Jesus as King**: 'Son of David' (1.1; 9.27; 12.23; 15.22; 20.30, 31; 21.9, 15; 22.42, 43, 45); 'Messiah' (1.1, 16, 17, 18; 2.4; 11.2; 16.16, 20; 22.42; 23.10; 24.5, 23; 26.63, 68; 27.17, 22, 25; 27.17); 'King' (21.5 [Zech. 9.9]); 'King of the Jews' (27.11, 29, 37); 'King of Israel' (27.42)].

III. Priestly aristocracy
High Priest Caiaphas (26.3, 57, 58, 62, 63, 65); **chief priests** (2.4; 16.21; 20.18; 21.15, 23, 45; 26.3, 14, 47, 51, 59; 27.1, 3, 6, 12, 20, 41, 62; 28.11); **priests** (8.4; 12.4, 5); **Sadducees** (3.7; 16.1, 6, 11, 12; 22.23, 34).

IV. Lay aristocracy
elders (15.2; 16.21; 21.23; 26.3, 47, 57; 27.1, 3, 12, 20, 41; 28.12); **'landowner'** (21.33).

V. Merchants (10.29; 13.44, 45).

VI. Retainers
Toll-collectors (5.46, 47; 9.10, 11; 10.3; 11.19; 18.17; 21.31, 32); **general military personnel** (3.14; 5.25); **Roman centurions** (8.5, 8, 13; 27.54); **High Priest's guards** (26.58; 28.11; 27.65, 66; 28.11; **scribes** (2.4; 5.20; 7.29; 8.19; 9.3; 12.38; 13.52; 15.1; 16.21; 17.10; 20.18; 21.15; 23.2, 13, 15, 23, 25, 27, 29, 34; 26.57; 27.41); **'Ruler (of the synagogue)'?** (9.18, 23); **Pharisees** (3.7; 5.20; 9.11, 14, 34; 12.2, 14, 24, 38; 15.1, 12; 16.1, 6, 11,12; 19.3; 21.45; 22.15, 34, 41; 23.2, 13, 15, 23, 25, 26, 27, 29; 27.62) .

VII. Artisans (13.55); **fishermen** (4.18–22; 13.47–50); **day-labourers** (20.1, 2, 8; perhaps 9.37, 38; 10.10).

VIII. Peasants and urban poor and destitute (overlaps with expendables and unclean)
Crowds (50 references!); **the anxious** (6.25–34); **labourers of the harvest** (9.37–38); **tenant farmers** (21.33); **sower** (13.3–8, 18–23, 24–30, 31–32, 33, 36–43); **'poor'** (5.3; 11.5; 19.21; 26.9, 11); **receivers of alms** (6.1–6; 19.21).

IX. Herders (9.36; 25.32; 26.31 [Zech. 13.7]) (one can view them as belonging to a separate social structure).

X. Slaves (8.9; 10.24, 25; 13.27, 28; 18.23, 26, 27, 28, 32; 20.27; 21.34, 35, 36; 22.3, 4, 6, 8, 10; 24.45, 46, 48, 50; 25.14, 19, 21, 23 [x2], 30; 26.51; *pais*: 8.6, 8, 13; 12.18 [Isa. 42.1]; 14.2; 17.18; 21.15?); **forced labourers** (implied): (5.37).

XI. Expendables and unclean (samples: overlaps with peasants, urban poor and destitute)
Eunuchs (19.12, [x3]); **ritually unclean**: (Jesus and) certain disciples (15.2); lepers (8.2; 10.8; 11.5; 26.6); **certain women** (5.32; 15.19; 19.9; cf. 1.19); **woman with haemorrhage** (9.20–22); **women outside their usual home 'space' who follow Jesus**: those with 'every disease and every infirmity' (4.23 and 9.35); with 'various diseases and pains'

(4.24; **'all who were sick'** (8.16); **'their sick'** (14.14); **'sick'** (14.35); **blind** (9.27, 28; 11.5; 12.22; 15.14 [x2];); 15.30; 15.31; 20.30; 21.14); **dumb** (9.32, 33; 12.22 [x2]; 15.30, 31; 20.30; 21.14); **lame** (11.5; 15.30, 31; 18.8; 21.14); **deaf** (11.5); **maimed** (15.30, 31); **withered hand** (12.9–14); **paralytics** (4.24; 8.6; 9.2 [x2], 6); **demoniacs** (4.24; 8.16; 8.28–34; 12.22, 43–45; 15.21–28); **epileptics** (4.24); **lepers** (8.1–4; 10.8; 11.5); **bandits** (21.13 [Jer 7.11]; 26.55; 27.38, 44); **thieves** (6.19–20); **prostitutes** (21.31, 32).

It would be desirable to examine each of these eleven strata from various times, places and levels of abstraction (e.g., the distributive system). Elsewhere I have developed an analysis of the scribes.[74] Here it is possible to offer as an illustration some theory and modelling of the peasantry.

3.7 *The Peasantry*

3.7.1 *'Commercialized' empires and peasants*

John Kautsky's views are much indebted to Lenski's and are sometimes correlated with Lenski's perspective in New Testament interpretation.[75] Kautsky develops three types of society in human history, although he does not think that they are necessarily sequential. He calls them 'primitive societies', 'traditional aristocratic empires' and 'modern societies'. He offers a simplified model of his evolutionary scheme.[76]

The key concepts in Kautsky's analysis are 'aristocracy' and 'aristocratic empire':

> An *aristocracy* ... is a ruling class in an agrarian economy that does not engage in productive labor but lives wholly or primarily off the labor of peasants. Hence *aristocratic empires* must contain not only aristocrats but also peasants who, in turn, live in agrarian primitive societies. Because ... it takes many peasants to support one aristocrat, this also implies that aristocratic empires are necessarily a good deal larger than primitive societies.[77]

For Kautsky, ancient Egypt, Mesopotamia and early medieval Europe are typical '*traditional* aristocratic empires'. Empires in which aristocrats have given up some of their power to a class of merchants, financiers and tax

---

74. 'Matthew as a Marginal Scribe', 520–75.

75. *The Politics of Aristocratic Empires* (Chapel Hill, NC: University of North Carolina Press, 1982). Kautsky's work was first introduced to New Testament scholars by Richard Horsley in the 1980s; Kautsky was a guest of the Society of Biblical Literature's Social-Scientific Criticism of the New Testament section in 2000.

76. *The Politics of Aristocratic Empires*, 21–7.

77. *The Politics of Aristocratic Empires*, 24 (italics added).

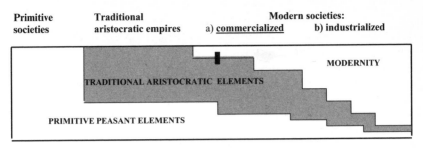

(█ = Roman Empire)

Model 5   John Kautsky's Societies Representing the Three Phases of History
Source: Kautsky, *The Politics of Aristocratic Empires*, 27 (slightly adapted)

collectors, or have become merchants themselves are called '*commercialized* empires'. The Roman Empire belongs in this modified type,[78] although it still retains some 'primitive peasant elements'. What this commercialism means in the Roman Empire is succinctly summarized by Dominic Crossan:

> Put bluntly: in a traditional agrarian empire, the aristocracy takes the (agricultural) *surplus* (of the land) from the peasantry; in a commercializing agrarian empire, the aristocracy takes the *land* (itself) from the peasantry. The former devours the industry and productivity of the peasantry; the latter their very identity and dignity. Commercialization moves (. . . the peasant) in increasing numbers down the terrible slope from small freeholder to tenant farmer to day-laborer to beggar or bandit.[79]

Or to peasant resistance!

3.7.2 *Peasant resistance*
Kautsky emphasizes that aristocrats claim reciprocity but in reality exploit peasants. Here I mention three forms of peasant resistance relevant for the historical context of the Roman Empire and Matthew: millennial movements, peasant revolts and everyday nonviolent resistance.[80]

78. *The Politics of Aristocratic Empires*, 159–82.
79. Crossan, *The Birth of Christianity*, 157–8.
80. Crossan, *The Birth of Christianity*, 159; Kautsky, *The Politics of Aristocratic Empires*, 280–308.

3.7.2.1 *Millennial movements*

The term 'millennialism' is derived from the description of the 1000-year reign of Christ and the martyrs in Revelation 20.4–8 (Latin *mille*, 1000). Millennial (or apocalyptic) movements view the present order as oppressive (natural or social), as being in crisis. Some causes are flood, drought, *coup d'état*, military conquest, cultural oppression, and the like. The present order will soon end, usually by some cataclysmic event, and it will be replaced by a new, perfect, blissful and trouble-free world (*Endzeit*: end-time), often believed to be a restoration of some perfect time and place, usually 'of old' (*Urzeit*: original time, golden age). This ideology can be so intense that those who believe it can prepare for the new age or attempt to force its coming by radical political activity. Typically a prophet or messiah emerges, sometimes preceded by a forerunner. This figure usually experiences altered states of consciousness; (s)he crystallizes common experiences and offers a new solution to social problems. (S)he attracts followers (Weber's 'charismatic leader') who also have such experiences and either await the coming new order or attempt to bring it about by political activity (see further below). Such groups are usually loosely organized and sometimes splinter. On rare occasions they become organized with hierarchical leaders (Weber: 'routinization of charisma'). If the movement is successful, the population at large adopts their views as normative. Cultural transformation occurs, eventually accompanied by doctrine, ritual and a social programme. This becomes the new social system.[81]

Millennial ideology was very widespread in Judaean circles of the Hellenistic and Roman periods. An excellent illustration is the *Assumption (Testament) of Moses* 10, usually considered to have a first-century Palestinian provenance. In this text God's *basileia* ('rule', 'kingdom', 'empire') will replace that of the enemies, the idolatrous Gentiles will be punished and Israel will be happy and exalted to the heavens, and she will give thanks.[82]

In the canonical gospels, including the Gospel of Matthew, Jesus's central teaching is remembered as the 'rule/kingdom/empire of heaven'. Many New Testament scholars have seen Jesus's teaching as a form of millennialism.[83]

---

81. D.C. Duling, '*BTB* Readers' Guide: Millennialism', *BTB* 24 (1993), 132–42; 'Millennialism' in R.L. Rohrbaugh (ed.), *The Social Sciences and New Testament Interpretation* (Peabody: Hendrickson, 1996), 183–205.

82. D.C. Duling, 'Kingdom of God/Heaven (OT, Early Judaism, and Hellenistic Usage)', in D.N. Freedman (ed.), *Anchor Bible Dictionary. Vol. 4* (New York: Doubleday, 1992), 51.

83. Probably the dominant emphasis in the twentieth century. On Matthaean sectarianism, see D.C. Sim, *The Gospel of Matthew and Christian Judaism: The History and Social Setting of the Matthean Community* (SNTW; Edinburgh: T&T Clark, 1998).

3.7.2.2 *Peasant rebellion*

Millennialism sometimes becomes the ideology of peasant rebellion. In peasant rebellion local elites – landlords, village leaders, local scribes – join forces with peasants in revolt, indeed help to lead it.[84] Whether against native ruling strata or foreign occupying powers, or both, peasant revolts do not often succeed, mainly because their enemies are too powerful and well organized. In the case of empires another reason is that local elites (periphery) benefit enormously as collaborators with imperial elites (centre) and therefore do not ordinarily join in alliances against them.

With respect to the Roman Empire, Stephen Dyson has studied various native revolts.[85] He has isolated two patterns of resistance. In the Western Empire, conflict between Rome and tribal peoples centred mainly on payment of taxes in coin, a Roman policy that introduced an alien and distrusted monetary economy and fostered abuses by tax collectors.[86] Also, Roman agricultural settlements meant loss of land and conflict between Roman agricultural and local pastoral economies.[87] Strong pockets of resistance emerged in the mountainous buffer-zones between Roman agricultural settlements and remote, more independent tribal communities. While Romanized native aristocracies supported the Roman occupation, native religions tended to perpetuate traditional values, and when extremist religious rebels emerged, they were simply eliminated

More familiar to scholars of Graeco-Roman antiquity is the second pattern, which was typical of the Eastern Empire, especially in Greece and Judaea.[88] The primary factor that led to resistance in the East, says Dyson, was rapid acculturation (Hellenization and Romanization). As in the West, natives had to adjust to a 'colonial' administrative structure that forced upon them taxes, governors and soldier-farmers who confiscated their land. Rebellions usually occurred just when imperial powers had come to think that the major problems of conquest had been solved.[89] It is possible to see the Judaean rebellion against Rome in 66 CE in this light. The Gospel of Matthew was written in the following generation.[90]

---

84. S. Naquin, *Millenarian Rebellion in China: The Eight Trigrams Uprising of 1813* (New Haven, CT: Yale University Press, 1976).

85. S. Dyson, 'Native Revolt Patterns in the Roman Empire' in H. Temporini (ed.), *Aufstieg und Niedergang der römischen Welt. II.3* (Berlin: de Gruyter, 1975), 138–75.

86. Revolts in Spain, 197 BCE and among the the Nasamones (86 BCE) and Frisians (28 CE).

87. Especially in North Africa.

88. S. Dyson, 'Native Revolts in the Roman Empire', *Historia* 20 (1971), 239–74.

89. E.g., Arminius, Batavian, Boudicca, the Pannonian-Dalmatian and Vercingetorix.

90. For analysis of the Judaean social and economic context, see K.C. Hanson and D. Oakman, *Palestine in the Time of Jesus. Social Structures and Social Conflicts* (Minneapolis, MN: Fortress, 1998).

A further word about theory is in order. Daniel Little has written a paper highlighting two models of peasant rebellion: the class-conflict model and the local politics model.[91] The class-conflict model, which goes back to Marx, stresses 'the property system': that is, rural property arrangements determine class relations among landlords, tenants, labourers and the imperial occupation. Peasants experience exploitation when the agricultural surplus is extracted by elites in the form of rents, interest, corvée labour, taxation and tribute. They develop 'class consciousness' and are motivated to collective political action whenever sufficient political resources and organization are present. Thus, '[r]ebellions and popular collective action are rational strategies of collective self-defense on the part of subordinate classes'.[92]

Little recognizes that the class-conflict model has great explanatory power, but he thinks that it usually operates at too general a level to take account of local politics, which becomes the basis for his second model. In China, for example, political resistance has been different in wet-rice regions and dry-cropping areas. Also, it is necessary to take account of 'non-class' factors: religion, intervillage conflict and kinship and religious organizations. Little's critique is similar to that observed in previous discussions: general modelling can obscure variables related to the distribution system, temporal changes and local conditions. In short, the interpreter must be conscious of levels of abstraction and aware of exceptions. This critique is also present in the following analysis.

3.7.2.3 *Everyday peasant resistance*

Political scientist James C. Scott has analysed a peasant village, which he calls 'Sedaka' (not its real name), in the 'rice bowl' of Malaysia.[93] His procedure is to paint a social 'landscape': background, middle-ground and foreground.

The *background* is post-colonial Malaysia's attempt to insure a self-sufficient supply of rice, raise the standard of living and avoid civil strife, all by building an infrastructure, sponsoring peasant resettlement schemes

91. D. Little, 'Local Politics and Class Conflict: Theories of Peasant Rebellion in Nineteenth-Century China' (Paper of the Bellagio Conference on Peasant Culture and Consciousness, January 1990): *http://www-personal.umd.umich.edu/~delittle/BELLAGI2.PDF* (accessed 15 April 04). Little, now Chancellor at the University of Michigan, Dearborn, wrote this paper as a visiting scholar and associate at the Harvard University Center for International Affairs in 1989.

92. Little, 'Local Politics and Class Conflict', 3. For yet another Marxist-oriented view of the peasantry, see E. Wolf, *Peasants* (Englewood Cliffs, NJ: Prentice Hall, 1966).

93. J.C. Scott, *Weapons of the Weak: Everyday Forms of Peasant Resistance* (New Haven, CT: Yale University Press, 1985); *Moral Economy of the Peasant: Rebellion and Subsistence in Southeast Asia* (New Haven, CT: Yale University Press, 1977); *Domination and the Arts of Resistance: Hidden Transcripts* (New Haven, CT: Yale University Press, 1992).

and introducing a second crop ('double cropping'). The *middle-ground* is regional, namely, the Muda region of Kedah (northwest Malaysia) from 1970 to 1980, which was the 'beneficiary' of an irrigation programme that included dams and canals; new high-yielding, fast-growing strains of rice; fertilizers; double-cropping; mechanization; credit bureaux; and milling and marketing opportunities. The programme immediately increased Malaysian rice production by about 250 per cent and the region became a showpiece of Southeast Asia's 'Green Revolution'. Scott's *foreground* is Sedaka. Double-cropping was introduced in 1971 and harvest combines appeared in 1976. Scott describes the unintended effect of the Green Revolution in Sedaka:

> Before, large landowners rented land out to poorer tenants; now they rent increasingly to wealthy entrepreneurs (some Chinese) or farm their land themselves with machinery. Before, large farmers hired poorer neighbors to plough and harrow their fields with water buffalo; now they hire poorer neighbors (only) to prepare their land. Before, larger farmers hired poorer neighbors to transplant their paddy; now many of them broadcast their own seed (scattered rice is more difficult to cultivate than rows). Before, these same farmers hired the poor to reap and thresh their crop; now they hire wealthy combine owners for the same job. Before, well-to-do villagers had good reason to provide advance wages and give *zakat* payments to their work force; now, if they have a work force at all, they see no need to be as openhanded. Before, the village rich had good reason to build a reputation with lavish feasts; now many of them regard such large feasts as a waste of money. Taken together, these reversals call into question virtually every assumption that governed the social relations of production before double-cropping.[94]

In short, there had been inequities before, but also cooperation, reciprocity and mutual interdependence rooted in kinship, neighbourhood and religion; with agricultural innovations much of that vanished. Modern capitalistic developments served to disrupt the moral economy of the peasants.[95]

How did the peasants of Sedaka respond? In contrast to much of southeast Asia, '[t]here [were] no riots, no demonstrations, no arson, no organized social banditry, no open violence'.[96] Rather, they resorted to grumbling, foot-dragging, dissipation, false compliance, pilfering, petty theft, arson, sabotage, feigned ignorance, malicious gossip, slander, rumourmongering, jokes, offhand comments, innuendoes, flight to

---

94. *Weapons of the Weak*, 179–80.
95. *Weapons of the Weak*, 74.
96. *Weapons of the Weak*, 273.

another village and a nostalgic appeal to the not-so-good 'good old days'.[97] They avoided thoroughly threshing every bundle of cut paddy, stuffed their pockets with rice at the end of the day and left some bundles for family members to glean later. They threatened to go on strike. They engaged in night-time petty theft of the rich. Occasionally they murdered their farm animals. They told stories about famous 'social bandits' of former times.[98]

Why did resistance take these seemingly placid forms? Scott offers a few explanations: the changes in Sedaka were gradual; the conditions of wealthier villagers did in fact improve;[99] poor people did not actually starve; two-thirds of land tenancies were still kinship-based; and village relations were in part still rooted in friendship, faction, patronage and ritual.

Routine, everyday forms of peasant resistance raise important theoretical issues. Marxists like Antonio Gramsci explain such apparent proletarian passivity by the concept of 'hegemony',[100] that is, the ruled stratum accepts the ideology of the ruling stratum as natural, as given ('the dominant ideology thesis'). This passivity is an institutional form of Marx's 'false consciousness', which inhibits social change. For Scott, however, Gramsci's generalized Marxist views do not sufficiently take into account the mediation of real-life class experience which, as E.P. Thompson says, 'gives a coloration to culture, to values, and to thought; it is by means of experience that the mode of production exerts a determining pressure upon other activities ...'[101] The interpreter needs to take into account the more subtle aspects of language and social relations, that is, proverbs, folksongs, history, customs, ritual and religion. It is necessary to understand not only what is said publicly ('onstage'; the 'partial transcript'), but privately, among family, friends and work-companions ('offstage'; the 'full transcript'). Scott himself calls his method 'phenomenology' and 'ethnology';[102] it may be best understood as an example of what anthropologist Clifford Geertz calls 'thick description' of

97.   *Weapons of the Weak*, 280.

98.   See C.B. Kheng, *Social Banditry and Rural Crime in Kedah, 1910–1929* (Oxford: Oxford University Press, 1988).

99.   *Weapons of the Weak*, 147.

100. *Selections from the Prison Notebooks* (ed. and trans. Q. Hoare and G.N. Smith; London: Lawrence & Wishart, 1971).

101. *The Poverty of Theory and Other Essays* (New York: Monthly Review Press, 1978), 98.

102. *Weapons of the Weak*, 46–7.

culture.[103] For Scott, as for other critics, general theory should be counterbalanced by contextual specificity.

It is impossible for scholars of ancient empires, thus the Roman Empire, to gain access to the 'full transcript' of ancient peasants to the degree that Scott does. Nonetheless, it is possible to gain *some* insight into ancient transcripts by looking carefully at storytelling, labelling, symbols and the like, and then to offer a reading with imperialist glasses. That reading can be a lens for understanding the peasant stratum of the Gospel of Matthew.[104]

3.8 *Roman Ethnic Identity and Imperial Ideology: Constructing 'Empire'*

As Doyle suggests, the Roman Empire had to control several kinds of polities and a vast array of peoples, beliefs, religions, laws and monetary systems. What ideology motivated Roman imperialists to hold it all together?

Greg Woolf offers an answer to this question: it is through a combination of Roman ethnic identity, or ethnocentrism, and imperial theology.[105] As an illustration, he cites the beginning of the famous 'Deeds of the Divine Augustus' (*Res Gestae Divi Augusti*), originally inscribed at Augustus's tomb in Rome and widely publicized throughout the empire:[106] 'These are the deeds performed by the deified Augustus, by which he subjected the entire world to the power of the Roman people (*imperio populi Rom*).'[107] Recall that the word *imperium*, 'power' or 'rule', in this inscription is the word for 'empire' and that it had roots in the Roman army. The inscription says more, however, for the *imperium* belongs to the Roman 'people' (Latin *populus* [Greek *ethnos*]), an ancient ethnie.[108]

Ethnic self-identity was corroborated by Roman 'imperial theology'.

---

103. 'Thick Description: Toward a Theory of Culture' in C. Geertz, *The Interpretation of Cultures* (New York: Basic Books, 1973), 3–30. For Scott's admiration of Geertz, see *Weapons of the Weak*, 45, 138–40.

104. See the study of John Riches in this volume.

105. 'Inventing Empire in Ancient Rome' in S.E. Alcock, T.N.D. Altroy, K.D. Morrison and C.M. Sinopoli (eds), *Empires: Perspectives from Archaeology and History* (Cambridge: Cambridge University Press, 2001), 311–22; see also Carter, *Matthew and Empire*, Ch. 2.

106. A copy is on a temple of Augustus in Ankara, Turkey.

107. *http://www.csum.edu/~hcf11004/resgest.html* (accessed 30 April 04). For Thomas Bushnell's translation, see *http://classics.mit.edu/Augustus/deeds.html* (accessed 30 April 04).

108. For the linguistic field, see D.C. Duling, '"Whatever Gain I Had...": Ethnicity and Paul's Self-Identification in Phil. 3.5–6' in D.B. Gowler, L.G. Bloomquist and D.F. Watson (eds), *Fabrics of Discourse: Essays in Honor of Vernon K. Robbins* (Harrisburg, IL: Trinity Press International, 2003) 222–41.

Divine sanctions were given to both the Julio-Claudian and Flavian emperors. In the first words of the *Res Gestae* the emperor was publicized as the '*divine* Augustus'. Literature portrays Roman emperors as the elect mediators of the gods. Roman coins portrayed them as rulers of the whole world.[109] The imperial cult in the East acclaimed them as divine. Divine election was also attributed to the Roman people. Virgil claims that the god Jupiter appointed Romulus to found Rome and that the Romans were destined to be 'lords of the world'.[110]

In short, the Romans believed that they were God's chosen people and that if their leaders, especially the emperor, maintained the appropriate virtue and piety their mandate to rule the world was a mandate from heaven.[111]

3.9 *Conclusion*

Theories and models of empire are implicit in any utterance about empire, ancient or modern. Cases in point are where ancient narrators tell stories with a religious purpose and where modern interpreters proceed empirically with the intent of historical description. It is therefore helpful – I would say imperative – to make theories and models as explicit as possible as a means to better understanding.

In this chapter I have attempted to present the importance of the empire discussion, definitions of empires, theories of their origins, models of their vertical social arrangements, models of their horizontal extension, models of their impact on the peasant strata and some discussion of ethnocentric and ideological justification on the part of imperialists who wield power. In all sections, I have done so with a view to offering plausible scenarios for understanding the Roman Empire as the context for a single story, the Gospel of Matthew. I hope thereby to have laid a foundation for reading this gospel with empire lenses and for studying and interpreting it from more specific perspectives.

---

109. Carter, *Matthew and Empire*, 20–29 offers many examples.
110. *Aeneid* 1.254, 278–9, 282; Carter, *Matthew and Empire*, 22.
111. 'Inventing Empire in Ancient Rome', 319. Similar ideas are found in Deuteronomic views of the Davidic kings.

A State of Tension: Rome in the New Testament

Peter Oakes

Richard Cassidy has recently made an interesting suggestion about Paul's attitudes to Rome. Cassidy suggests that Paul viewed Rome in positive terms when he wrote Romans 13 but that his subsequent experience, especially his imprisonment, made him negative about Rome by the time he wrote Philippians.[1] The elegance of this suggestion lies in its defusing of an apparent Pauline contradiction by appeal to a palpably reasonable process: anyone would be likely to be embittered against the authorities by a long period of imprisonment.

The difficulty with Cassidy's thesis is that the Pauline contradiction that Cassidy is trying to deal with is implicitly present in the letter to the Romans itself (and, I would also argue, in Philippians).[2] In particular, the criticism directed against the idolatrous world in Romans 1.18–32 is so comprehensive that it condemns the Roman system of thought and authority at its core.

In fact, many writers have noted elements of Paul's implied critique of Roman authority. Their consequent move has been to argue that an apparently positive passage, such as Romans 13.1–7, must be essentially tactical or, in fact, rather negative. Some writers have suggested that the

---

1. On Romans 13.1–7, Cassidy writes: 'Paul's position in these verses is one of virtually unqualified support for the authorities of the Roman Empire.' Cassidy further expresses this as 'the startling level of affirmation and support that Paul affords to the existing authorities'. In describing the contrast with Philippians Cassidy writes: 'a dramatic shift occurs in Paul's outlook between Romans and Philippians. In effect, Philippians contains a critical perspective regarding the Roman authorities that Romans simply does not possess.' R.J. Cassidy, *Paul in Chains: Roman Imprisonment and the Letters of St Paul* (New York: Crossroad, 2001), 18, 5.

2. For discussion of Philippians in relation to Rome (although not on this particular issue) see P. Oakes, *Philippians: From People to Letter* (SNTSMS 110; Cambridge: CUP, 2001), esp. Ch. 5, 'Christ and the Emperor'; P. Oakes, 'God's Sovereignty over Roman Authorities: A Theme in Philippians' in P. Oakes (ed.), *Rome in the Bible and the Early Church* (Carlisle/Grand Rapids, MI: Paternoster/Baker, 2002), 126–41.

passage merely promotes a survival strategy of conforming behaviour.[3] Others have seen Paul as wishing to sound positive because of suspicion that he was disloyal.[4] Yet others have argued that the underlying idea is the restriction of Rome's authority, since it is a provisional institution and fundamentally not of divine nature.[5]

I would suggest that, although such points have some validity, the attempt by these writers and Richard Cassidy to remove the tension between positive and negative comments on Rome in Paul's writings is unnecessary. Paul's writings represent a pattern seen in the New Testament as a whole: a pattern of fundamental tension inherent in early Christian attitudes to Rome.

In preparing a recent article[6] I began thinking about how to model the attitudes of Christians to Rome at the time of Paul's letter sent to the city. At that period (the late 50s), Christianity was a provincial religious movement rooted in Jewish beliefs, practice and history. This suggested that it would be illuminating to model Christian attitudes as a combination of prominent aspects of provincial, Jewish and distinctively Christian (e.g. christological) attitudes to Rome.

Looking at provincial evidence gave me a list of three prominent attitudes: awe at Rome's prestige, power and wealth; appreciation of the *pax romana* for the stability and economic prosperity it brought; resentment at payment of taxes. My Jewish list contained: appreciation of Rome's (partial) protection of Diaspora communities and of laws permitting Jewish practice; resentment at occupation of Israel and recent poor governing of Judea; contempt for Roman religious beliefs and certain aspects of morality. Jews would also share the provincial attitudes above. Christians' experience of Rome, as Christians *per se*, was probably too limited at that period to have a great effect on Christian attitudes. However, Christian beliefs (in common with those of some other Jewish groups) sharpened certain elements of Jewish theology so as to produce more emphatic attitudes of denying Rome's ultimate authority and expecting the overthrow of the Roman social and political system. This sharpening stemmed especially from fundamental Christian

---

3. R.A. Horsley and N.A. Silberman, *The Message and the Kingdom: How Jesus and Paul Ignited a Revolution and Transformed the Ancient World* (Minneapolis, MN: Fortress, 1997), 191; J. Friedrich, W. Pöhlmann and P. Stuhlmacher, 'Zur historischen Situation und Intention von Röm 13.1–7', *ZTK* 73 (1976), 131–66, here 165.

4. K. Wengst, *Pax Romana and the Peace of Jesus Christ*, trans. J. Bowden (Philadelphia, PA: Fortress Press, 1987), 82–3.

5. O. Cullmann, *The State in the New Testament* (London: SCM Press, 1957), 67; cf. J.J. Meggitt, *Paul, Poverty and Survival* (Edinburgh: T&T Clark, 1998), 185–6.

6. P. Oakes, 'Christian Attitudes to Rome at the Time of Paul's Letter', *Review and Expositor* 100 (2003), 103–11.

ideas about the authority of the Messiah and the advent of God's kingdom.[7]

In total, my list of expected Christian attitudes in the mid-50s had six broad elements: awe, appreciation, resentment, contempt, denial of ultimate authority, expectation of overthrow. My conclusion was that a list full of tension, such as this six-element list of attitudes, had deep and wide-spreading roots in the thought-world of the earliest Christian writers.[8] Attempts to defuse such tension are likely to lose connection with these roots at some point.

To what extent is this conclusion about expected attitudes borne out by evidence of actual attitudes seen in the New Testament writings? Is tension inherent in each writing or, as Cassidy and others argue, do various books represent various elements of it? To what extent is there change over time or space in the nature of the tension? Is there ever resolution of the tension in favour of either its positive or negative pole?

To attempt to reach even provisional conclusions on these questions we must deal in some way with a substantial complicating factor. My previous model of attitudes was in principle a snapshot for about the year 57 CE. If we move either backwards or forwards from this date, the picture changes.

4.1 *Continuities and Discontinuities in Attitude*

In the years between Jesus's crucifixion and 57, provincial attitudes to Rome probably changed little. Caligula's eccentricity had only a limited general effect, and the solidity of Claudius's reign would have re-established the impression of smoothly running Roman power and progress. After 57, Nero's decline was probably not a significant factor. He seems to have remained popular in the eastern half of the empire, where our interest lies. News of the catastrophic fire in 64 must have dented Rome's appearance of invulnerability. This must have been even more true of the 'year of the four emperors', 69, and the difficulty that Rome had in suppressing the Jewish revolt (66–70). However, once the Flavian dynasty was installed and the revolt in the east put down, Rome's prestige and stability would have remained secure through to the end of the period of production of the NT writings. Although we know of some trouble over taxation under Nero and that there were famines and some other calamities at other points in the first century, the provincial mixture of awe, appreciation and resentment was probably relatively constant over the course of the century as a whole.

7. Oakes, 'Christian Attitudes to Rome', 105–9.
8. Oakes, 'Christian Attitudes to Rome', 110.

The same cannot be said of Jewish attitudes to Rome. The reign of Agrippa I (41–4), placed on the throne of Judea by an emperor who was his friend, probably represented a high-point in Jewish attitudes to the Roman Empire. Direct Roman rule, the pattern for the rest of the period, was characterized by a long series of episodes of mismanagement, such as the string of problems under Ventidius Cumanus (48–52).[9] Such problems would primarily have annoyed Judaean Jews, but Diaspora interest in the fate of Judea must have meant that bad governors affected attitudes in the Diaspora communities too. These communities owed their economic welfare to the *pax romana*, but they also had their own difficulties in terms of periodic conflicts with other groups in the cities, most seriously in Alexandria in the late 30s. Jews blamed the Roman authorities for mismanagement of such conflicts (e.g. Philo, *In Flaccum*).

There are, therefore, some potential sharp short-term variations in Jewish attitudes. However, for the purposes of our model it is probably worth simplifying all this to say that, up to the mid-60s, both Diaspora and Judaean Jewish communities broadly held the combination of attitudes (appreciation, resentment and contempt) described in the 57 CE model above.

The Jewish war changed that. Even if some Jews saw responsibility for the war as lying with certain hot-headed Jewish groups, and saw Rome's crushing of the rebellion as political common sense (from a Roman viewpoint), the manner of Rome's action must have engendered great bitterness for a long time afterwards. Rome killed thousands and enslaved far more. Rome demolished the Temple and, indeed, the whole of Jerusalem. Rome gloried in its triumph over the Jews. There must have been great resentment at the *judaea capta* coins and, particularly, at the parading of the Temple artefacts in Rome and their subsequent representation on the Arch of Titus. Most Jews would not have travelled to Rome but many would have heard that a new architectural centre-point of the city was a depiction of the carrying-off of the Menorah. The war also saw fresh disturbances between some Diaspora communities and their neighbours, especially in Alexandria (Josephus, *War* 2.18.7–8).[10] Both in terms of Jewish experience of Rome and in terms of the offence to Jewish theology, post-war attitudes to Rome must have been very negative. Evidence for this is clear in apocalyptic texts such as 4 Ezra, 2 Baruch and Sibylline Oracle 4, but it was surely also more generally true. Looking back at my list, Jewish attitudes to Rome must still have included awe but appreciation had probably gone. Resentment and religious and moral contempt were still there. Jewish groups that particularly denied

---

9.   L.L. Grabbe, *Judaism from Cyrus to Hadrian* (London: SCM Press, 1992, one-vol. edn), 440.

10.   Grabbe, *Judaism*, 439.

Roman authority or expected Rome's overthrow had largely been crushed, although apocalyptic writing continued to be produced and more actively military groups reappear after the NT period. I would think that, between 70 and 100 CE, awe, resentment and contempt were the predominant attitudes.

My method for arriving at specifically Christian attitudes in 57 was to look at the evidence up to that point; therefore I cannot distinguish between Christian attitudes in 57 and those prior to 57. Moving beyond 57, we have three major factors to consider: the first identifiable persecution of Christians as a distinct group, by Nero in 64; the Jewish war and its outcome; and the increasing separation of Christianity from Judaism.

The killing of Christians by Nero, and any further persecution by Roman authority figures in the remainder of the century, must have introduced a new element – that of resentment against persecution – into Christian attitudes to Rome. Christians' experience of Rome, as Christians, was no longer neutral. However, government action against Christians was not at all on the scale of government action against Jews. There is nothing like the mass slaughter and mass enslavement that Jews experienced during the war. Government persecution of Christians was probably not sufficiently widespread to extinguish all appreciation of the benefits of the *pax romana*. Some such appreciation of the benefits that the authorities brought would generally have sat alongside resentment at stories of persecution.

The Jewish war and the increasing separation of Christians from Jews need to be taken together. The basic separation at this point is in experience. The war was a catastrophic trauma for Jews but not, to anything like the same extent, for most Christians. Conversely, the Neronian persecution and any aftermath of it affected Christians, not Jews. The experience-based attitudes to Rome of each community must have been becoming fairly independent of each other at this period. Whether Jews appreciated or resented Rome no longer directly affected Christian attitudes.

On the other hand, there is clearly still continuity in theological views about Rome between Jews and Christians. The texts of 4 Ezra, 2 Baruch and Sibylline Oracle 4 show that at least certain groups of post-war Jews shared the expectation of Rome's overthrow by God that is also seen in Christian texts of the period. More broadly, Jews and Christians continued to hold basic theological views, such as contempt for Roman religious ideas, that they had shared since the earliest days of the Jesus-movement.

Let us take the events of 64 together with those of 70 and try to characterize Christian attitudes in two periods, before and after 70. The overall list of expected attitudes is probably the same pre- and post-70:

awe, appreciation, resentment, contempt, denial of ultimate authority, expectation of overthrow. However, this similarity masks two important differences. First, resentment now includes resentment against Roman persecution of Christians. Even if persecution was limited, stories of such events clearly circulated widely. Second, the post-70 Christian attitudes are more detached from Jewish attitudes than were the pre-70 ones. There is much continuity in theology, especially in apocalyptic texts, but the two groups' experiences of Rome are now rather divergent.

Let us now look at five test-cases: 1 Thessalonians, Romans, Mark, Acts and Revelation. These are five of the texts that tell us most about early Christian attitudes to Rome. Two of these are firmly pre-70. Mark probably dates from around 70 but certainly includes earlier traditions. Acts is usually seen as post-70, although some scholars place it in the 60s and, again, it includes earlier traditions. Revelation is almost universally seen as considerably later than 70. In fact, many scholars place it in the early second century. However, that does not affect our model of attitudes since, for our model, the end of the first century is not a sharp cut-off point.

4.2 *1 Thessalonians*

1 Thessalonians begins on a note of suffering. The Thessalonians have suffered (1.6; 2.14), as have Paul and his entourage, both in Thessalonica and Philippi (2.2, 17). However, unlike in 2 Thessalonians (1.6–8), this does not lead into the issuing of apocalyptic warnings about the fate of the persecutors as such. They will get caught up in the trouble of 1 Thessalonians 5.3 but there is no assertion there that the authorities, Greek or Roman, are destroyed because of their persecution of Christians. However, the rhetoric about suffering does imply a view of the social environment as hostile. Politically, in Thessalonica, that environment is one of Greek rule under Roman supervision. We should probably describe the attitude encapsulated by the rhetoric on suffering as being one of distrust and distance. However, this is directed essentially at the local society and authorities. It is not clear that we can yet draw Rome itself into its scope.

Jewish dismissal of the Graeco-Roman religious system is clear in the fundamental description of conversion in 1 Thessalonians 1.9: 'you turned to God from idols to serve the living and genuine God'. *Pietas*, right behaviour towards ancestors and the gods, was central to the Romans' concept of their identity and of why their empire succeeded. For Paul to show contempt for gods (and hence ancestral traditions) as false, worthless things to be abandoned meant contempt for Rome, even if he was a citizen. Of course, the Romans were used to Jewish denigration of the gods. However, for Paul to found predominantly Gentile communities on that basis, as 1.9 implies, was going far further.

If 2.16c, 'wrath has come upon them', is original to the letter, it could refer to some sort of Roman action that went against Jewish interests.[11] In that case, Paul would be responding to that action by giving it some sort of theological legitimation, rather than simply condemning it as one would expect a Jew of the time to do. Admittedly, Paul does not explicitly sanction the action that may lie behind 2.16. However, the rhetoric is more what one would expect of a post-70 attitude than a pre-70 one. Indeed, this argument has been used by some scholars to back the idea of the text being a post-70 interpolation.[12] However, the lack of text-critical evidence for interpolation makes one reluctant to accept the suggestion. From the point of view of this essay, the interesting way to read the verse is as a possible sign of very early Christian development towards a kind of rhetoric, in relation to Rome's treatment of Judea, that became full-blown once Christianity and Judaism moved further apart.

Paul urges the Thessalonian Christians to work and lead a quiet life, so as to seem respectable to outsiders (4.11–12). As with Romans 13, some scholars argue that this is a tactical, defensive measure. I agree that the practical imperatives of the Thessalonians' situation make it important. However, we should also see it as expressing a certain amount of respect for the Graeco-Roman social status quo. Paul presents this as one in which quiet hard work can be expected to generate adequate income (4.12). There is nothing directly about Rome here but I think we should see a corollary of this passage as being that Paul does appreciate the socio-economic system sustained by the *pax romana*. One can contrast this with Revelation 18 in which the Roman economic system is seen as working for the benefit of people such as merchants rather than that of ordinary people such as the Christians.

The text of 1 Thessalonians 4.13–5.11 presents an event that changes the world order. We do not see Rome crashing down in flames. This is not the Book of Revelation. However, the parousia in 1 Thessalonians is bound to be seen as overthrowing the Roman order. The apocalyptic language of commands, archangels and trumpets in 4.16 signals an intervention by God to change the world radically, to end the present age. The political overtones[13] of the description of Christ's return in 4.15–17

---

11. A.J. Malherbe, *The Letters to the Thessalonians* (Anchor Bible; New York: Doubleday, 2000), 178, gives several possibilities, such as the killing of thousands of Jews in 49 CE (citing Josephus, *Ant.* 20.102, 112–17; *War*, 2.225–7).

12. Most notably, B.A. Pearson, '1 Thessalonians 2.13–16: A Deutero-Pauline Interpolation', *HTR* 64 (1971), 79–94, at 82–4.

13. K. Donfried, 'The Cults of Thessalonica', *NTS* 31 (1985), 336–56, at 334.

suggest Christ taking up some position of great authority. Above all, the destruction in 5.3 must sweep away the current system.

How specifically this relates to Rome depends on the interpretation of *eirênê kai aphaleia*, 'peace and safety', *pax et securitas* (5.3). Malherbe is sceptical about political readings of this. He takes the slogan as summarizing the view of false teachers at Thessalonica, with Paul characterizing their message both in terms of the false prophets of Jeremiah's day who cried 'Peace!' (Jeremiah 6.14; 8.11) and of the Epicurean promise of 'security' (Epicurus, *Principal Doctrine* 14).[14] A weakness in Malherbe's suggestion lies in the need to draw the two terms from different spheres. Vom Brocke has recently given a robust defence of Ernst Bammel's drawing of both terms from the slogans of Roman politics.[15] Because this is a single sphere of discourse, this suggestion would, in principle, be stronger than that of Malherbe even if, in politics, the terms never occurred together. The popular spread of the terminology, seen especially in Claudius's *PACI AUGUSTAE* coins and the *SECURITAS AUGUSTI* ones of Nero, was also far wider than that of the Epicurean usage. The terms do, in fact, sometimes occur together. Velleius sees Tiberius as having restored *Asiae securitatem, Macedoniae pacem* (Velleius Paterculus 2.98.2). A first-century BC inscription at Troas celebrates Pompey's restoration of *[eir]ênên kai tên asphaleian*.[16] Klaus Wengst and Holland Hendrix give further examples.[17]

I doubt whether Paul is thinking specifically of the Roman authorities as those who say 'Peace and safety'. In the context of the letter it looks more likely to be the general non-Christian population of Thessalonica.[18] Cocooned by the Roman peace, they assume that nothing will disturb their lives, a state which Paul characterizes as 'sleep' – in an ironic juxtaposition to the state of the Christian dead (5.6–7, cf. 10). This illusory peace will be swept away by the arrival of the Lord 'like a thief in the night' (v. 2). This is bound to involve the Roman system being overthrown along with its *pax*. Paul seems to have Thessalonians rather than Romans at the centre of his focus in 5.3, but he does seem to expect Rome's overthrow.

In 1 Thessalonians, Paul does not directly write about Rome. However,

---

14. Malherbe, *Thessalonians*, 292, 304.

15. E. Bammel, 'Ein Beitrag zur paulinischen Staatsanschauung', *ThLZ* 85 (1960), 837–40; C. vom Brocke, *Thessaloniki – Stadt des Kassander und Gemeinde des Paulus* (WUNT 2.125; Tübingen: Mohr Siebeck, 2001), 167–85.

16. E. Schwertheim, *Araştirma Sonuçlari Toplantisi* 7 (1990), 230. For all the above references see vom Brocke, *Thessaloniki*, 177–9.

17. Wengst, *Pax Romana*, 19, 21; H.L. Hendrix, 'Archaeology and Eschatology at Thessalonica' in B.A. Pearson (ed.), *The Future of Early Christianity: Essays in honor of Helmut Koester* (Minneapolis, MN: Fortress Press, 1991), 113–14.

18. Cf. vom Brocke, *Thessaloniki*, 184–5.

several of the points that he makes indicate attitudes that he has towards Rome. The advice to live quietly and work, and the confidence that this will avoid dependence, suggest confidence in the Graeco-Roman socio-economic order. However, the concern about suffering implies a picture of the surrounding society as hostile. His view may be that hostility towards Christians is a bad element in a generally beneficent system. There is no indication of resentment directed against Rome on this account, nor on account of harsh Roman treatment of Jews, if that is what is behind 2.16. There is clear contempt for the Graeco-Roman religious system. There is expectation of the overthrow of the current world order but, although Roman political language is used, attention is not drawn to Rome as a particular power to be done away with. Paul's attitudes to Rome implied by the text lie broadly across the range that we are using.

4.3 *Romans*

Several scholars working on this letter are currently studying a wide range of material that may relate to Rome. I too have interests in this area. At present, I want to reinforce my comments on the tension between 1.19–32 and 13.1–7. Roman writers would regard Paul's combination of views as bizarrely paradoxical. They would agree that Rome was God's servant (13.4; Roman writers are happy to use monotheistic language in this kind of context, e.g., Seneca, *De Beneficiis* 4.32.3) but they would see the centre point of that service as being the maintenance of *pietas*. Rome's other good actions, such as praising good people and punishing the bad (Romans 13.3–4) would be seen as outworkings of this *pietas*. But, in Chapter 1, Paul sees Roman *pietas* as the very cause of all immorality (1.21–32)!

Paul shows appreciation of Rome's judicial role. He even shows a kind of awe in giving Rome the distinction of being God's servant in this way. Yet Paul displays contempt for Roman religion and aspects of Roman moral behaviour. We must not bracket off this religious contempt as though Paul were criticizing only an incidental part of Roman life. From the taking of auguries before Senate meetings, to the Fetial Law (a complex system of ideas and ritual actions that governed warfare), to the religious role of the paterfamilias, to the way in which the Imperial Cult expressed provincial loyalty, religion lay at the heart of the functioning of the Roman Empire.[19] The tension inherent in Paul's view is powerfully illustrated in the incomprehension of Roman officials in many of the later martyr accounts. To honour Rome while dishonouring Rome's gods was a contradiction in terms. Paul inherited this contradiction as part of his

---

19. Meggitt, *Paul, Poverty and Survival*, 118.

Judaism. For Gentile converts to Christianity it must have seemed very strange. Surely, they might think, if Romans 1 shows us that Graeco-Roman life is a progress from idolatry to immorality, Romans 13 should say that the Roman authorities serve demons. The authorities' very operation is by means of idolatry. How does God suddenly come into the equation? There is a tension in early Christian thought here.

There is, of course, a biblical pattern to all this. Figures like Nebuchadnezzar could be seen as God's instruments even though Babylonian religious beliefs were still attacked. Something of the tension that was present in early Christian attitudes to Rome was also present in earlier Israelite attitudes to other dominant political powers.

4.4 *The Gospel of Mark*

'Your manner of life must not be like that of those who are regarded as ruling the Gentiles.' If we précis Mark 10.42–44 in that way we can see a sharp potential critique of the Roman model of rule.[20] Furthermore, the thing that will arrive in the Temple is 'the abomination of desolation' (Mark 13.14). The fact that this is an allusion to Daniel's portrayal of the aweful events under Antiochus Epiphanes (Dan. 9.27; 11.31; 12.11) makes it very pointed. Mark also gives us our first view of Pontius Pilate. His administration of justice is clearly unfair and brutal. Mark makes no attempt to signal that Pilate's actions are not typical of Roman governors.

On the other hand, a climactic theological assertion in the book is given to a centurion: 'Truly this man was a son of God' (Mark 15.39). This is a Roman executioner being given a key positive role! There is also the question and answer in the Temple. Jesus looks at the head of the Emperor on a denarius and says, 'Give the things of Caesar to Caesar and the things of God to God' (12.15–17). Jesus's reference to the denarius and the use of *kai*[21] in 12.17 make it difficult to follow Horsley and Silberman in seeing the reference to God as effectively nullifying that to Caesar.[22] Mark's Jesus is supporting economic cooperation with the Romans.

In between those negative and positive points, some ambiguous issues raise far-reaching questions. Should we link to Rome the use of the term 'gospel' (1.1), or of the expression 'son of God' (1.1; 13.14)? Should we read anything into the demons being called 'Legion' (5.9)?[23] How

---

20. Wengst, *Pax Romana*, 56.
21. R.T. France, *The Gospel of Mark* (NIGTC; Grand Rapids, MI: Eerdmans, 2002), 469.
22. Horsley and Silberman, *The Message and the Kingdom*, 84.
23. G. Theissen, *Miracle Stories of the Early Christian Tradition* (Edinburgh: T&T Clark, 1983), 255.

indicative of the nature of Rome should we see Pilate's behaviour as being?

If Mark's Gospel is written during the momentous events of the 60s, either in Rome or near Judea, we might tend to expect a direct engagement with the issue of Roman power and Rome's attitudes. It could possibly be that the engagement stares us in the face. We take the general structure of Mark for granted, but it may be that we should see the long description of Jesus's passion as carrying an extended comment on the interaction between innocence and Roman power. Moreover, the hinge of the Gospel is the revelation at Caesarea Philippi of Jesus's messiahship, a revelation that is immediately tied into a passage that culminates in an implied call to the reader to be willing to face martyrdom (8.31–38).

But such a reading cannot be completely convincing. The elaborate interactions of the week of the Passion are mainly played out between Jesus and various Jewish groups, or between Jesus and his disciples. Politically, Mark is tantalizing. So many elements could be read in relation to Rome but the prominence of other issues makes one wonder whether many of these elements point another way. For example, how much should be read in terms of a more cosmic conflict? – although, in turn, the cosmic conflict could, of course, relate to politics.

Mark's attitude to Rome is more a puzzle than a clear tension. However, we can see aspects of our model of attitudes. The course of the discussion on paying tax depicts Rome's ability to impose its economic and iconographic system on God's people. There is an element of awe implied here. There is, however, no obvious appreciation of the *pax romana*. On the contrary, the portrayal of Pilate implies resentment at the rule of this governor at least. The prophecy of the events of 70 CE also conveys deep resentment at the way in which the attackers will behave. There is considerable stress on allegiance to the authority of Jesus being more important than that of those who might promise 'life' and 'the whole world' (8.35–36). His arrival with his father's glory and the holy angels (8.38) presumably represents the end of the present order. Mark does think about Rome – and the implied attitudes are generally negative. However, in the appreciation of the potential openness of the centurion at the Cross, and in the instruction to give Caesar whatever is properly his, I still get a sense of the thought-world of 1 Thessalonians. The call is radical but with a pervasive strand of quietism. Any book that can say 'Give to Caesar the things that are Caesar's' cannot be wholly on the negative side of the equation in relation to Rome. I think we can see enough to conclude that the tension that we are considering is at work in Mark's Gospel, although its effects are enigmatic.

4.5 *The Book of Acts*

The ground here is very well worn. Steve Walton has recently surveyed various approaches and argued persuasively that Luke maintains a stance of critical distance towards Rome. Luke will effectively commend Rome when it does well but is always aware that it may do badly.[24] This is not quite the same as the tension that I am arguing for, although the two approaches can coexist. If Luke holds a mixture of positive and negative attitudes to Rome (my view) then one would expect him to evaluate Rome's actions and judge them as good or bad (Walton's view). By contrast, if Luke held a firmly negative view of Rome, one would expect him to prejudge all of Rome's actions as negative.

Roman officials abound. Cornelius the Italian centurion is a very positive character (Acts 10). Even before conversion to Christianity he is described as 'devout and God-fearing' (10.2). His actions in Acts 10 play an important positive role in the forward movement of Luke's story. The governor Sergius Paulus is also presented positively. He is 'intelligent' and open to Christianity (13.6–12). Gallio judges in favour of the Christians (18.12–16), although the description of his lack of concern about the synagogue ruler being beaten up in front of him could carry a note of censure (18.17). The centurion in the shipwreck behaves well (27.32, 43). The chief magistrate on Malta is generous to Paul (28.7). The conditions of Paul's imprisonment at Rome seem very favourable (28.30–31).

Felix is an ambiguous character but, on balance, seems negative for Luke. Felix conducts an orderly hearing and certainly does not jump to conclusions! However, the ensuing two-year hiatus is clearly a scandal and, although his desire to talk repeatedly with Paul would look positive in itself, it becomes negative in Luke's note that Felix's motive is the hope for bribery (24.26). Festus is also ambiguous but does not have the obvious negative edge that Felix has. At the instigation of Paul's opponents among the Jewish authorities, Festus tries to resolve Paul's case (25.2–5). Festus's desire to 'do the Jews a favour' inclines him to send Paul to Jerusalem (25.9). Luke's reader knows that this would lead to an ambush, but Luke's Festus is clearly not complicit in this. In any case, Paul solves Festus's problem by appealing to Caesar. The hearing involving Agrippa and Berenice, prior to Paul being sent to Rome, shows Festus as generally reasonable, although his outburst at Paul (26.24) suggests some intemperance.

Another ambiguous case of Roman behaviour is the conduct of the troops who arrest Paul. They stop him being beaten by the mob in the Temple court (21.32) but immediately chain him (v. 33). Surprisingly, the

---

24.   S. Walton, 'The State they Were in: Luke's View of the Roman Empire', in Oakes (ed.), *Rome in the Bible and the Early Church*, 1–41, at 33–5.

tribune then permits Paul to deliver a speech to the crowd (v. 40). When this ends in chaos, the tribune orders the flogging and questioning of Paul (22.24) but cancels the order in alarm on discovering Paul's Roman citizenship (v. 29). The tribune then organizes a hearing before the Sanhedrin. His motive is the positive one of wanting to understand the case properly (v. 30). He then intervenes again to rescue Paul at the end of that meeting (23.10). Finally, the tribune listens to the report of the plot against Paul and takes careful steps to preserve his life and refer his case to the governor (23.19–33).

The final example is the negative one of the behaviour of the Roman authorities at Philippi. In response to charges of un-Roman teaching and to clamour from the forum mob, they peremptorily order the heavy beating and close imprisonment of Paul and Silas (16.20–24). Discovering the next morning that they had illegally beaten Roman citizens, the magistrates show fear and some servility (16.35–39). They compound the bad impression by tacitly reinforcing their original unjust action by asking Paul to leave Philippi (v. 39). This incident stretches Wengst's argument that Luke depicts Rome and its representatives 'in an explicitly favourable light'.[25] His view of the Philippi narrative is that Luke was faced with an unavoidable negative incident and toned down the magistrates' violence by appeal to points such as their lack of understanding.[26] On the contrary: Luke's narrative seems designed to highlight the arbitrariness and violence of the magistrates. They themselves tear off the apostles' clothes (*contra* NRSV, etc.) and order a particularly heavy beating and unnecessarily onerous imprisonment (16.22–23).

Looking through the series of incidents involving Roman officials in Acts leads to the conclusion that they are portrayed in varying ways, both positive and negative. This tells against views, such as that of Wengst, in which Luke is seen as attempting to portray Rome in a uniformly positive light. It would fit the opinion of Cullmann and others, who see Luke as portraying a range of officials whose character and behaviour varies. This view can be close to that of Wengst because the variation can be read in terms of some officials properly representing Rome, while others slip from the generally high standards which Luke sees Rome as having.

However, it may be that we should look at this evidence differently. We could read the officials as uniformly representing Rome, but a Rome that was, in Luke's eyes, a paradoxical mixture of good and bad. Felix's love of bribery was as much a part of the common behaviour of Roman governors as was Gallio's dismissal of the case against Paul. Luke knew that Rome was like that. As Walton argues, Luke could see Rome (itself) as sometimes acting well and sometimes badly. As I would put it, this is

---

25. Wengst, *Pax Romana*, 90.
26. Wengst, *Pax Romana*, 95–6.

simply the converse of Luke having a view of Rome in which there is tension between appreciation and resentment. The evidence in Acts does not show Luke's Rome as wholly positive. Luke's Rome is a mixture of efficiency, openness, justice, cruelty and corruption.

4.6 *The Book of Revelation*

Surely there is no paradox and tension here? Surely the attitudes to Rome are purely on the negative side – resentment, contempt, denial of ultimate authority, expectation of overthrow – without a hint of awe or of appreciation of the *pax romana*?

The negative aspects of Revelation's attitude to Rome scarcely need documenting. There is impassioned resentment at persecution and the persecution is laid specifically at Rome's door (Rev. 17.6; 18.20, 24). There is resentment at the nature of the Roman empire. Rome 'corrupted the earth' (19.2). The repeated emphasis on Rome's luxury (17.4; 18.3, 7, 11–14, 16) presumably implies an idea of economic exploitation of the empire. The long list of traded goods probably implies this too, especially since the list ends with slaves (18.11–13). Contempt for Rome is most graphically shown by the depiction of the city as a drunken, bejewelled prostitute riding a beast (17.3–6). There is more specific moral contempt in references such as those to luxury and the slave-trade. A major thrust of the Book of Revelation as a whole is to persuade its hearers not to submit to certain aspects of Roman authority. This is shown particularly by the insistence on refusing to receive the mark of the name of the beast (14.11). Expectation of Rome's overthrow in Revelation really does need no documenting.

On the positive side of our list of attitudes, the writer of Revelation expresses awe at Rome's wealth and power. Rome glitters 'with gold, precious stones and pearls' (18.16). The list of goods of which Rome is the principal buyer is long and detailed (18.11–13). 'Was there ever a city like this great city?' cry the seafarers (18.17–18). The angel calls Rome 'the great city that has sovereignty over the kings of the earth' (17.18). The writer seems genuinely struck by the extent of Rome's riches and might. This stands in some tension with the derision expressed in the depiction of the prostitute on the beast. The seer holds together awe and contempt.

The writer also describes the Roman empire as bringing economic benefits. 'The merchants of the earth grew rich' (18.3). They sold the goods in the list of 18.11–13. Ship-owners too became wealthy (18.19). However, the crucial point is that the writer of Revelation does not identify himself or his community as benefiting from these economic gains. The writer represents a group that sees itself as standing outside the benefits that many other people in the empire are enjoying. If we compare

Luke's Roman empire with that of Revelation, the Roman empire of Revelation is a more exploitative place for most of its inhabitants. However, the greater structural difference between Luke and Revelation is that, for Revelation, Christians are not able to benefit from aspects of the empire that bring good to some subjects.

There is no tension in the seer's outlook between appreciation and resentment of the empire, even though the seer understands that the empire brings benefit to some people. There is no tension in the writer's assessment of whether Rome is good or bad. It is bad. The only tension in the attitudes in Revelation is probably between awe at 'the great city' and derisive contempt at 'the prostitute'. One could certainly argue that in Revelation the tension between positive and negative elements in the evaluation of Rome is resolved in favour of the negative. However, even here there is the occasional air of the awe-struck provincial, gaping at the splendour of the city. One might even say that it is the positive element of awe that lends sharpness to the negative catalogue of Rome's faults and impending disaster.

4.7 *Conclusions*

Horsley and Silberman, in their book, *The Message and the Kingdom*, present early Christian attitudes to Rome as a trajectory, from the radical Jesus and Paul to the accommodating Luke. I agree that there are trajectories in operation. Two that we have noted in this article are the changing attitudes towards Rome's action in Judea and the changing place of persecution as a factor in Christian attitudes. However, the argument of this article is that, alongside any trajectories in attitudes, there is a fundamental and persistent element of tension between positive and negative factors within Christian attitudes to Rome. A corollary of this is that scholars' depictions of trajectories have generally been over-played by ignoring the constant factor of tension.

The New Testament texts differ in the topics that they address and hence in the ways in which some of these topics relate to attitudes to Rome. This means that the nature of the indicators of attitude to Rome vary from text to text. However, the clues in each text add up to an element of tension. In 1 Thessalonians there is a tension indicated by the combination of Paul's confidence in his prescription of quietism and his apocalypticism with regard to *pax et securitas*. In Romans there is a tension in the depiction of Rome's relationship to God. The state, whose government is driven by an idolatry that inevitably produces moral degradation, is also God's servant for praising the good and punishing the bad. In Mark there is tension between a Caesar to whom his due must be rendered and a Caesar whose arrival in the Temple is like the 'abomination of desolation' of Antiochus Epiphanes. In Acts there is a tension evidenced by the range of behaviour of the many Roman authority-figures in the book. Even in the Book of Revelation, where the moral evaluation of Rome is wholly negative, there is evidence of tension between awe at Rome's power and contempt at its corruption and at its ignominious fate.

Our sixfold model of expected early Christian attitudes to Rome – awe, appreciation, resentment, contempt, denial of ultimate authority, expectation of overthrow – is far from being the only list that could be made. However, it does appear to be a useful checklist for considering New Testament texts. None of the texts, except maybe the Book of Revelation, discuss Rome explicitly enough to give us direct evidence of the presence or absence of every one of the six factors. However, in many of the texts there are enough clues to suggest that such a list of expected attitudes is not too far from a list of actual attitudes. There seems to be sufficient evidence to suggest that tension, such as that existing between elements of that list, is present in Christian attitudes to Rome in all of the New Testament.

ROME IN MATTHEW'S ESCHATOLOGY

David C. Sim

5.1 *Introduction*

Modern Matthaean scholarship has devoted a great deal of attention to the social setting of the evangelist and his community. For the most part this has involved an analysis of this group's interaction with the Jewish world, which has developed in the last decade or so into a debate over whether Matthew and his Christian group still identified themselves within Judaism.[1] The focus on this theme has raised further questions concerning the relationship between the Matthaean community and the Gentile world[2] and between this group and the Pauline churches.[3] Although this previous work is doubtless important for establishing the type of community that Matthew represented and the circumstances that

---

1. For recent contributions to this debate, see D.C. Sim, *The Gospel of Matthew and Christian Judaism: The History and Social Setting of the Matthean Community* (SNTW; Edinburgh: T&T Clark, 1998), 109–63; J. Riches, *Conflicting Mythologies: Identity Formation in the Gospels of Mark and Matthew* (SNTW; Edinburgh: T&T Clark, 2000), 202–28, 316–24; D.R.A. Hare, 'How Jewish is the Gospel of Matthew?', *CBQ* 62 (2000), 264–77; P. Luomanen, 'The "Sociology of Sectarianism" in Matthew: Modelling the Genesis of Early Jewish and Christian Communities' in I. Dunderberg, C. Tuckett and K. Syreeni (eds), *Fair Play, Diversity and Conflicts in Early Christianity: Essays in Honour of Heikki Räisänen* (Leiden: Brill, 2003), 107–30; D.A. Hagner, 'Matthew: Apostate, Reformer, Revolutionary?', *NTS* 49 (2003), 193–208; and P. Foster, *Community, Law and Mission in Matthew's Gospel* (WUNT 2/177; Tübingen: Mohr Siebeck, 2004).

2. See D.C. Sim, 'The Gospel of Matthew and the Gentiles', *JSNT* 57 (1995), 19–48; Sim, *Matthew and Christian Judaism*, 215–56; D. Senior, 'Between Two Worlds: Gentiles and Jewish Christians in Matthew's Gospel', *CBQ* 61 (1999), 1–23; B. Byrne, 'The Messiah in Whose Name "The Gentiles Will Hope": Gentile Inclusion as an Essential Element of Matthew's Christology', *ABR* 50 (2002), 55–73; D.C. Sim, 'Matthew and the Gentiles: A Response to Brendan Byrne', *ABR* 50 (2002), 74–9; and W. Carter, 'Matthew and the Gentiles: Individual Conversion and/or Systemic Transformation?', *JSNT* 26 (2004), 259–82.

3. Sim, *Matthew and Christian Judaism*, 165–213. Cf. too D.C. Sim, 'Matthew's Anti-Paulinism: A Neglected Feature of Matthean Studies', *HTS* 58 (2002), 767–83.

influenced it, it is clear that there has been a large gap in the discussion. That gap concerns the relations between Matthew's group and the Roman Empire, and the manner in which Rome is treated in this gospel.

Warren Carter has drawn attention to this point in his important monograph devoted to this theme.[4] According to Carter, Roman imperialism was such a dominant reality in the daily lives of all those who lived within the empire that it must have made some impression on the evangelist and his intended readers. This is even more the case if, as most scholars argue, Matthew was written in Antioch on the Orontes, the capital of the Roman province of Syria.[5] Carter has spelt out just how omnipresent was the Roman presence in this city at the time of the gospel's composition.[6] The city was overseen by a Roman governor who was responsible for the troublesome eastern sections of the empire. At his disposal were four legions, or around 20,000 troops, which were permanently based in the city. Antioch was the base from which the Romans launched their counter-attack during the Jewish uprising in 66–70 CE. The Roman general in charge of this operation, Vespasian, returned to Antioch in 69 on his way to Rome to be confirmed as emperor. His son Titus, who successfully finished the campaign against the Jews the following year, also visited Antioch and displayed the spoils of his victory. He paraded Jewish prisoners, destroyed a Jewish synagogue and built in its place a theatre with a statue of his father, and erected other monuments to reinforce the power of Rome and the humiliation of the Jews. Like other Jews in Antioch, Matthew's Christian Jewish community shared this humiliation at the hands of the Romans.[7]

Carter argues that since Roman power and authority were an everyday reality in the lives of the evangelist and his community, we would expect that their views about Rome would be given expression in the gospel. He makes a solid case that Matthew's narrative about Jesus contests Rome's claim to sovereignty over the world by emphasizing that the world belongs to the God of Israel and Jesus, his messiah. Ultimately God will demonstrate his power over Rome by destroying it completely. This final point, the fate of Rome in Matthew's eschatological scheme, will be the topic of this study.

4. W. Carter, *Matthew and Empire: Initial Explorations* (Harrisburg, IL: Trinity Press International, 2001).

5. For detailed discussion of the provenance of Matthew, see Sim, *Matthew and Christian Judaism*, 40–62.

6. Carter, *Matthew and Empire*, 37–46.

7. Sim, *Matthew and Christian Judaism*, 234–6.

5.2 *Rome in Matthew's Dualistic Scheme*

In an earlier study of the gospel's eschatological scheme, I argued that the evangelist had embraced a comprehensive apocalyptic–eschatological viewpoint.[8] Amongst other things, I presented a case that the gospel reflects a developed dualism that was comparable to the schemes in the Dead Sea Scrolls and the Christian Book of Revelation. This dualism involves a strict division in the cosmic order between the forces of good and evil, which are engaged in a fierce battle for supremacy. Humans are inevitably caught up in this supernatural conflict, and individuals can choose either to side with God (and Jesus) or to side with Satan and his army of fallen angels; there is no middle ground. The advanced dualistic perspective is found throughout the gospel, but it is most clearly articulated in the interpretation of the parable of the tares (Matt. 13.36–43) where one is either a son of the kingdom aligned with the Son of Man (Jesus) or a son of the evil one (Satan).[9]

One point, however, that I had not fully appreciated in that discussion of the gospel's dualism is that Matthew inextricably connects Satan and the Roman Empire. In the context of the cosmic battle between God and Satan, the Romans have opted to throw in their lot with the latter. This theme is clearly spelt out in the temptation narrative (Matt. 4.1–11). On his third attempt to divert Jesus from obeying the will of God, Satan takes him to a high mountain and shows him all the kingdoms of the world and their glory. He tells Jesus that he will give all of these to him if he falls down and worships him. Jesus rejects this offer by telling Satan that he is to worship and serve God alone, and he dismisses Satan from his presence (vv. 8–10). The important point for our purposes is Satan's offer to give Jesus all the kingdoms of the world. The Roman Empire, the dominant power in the settings of both Jesus and Matthew, must be included within this reference. This means, as Carter rightly points out, that Rome comes directly under the power and control of Satan and serves his evil interests.[10]

This Matthaean theme finds a close parallel in the Book of Revelation, especially in the mention of the dragon and the two beasts in Chapter 13. The first beast is doubtless the Roman Empire, which is given power and authority by the dragon (13.2, 4) who is identified earlier as Satan (12.9; cf. 20.2). The second beast, which makes people worship the first beast (13.12), is a clear reference to the cult of emperor worship, which began

8.   D.C. Sim, *Apocalyptic Eschatology in the Gospel of Matthew* (SNTSMS 88; Cambridge: Cambridge University Press, 1996).

9.   Sim, *Apocalyptic Eschatology*, 75–87. For an alternative view of Matthew's dualistic scheme, see Riches, *Conflicting Mythologies*, 199–200, 264–9.

10.   Carter, *Matthew and Empire*, 62–3. See too W.D. Davies and D.C. Allison, *A Critical and Exegetical Commentary on the Gospel According to Saint Matthew* (ICC; 3 vols; Edinburgh: T&T Clark, 1988, 1991, 1997), I, 371.

with Augustus and was firmly entrenched by the end of the first century CE. It is well accepted that in Revelation all aspects of the Roman Empire – the military, the religious, the economic and the social – serve the interests of Satan and oppose the purposes of God. Matthew's view of Rome, though not spelt out in the same detail, is just as critical.

5.3 *Rome in Matthew's Eschatological Scenario*

Matthew provides a good deal of information about the conflict between Jesus and Satan, which he introduced in the temptation narrative. This battle continues throughout the current age. Jesus performs many exorcisms during the course of his mission (Matt. 8.16, 2–24; 9.32–4; 12.22–30; 15.22–8; 17.14–21; cf. 11.5) and his actions are repeated by the disciples (Matt. 10.8). But these successful exorcisms, important as they are, do not signal the ultimate defeat of Satan and his army of unclean spirits. In line with many contemporary apocalyptic–eschatological schemes, the final and definitive victory over the forces of evil will take place at the end of the age when the universal judgment takes place (cf. 25.31–46). For Matthew, this judgment will be presided over by Jesus the Son of Man after he returns from heaven in glory (19.28; 25.31). At this time Satan and the other fallen angels will be condemned and then cast into the eternal fires of Gehenna (25.41).

The evangelist specifies that this grisly fate also awaits those who have aligned themselves with Satan. He emphasizes more than any other New Testament author that the human wicked as well will face punishment by eternal fire (3.7–12; 5.22; 7.19; 13.40–42, 49–50; 18.8–9; 25.41) where they will be tortured forever (18.23–35; cf. 8.28–34).[11] By contrast, the righteous who have sided with Jesus and God in the cosmic battle will receive eternal rewards. Matthew reflects a strong apocalyptic–eschatological tradition that the righteous will be transformed into (heavenly) angels for their loyalty and endurance (22.30; cf. 5.8; 13.43; 22.11–13).[12] The evangelist's view that the judgment has only two possible results – transformation into an angel or eternal torture by the fires of Gehenna – reinforces his advanced dualistic perspective. Just as there are two sides in the battle between God and Satan, so there are only two options following the universal judgment.

Having established this point, we may now turn our attention to the Roman Empire in Matthew's eschatological expectations. Given that Rome is inextricably linked with Satan in the temptation narrative, we would expect Matthew to have believed that the Roman Empire was also

---

11. For more detailed discussion of this theme, see Sim, *Apocalyptic Eschatology*, 129–40.
12. Sim, *Apocalyptic Eschatology*, 140–5.

destined for condemnation and punishment when Jesus returns in glory at the end of the age. This is precisely what we find when we examine the gospel. The evangelist specifies that the last event in history will be a major war between the righteous and the forces of evil, the result of which will be the complete defeat of Rome and its oppressive military machine.

The belief that the end of the age would be marked by a terrible conflict was common in contemporary apocalyptic–eschatological schemes (cf. Dan. 11.40–45; 1 En. 56.5–7; 90.10–19; 91.11; Sib. Or. 3.63–74; 4.137–52; 5.93–109, 214–27, 361–74). In those traditions which reflect a developed dualism, the battle involves the two opposing sides and includes both the human and the supernatural worlds. This war is brought to an end by the arrival of a heavenly saviour figure who relieves the situation of the righteous by defeating the forces of evil, which in turn prepares the way for the final judgment.

In the Qumran War Scroll, the righteous community will be engaged in a 40-year conflict against the powers of darkness, comprising Satan (Belial) and his company of evil angels as well as the human armies who are allied with them (1QM 1.1–4). The holy angels led by the archangel Michael will come to the assistance of the Qumran community (1QM 13.9–10; 17.5–8), but victory will result only when God himself enters the battle (1QM 1.14; 14.15). The Book of Revelation envisages a similar scenario, although in this Christian text the returning Jesus plays a significant role in the events. In this document the supernatural forces of evil will rise from the bottomless pit to wreak havoc among the righteous (6.8; 9.1–11; 11.7; 17.8; cf. 20.7–8). At the very end of the age, the dragon (Satan), the beast (Rome) and the false prophet will summon the kings of the world and their armies for the final battle at Armageddon (16.12–16; 19.19). They will be opposed by Jesus who will appear from heaven on a white horse prepared for war. A sharp sword will issue from his mouth to smite the nations who oppose him, and he will lead the armies of heaven against his enemies (19.11–16). The beast and the other military forces will engage the heavenly host, but the beast will be captured and thrown into the lake of fire (19.20). Satan too will be captured and then imprisoned for one thousand years. At the end of this time he will be released, but he too will be cast into the fiery lake (20.1–10). In this way the unholy allies of Rome and Satan will be defeated and will share the same eschatological punishment.[13]

---

13. It is important to note that other apocalyptic–eschatological texts contemporaneous with Revelation depict the endtime defeat of Rome, even though they do not necessarily link the Roman Empire with Satan. The Sibylline Oracles denounce Rome for its great sins, and prophesy its destruction and/or eternal punishment (3.46–62; 5.162–78, 386–96). In similar vein, 4 Ezra presents the messiah condemning, judging and destroying the Romans at the end of the age (11.1–12.35).

The Gospel of Matthew, written at roughly the same time as the Christian apocalypse, presents a strikingly similar view of the final cosmic battle and its participants. I have argued this point previously,[14] and the arguments presented in that discussion can be summarized here. In the redactional verse 16.18, the Matthaean Jesus tells Peter that he will be the rock upon which the church will be built, and not even the gates of Hades will be able to prevail against this church. The 'gates of Hades' here probably refers to the final assault upon the righteous by the demonic forces who will advance from the underworld (cf. Rev. 6.8; 9.1–11; 11.7; 17.8). This conflict and its aftermath are spelt out in more detail in Matthew's eschatological discourse, specifically in 24.15–31.

At the very end of the age, the righteous will experience a great and unparalleled tribulation (vv. 15–21). This event includes the unleashing of the evil forces against the righteous mentioned in 16.18, but it involves other evil combatants in addition to these whose identity is provided in 24.28. In this verse Matthew states that wherever the corpse is, there the eagles (*aetoi*) will be gathered together. The corpse may be a reference to Satan himself or to an antichrist figure, but the eagles almost certainly refer to the Roman Empire and its armies. This is suggested by the fact that the eagle was a well-known symbol for Rome and appeared on the standards of the legions. It is noteworthy that 4 Ezra, an apocalypse written slightly later than the gospel, uses this very symbol to represent the Roman Empire (Chapters 11–12). On this understanding of v. 28, Matthew envisages the great tribulation that the righteous experience as the result of an unholy coalition between the satanic forces and Rome. These human and demonic forces will attack the righteous in a full-scale assault.

All of this acts as a prelude to the next decisive eschatological event: the arrival of Jesus the Son of Man from heaven. The arrival of Jesus will be preceded by a number of cosmic signs: the sun will be darkened, the moon will fail to give light, the stars will fall from heaven and the powers of the heavens will be shaken (v. 29). Immediately following these events, the sign of the Son of Man will appear and the tribes of the earth will mourn as they see the Son of Man coming on the clouds of heaven with power and great glory. He will send out his angels with a trumpet call to gather his elect (vv. 30–31).

Because Jesus returns in the context of a battle between the righteous and the forces of evil, the evangelist describes his appearance in military terms. Jesus returns from heaven at the head of an angelic army. This point is not specified in the immediate context, but in 26.53 the Matthaean Jesus refers to more than twelve legions of angels at his disposal. It is presumably these angels who accompany him at the eschaton. The sign of

---

14. See Sim, *Apocalyptic Eschatology*, 100–8 and literature cited there.

the Son of Man which precedes Jesus and his heavenly forces is therefore his military standard. That this is the correct interpretation of this motif is confirmed by the later reference to the trumpet call in verse 31. The coupling of the military banner and the trumpet call was well established in Jewish eschatology (cf. Isa. 18.3; Jer. 6.1; 51.27). More importantly, these items play prominent and crucial roles in the eschatological battle depicted in the War Scroll from Qumran (1QM 2.15–4.17).

Thus Matthew's expectations of the final events – an assault upon the righteous by demonic and Roman forces followed by the appearance of Jesus at the head of an angelic army – has very close affinities with the account of the eschatological conflict in Revelation 19.11–19. But the evangelist, unlike the author of Revelation, offers no description at all of a battle between Jesus's holy army and its wicked counterpart. It is likely that Matthew, for reasons which are not entirely clear, believed that the forces of evil would immediately surrender once they were confronted by the Son of Man and his legions of angels. This is suggested by the reference that the tribes of the earth will mourn once they witness the standard of the Son of Man. Presumably the Romans and their allies will submit in the face of the superior heavenly force. They will mourn as they realize that, having thrown in their lot with Satan, they face certain defeat and future punishment.

In this earlier study I had therefore made a link between Satan and Rome in Matthew's description of the eschatological war, but I must admit that the treatment of this theme was more incidental than pointed. My major concern was to demonstrate that the evangelist had adopted the apocalyptic–eschatological motif of the endtime war, and I did not emphasize the involvement of Rome in this event. This gap in my discussion has been filled in a much more focused study of Rome in the Matthaean eschatological discourse by Warren Carter.[15] This recent offering is a further attempt by Carter to extend his pioneering programme of interpreting Matthew's Gospel within its imperial context. According to Carter, the crucial section in Matthew 24.27–31 is wholly devoted to the theme of Rome's defeat by Jesus and his heavenly angels. Carter graciously acknowledges that his work builds on my previous suggestion that the Roman army is in view in these particular verses,[16] and he accepts my arguments that Jesus in verses 30–31 is depicted as a military leader at the head of an angelic army.[17] But Carter's analysis goes much further than my own, and makes many more connections between

15.   W. Carter, 'Are there Imperial Texts in the Class? Intertextual Eagles and Matthean Eschatology as "Lights Out" Time for Imperial Rome (Matthew 24.27–31)', *JBL* 122 (2003), 467–87. See too his *Matthew and Empire*, 86–8.

16.   Carter, 'Are there Imperial Texts in the Class?', 486.

17.   Carter, 'Are there Imperial Texts in the Class?', 485–6.

these Matthaean verses and imperial Rome. His arguments can be summarized in the following manner.

Carter begins with the Greek term *aetoi* in 24.28, which is often translated and understood not as 'eagles' but as 'vultures'. This is of obvious importance. If Matthew here is referring to vultures rather than eagles, then any connection with Rome in these verses must be deemed implausible. But Carter, referring to a wide variety of contemporary texts, demonstrates conclusively that *aetoi* in this verse must be rendered as 'eagles'.[18] Next he investigates the identity of these eagles in Matthew, and concludes that they must be associated with Rome. In the LXX the eagle is often used to symbolize imperial powers used by God to punish his people, but which will in turn be judged and punished by God. Moreover, in the time of Roman imperialism the eagle was the definitive sign of Roman rule. It was the symbol of Jupiter; it appeared on the standards of the Roman legions and on Roman coins, and it was used to represent Rome in 4 Ezra. Carter concludes that in Matthew's imperial setting the eagles in 24.28 can only mean the standards of the Roman armies that represent and protect Roman interests.[19]

Having established this point, Carter moves to the issue of the corpse around which the eagles are gathered. He suggests that Matthew is describing the death of Rome and its legions as God's just punishment delivered by the Son of Man. In support of this interpretation, Carter reintroduces and expands an earlier point. The LXX uses the eagle as a symbol of those empires which God uses to chasten his people but who are in turn punished by God. Matthew follows this pattern. He considers Rome to be God's agent of punishment in its destruction of Jerusalem and the Jewish temple (22.7), which means that he must have anticipated the future punishment and destruction of Rome. This reading is consistent with the wording in 24.28, which uses *sunagô* (divine passive) and *ptôma*, both of which suggest a judgmental scenario. Further, in contemporary apocalyptic literature, Rome is often depicted as the victim of God's vengeance in the final eschatological battle.[20]

Carter sees further imperial references in the surrounding verses. In verse 27 the comparison of the coming of the Son of Man to lightning evokes a Roman image of imperial power. Lightning was associated with Jupiter, and symbolized that Rome was supported in its endeavours by the gods. Matthew's use of this imagery to describe the arrival of Jesus represents the counterclaim that God is sovereign over the world and that Jesus and not Rome enjoys divine favour. The same can be said of the coming or *parousia* of the Son of Man in this verse. This Greek term was

18. Carter, 'Are there Imperial Texts in the Class?', 469–72.
19. Carter, 'Are there Imperial Texts in the Class?', 473–6.
20. Carter, 'Are there Imperial Texts in the Class?', 477–80.

often employed to denote the arrival of the emperor, but its presence here once again emphasizes the majesty and authority of Jesus who represents and fulfils the will of God. Further imperial associations, according to Carter, appear in verse 29. The cosmic phenomena that precede the Son of Man's arrival refer to the destruction of Rome. While the Romans claimed that they enjoyed the blessings of the gods of the sun, moon and stars, the Son of Man demonstrates the falsity of this claim by bringing the cosmic order to an end. The falling of the stars from heaven may also indicate the defeat of Satan and his evil angels, since in Jewish thought the judgment of Satan and his demonic underlings is sometimes associated with falling stars (cf. 1 En. 86.1–3; 88.1–3; 90.24; Dan. 8.10; Jude 13; Rev. 12.4). Matthew is perhaps making the point that the return of Jesus the Son of Man entails the destruction of Satan as well as Rome, the unholy alliance he establishes in the temptation narrative.[21]

Carter's thorough study is clearly an important contribution to the subject of Rome in Matthew's eschatology. He has taken my earlier suggestion that Matthew envisages in the end time a confrontation between Jesus and his holy angels on the one side, and Satan and his Roman allies on the other, and strengthened it considerably with a wealth of further evidence. The Roman Empire with its divine pretensions and its oppressive measures against those who do the will of God will meet its match when Jesus returns at the end of the age. I am less convinced than Carter that Matthew anticipates the destruction of Rome and its armies at this point in time. It seems more likely to me that Rome surrenders to the Son of Man and survives, but this is not to say that the evangelist believes the Romans will be spared punishment. For Matthew, as I stated above, the major eschatological event is the universal judgment before the enthroned Son of Man (25.31–46; cf. 7.22–3; 19.28). Rome is therefore spared physical destruction so that it can be judged, condemned and then finally punished for its alliance with Satan and its crimes against the righteous.

Does the gospel refer to the judgment and punishment of Rome? In answer to this question, we may begin with the scene of universal judgment in 25.31–46. According to this text, when the Son of Man sits on his glorious throne all the nations will be gathered before him prior to their separation (vv. 31–32). This reference to all the nations recalls the mention of 'all the kingdoms of the world' that come under the influence of Satan in Matthew 4.8. Rome is therefore included in the final judgment before the Son of Man, even if it is not specifically mentioned. Moreover, as allies of Satan and oppressors of the righteous, the Romans are destined to be sent to the eternal fire prepared for Satan and his angels (v. 41). Just as we found in Revelation, the unholy alliance of Satan and

---

21. Carter, 'Are there Imperial Texts in the Class?', 480–85.

Rome in this age dictates that they will share the same eternal punishment in the age to come. Does Matthew say anything else concerning the judgment of the Roman Empire and those who serve her evil interests? I think he does.

5.4 *A Proleptic Judgment on Rome in Matthew's Crucifixion Scene*

Some ten years ago I published an article on the Roman soldiers at the foot of the cross who acknowledged that Jesus was the Son of God.[22] In that study I argued that the consensus view, which affirms that these soldiers make a solemn confession of Christian faith, was incorrect in terms of Matthew's intentions, and that we should understand their statement rather differently. It must be conceded that this critique of the common view has not been warmly embraced by other scholars. Later commentators have politely referred to this study and noted that it presents a contrary interpretation of the soldiers' words,[23] but to my knowledge no one has expressed any agreement with my view. Yet I would suggest that the argument I pursued in that study is much more consistent than the consensus position with the recent trend in Matthaean studies that highlights Matthew's intense opposition to Roman power and imperialism.

The statement of the soldiers is an integral part of the pericope in Matthew 27.51–4, which relates the events that immediately follow the death of Jesus in verse 50. After Jesus yields up his spirit, a number of supernatural events occur: the curtain of the Jewish temple is torn in two; an earthquake occurs which splits open rocks; and many saints who were dead are raised to life (vv. 51–53). The centurion and other Roman soldiers at the foot of the cross witness these events and become terrified. In response to what they see, they proclaim 'Truly this was the (or a) Son of God (*theou huios*)' (v. 54). In attempting to determine Matthew's purpose in this narrative, two points need to be established.

The first concerns the evangelist's characterization of these Roman soldiers. Matthew specifies much more clearly than his Marcan source that the soldiers who proclaim Jesus as Son of God were in fact the very soldiers who crucified him. This is made clear in two redactional sections. First, in 27.36 Matthew rewrites Mark and relates how the soldiers who crucified Jesus cast lots for his garments and then sat down to keep watch

---

22.   D.C. Sim, 'The "Confession" of the Soldiers in Matthew 27.54', *HeyJ* 34 (1993), 401–24.

23.   See, for example, Davies and Allison, *Matthew*, III, 635, n.139; C.S. Keener, *A Commentary on the Gospel of Matthew* (Grand Rapids, MI: Eerdmans, 1999), 688, n. 249; and W. Carter, *Matthew and the Margins: A Sociopolitical and Religious Reading* (Maryknoll, NY: Orbis, 2000), 607 n. 23.

over him. Second, in another redactional insertion in 27.54, the evangelist describes those who attest Jesus as the Son of God as the centurion and the others with him who were keeping watch over Jesus. These editorial alterations to Mark therefore identify explicitly the executioners of Jesus with those who affirm his status as Son of God. But these soldiers do not merely crucify Jesus. Matthew says a good deal more about these characters in the earlier section of his passion narrative. They are introduced into the story in 27.26–7.

Pilate has Jesus scourged and delivers him into the hands of the 'soldiers of the governor' who are responsible for his crucifixion. These soldiers parade Jesus before the whole battalion in the praetorium, dress him in a scarlet robe, place a crown of thorns on his head, give him a reed and then mock him as the king of the Jews. They then spit on Jesus, strike him with the reed and dress him in his own clothes in preparation for his execution. After forcing Simon of Cyrene to carry his cross, the soldiers then crucify Jesus and gamble for his garments before taking watch over him. Matthew has therefore quite deliberately identified the soldiers who acknowledge Jesus as Son of God not merely as his executioners, but also as the ones who humiliated and brutalized him prior to his crucifixion. They are depicted as willing instruments of the unjust Roman judicial system, who carry out their brutal work with extreme arrogance and cruelty.[24] From Matthew's point of view, they represent the very worst aspects of Roman imperialism. The way of Rome is the complete antithesis to the will of God, which demands justice and mercy (cf. 23.23).

The second point concerns the meaning of their statement that Jesus truly was the Son of God. On this issue the recent study of the *theou huios* formula in Matthew by R.L. Mowery is quite suggestive.[25] First of all, Mowery notes that this specific formula to denote Jesus as the Son of God appears only in Matthew, where it occurs three times (14.33; 27.43, 54).[26] Second, Mowery establishes that a number of Roman emperors were denoted as *theou huios*: Augustus, Tiberius, Nero, Titus and Domitian. In the case of Domitian, in whose reign the Gospel of Matthew was probably written, some 80 coins minted in the east of the Roman Empire refer to this emperor using this titular expression.[27] Mowery then argues that Matthew's community, which probably resided in Antioch, would have known of this imperial title. The imperial cult was widely practised throughout the empire and Antioch was the centre of Roman adminis-

---

24. Sim, 'The "Confession" of the Soldiers', 404–6.

25. R.L. Mowery, 'Son of God in Roman Imperial Titles and Matthew', *Biblica* 83 (2002), 100–10.

26. Mowery, 'Son of God', 100–1.

27. Mowery, 'Son of God', 101–5.

tration in the province of Syria.[28] Finally, Mowery shows that the three instances of *theou huios* in Matthew derive from the hand of the evangelist himself. He introduced the phrase into his Marcan source in both 14.33 and 27.43, while in 27.54 he has inverted the original *huios theou* in Mark 15.39. Since *theou huios* does not conform to Matthew's linguistic style, it must be concluded that he is imitating an existing formula.[29] Mowery concludes that 'this formula would have evoked Roman imperial usage for at least some members of his [Matthew's] community', and would have demonstrated that Jesus and not the emperor is in fact the Son of God.[30]

Mowery's article places the statement of the soldiers into its true imperial perspective. These members of the military were the defenders and the enforcers of the emperor and the empire, including the imperial cult which often referred to the reigning ruler as the Son of (a) God. When the soldiers who crucify Jesus in the Matthaean narrative acknowledge that Jesus truly was the Son of God, they are patently denying the divine status of the emperor and transferring that status to Jesus. Jesus is the Son of God and not Tiberius (the emperor at the time of Jesus) or Domitian (the emperor at the time of Matthew). Matthew's depiction of these soldiers therefore begins with their brutality and arrogance as they humiliate, beat and finally execute Jesus, and ends with their solemn proclamation that the one they have just crucified, and not the emperor, was in fact the Son of God. What was Matthew's purpose in presenting this particular portrayal of the centurion and his fellow soldiers?

According to many scholars, Matthew intends to describe a remarkable conversion experience on the part of those who executed Jesus. The evangelist in fact emphasizes their initial cruelty and their mocking of Jesus in order to highlight the magnitude of their conversion occasioned by the apocalyptic signs they witness.[31] On this view Matthew transforms them from negative into positive characters who make the Christian confession that Jesus truly is the Son of God (cf. the similar confession of the disciples in 14.33). As positive characters in the narrative, these soldiers now become representative of the Gentile world. Their coming to faith anticipates the Gentile mission that the risen Christ later initiates (28.16–20), and they themselves are therefore models of Gentile Christian faith.

28. Mowery, 'Son of God', 105–8.
29. Mowery, 'Son of God', 108–9.
30. Mowery, 'Son of God', 110.
31. For recent studies, see Davies and Allison, *Matthew*, III, 635; Carter, *Matthew and the Margins*, 537–8 and D.J. Weaver, ' "Thus You Will Know them by their Fruits": The Roman Characters of the Gospel of Matthew', in this volume. Cf. too a number of earlier studies; J.P. Meier, *The Vision of Matthew: Christ, Church and Morality in the First Gospel* (Mahwah, NJ: Paulist Press, 1979), 205 n. 249; and J.P. Heil, *The Death and Resurrection of Jesus: A Narrative-Critical Reading of Matthew 26–28* (Minneapolis, MN: Augsburg Fortress, 1991), 87.

I have argued previously, and in some detail, that this reading of the soldiers' words as a genuine confession of Christian faith following a conversion experience is based upon rather spurious evidence, and does not conform to Matthew's intentions in this text.[32] I do not propose to repeat all the arguments here; it is sufficient to restate only one of them briefly. The consensus view takes for granted that for Matthew belief in Jesus from a prior situation of unbelief can be generated through a miracle or supernatural event. In the case of the soldiers at the cross, they come to faith after witnessing the earthquake and the other terrifying apocalyptic occurrences. While it is true that in some early Christian traditions miracles or other manifestations of the divine do lead people to Christian faith (e.g. Acts 9.1–19; 13.6–12), this is never the case in Matthew.

In this gospel faith in Jesus always precedes the miracle and never results from it. This pattern is evident in the miracle stories of Chapters 8–9 – the centurion of Capernaum (8.5–13), the paralytic (9.2), the ruler's daughter (9.18–19, 23–25), the woman with the haemorrhage (9.20–22) – and is repeated in the later episode of the Canaanite woman (15.21–28). In 13.53–58 the Matthaean Jesus refuses to work miracles in his own country because of the unbelief of the people (13.53–58), which again reinforces the point that miracles are dependent upon the prior act of faith and cannot be used to generate faith. In similar vein, when the opponents of Jesus ask him to produce a sign or a miracle to prove his credentials, he refuses and states that only an evil and adulterous generation requires such signs (12.39–40; 16.1–4).[33]

Matthew's consistent view on the relationship between faith and miracles calls the consensus interpretation into question. The common understanding of the soldiers' words asks us to believe that the evangelist breaks the pattern that is found throughout the remainder of the gospel. In the single case of the soldiers at the foot of the cross, we find the miracle not only preceding faith but also generating faith. While Jesus refuses to produce a sign for his opponents earlier in the gospel, he (or God) happily does so for those who abuse, humiliate, brutalize and execute him. There is a serious inconsistency here, but its origin lies not with the evangelist but with his modern interpreters.

We might add a further point. It was noted above that many scholars claim that the evangelist uses these Roman soldiers as models of Gentile faith. By converting from paganism to belief in Jesus, they anticipate the success of the later Gentile mission. But how realistic is this proposal in the light of the recent studies that Matthew is vehemently opposed to Roman imperialism and those who enforce it? How valid is it in view of

32. Sim, 'The "Confession" of the Soldiers', 402–18.
33. Sim, 'The "Confession" of the Soldiers', 407–8.

Matthew's eschatological expectations that were spelt out earlier? If the evangelist envisages Rome to be in league with Satan, believes that the Romans and their demonic allies will terrorize the righteous prior to the parousia, and expects Jesus and his angelic army to bring the Roman forces to surrender, then how plausible is it that he would use members of the Roman army to anticipate Gentile faith in Jesus? This question is even more pointed once we realize that Matthew himself, in editing his Marcan source as he did, highlights the many crimes these soldiers committed against Jesus the messiah. It simply strains credulity to believe that Matthew would have used these particular soldiers, whose arrogance and brutality typify the worst excesses of the empire they serve, as models of Gentile faith. For this reason it is surprising to find that Warren Carter, who has done so much to bring to light Matthew's negative views concerning Rome and its abuse of imperial power, accepts the traditional interpretation of this pericope (see n. 31).

On the basis of the preceding discussion, we can reject the consensus view that Matthew describes the conversion of these soldiers who make a solemn confession of Christian faith. We need to find an alternative interpretation of this pericope which is more consistent with other aspects of the gospel. I have suggested such an alternative understanding of this episode,[34] which can be presented in the following summary form.

As Matthew's readers read the passion narrative, they would have formed a distinctly negative attitude towards the Roman soldiers who mocked, tortured and crucified their messiah. Since the evangelist gives no indication whatsoever that he intends to alter the characterization of these figures, their statement in 27.54 must be viewed as a reinforcement of their wickedness and not as a reversal of it. They witness the terrifying apocalyptic events that accompany the death of Jesus, and they come to the conclusion that Jesus was truly the Son of God. The soldiers used this particular term because they had heard passers-by deriding the dying Jesus and challenging him to prove that he is the Son of God (27.39–43). But their affirmation of Jesus's divine sonship at the expense of the emperor's claims does not indicate their conversion to belief in Jesus. Rather, it is an admission of guilt. This person whom they treated most shamefully and executed was indeed the Son of God. But their utterance of Jesus's true identity is also a cry of defeat. The supernatural events demonstrate the enormous power at Jesus's disposal and they concede their defeat in the face of this superior force. Their terrified proclamation that Jesus is the Son of God is not an expression of new Christian faith, but an acknowledgement that Jesus was right and they were wrong, and they stand condemned at the foot of the cross.

The crucifixion scene is important for Matthew in another way. It seems

34. Sim, 'The "Confession" of the Soldiers', 418–22.

to me that the evangelist has designed the events at the crucifixion to serve as a proleptic judgment scene. In Matthew's view of the eschatological processes, the cosmic order would be destroyed (24.29, 35) and recreated (19.28), and then Jesus the Son of Man would ascend his throne of glory and bestow eternal life for the righteous and eternal punishment by fire for the wicked (25.31–46). These elements are found in Matthew's crucifixion scene. The earthquake is a common sign of the endtime and anticipates the breakdown of the whole cosmic order at the end of the age, while the raising of the saints foreshadows the eternal life that awaits the righteous (cf. 19.16, 29; 25.46). The terror and the concession of defeat on the part of the soldiers anticipates the reaction of the Romans on the day of judgment once they realize the true identity of Jesus and the power and authority he possesses. On that terrible day they will learn precisely who Jesus is, but by then it will be too late. Their arrogance will be replaced by terror as they come to understand the horrible fate that awaits them in the fires of Gehenna. In short, the Romans at the cross symbolize the eschatological fate of imperial Rome.

This alternative understanding of the Matthaean pericope is consistent with the evangelist's editing of his Marcan source to emphasize the cruelty and arrogance of the Roman soldiers in the passion narrative. Unlike the common view, it does not involve the dubious proposition that Matthew would have used such wicked characters in his narrative as models of Gentile faith. Moreover, this interpretation is in line with the evangelist's view that Rome, the ally of Satan in the cosmic conflict, will be condemned and judged by Jesus the Son of Man. In this way the current trend in Matthaean studies to highlight Matthew's anti-Roman perspective supports my earlier study of the purpose of the crucifixion scene in the context of the gospel.

5.5 *Conclusions*

Matthew makes clear to his readers the true nature of Rome and its imperial system. The Roman Empire stands not on the side of God and the righteous but firmly in the camp of Satan and represents his evil purposes. This particular view of Rome, which is shared by the Book of Revelation, dictates the fate of Rome in Matthew's eschatological expectations. At the end of the age, the Roman armies will join their demonic allies and bring tribulation to the righteous. This unholy coalition will be met by an even greater military force, an angelic army led by the Son of Man on the clouds of heaven. The Romans will surrender and then take their place among the nations to await the judgment of the Son of Man on his throne of glory. As allies of Satan they will share the same fate: eternal torture in the fires of Gehenna. Once again there are

clear parallels with the eschatological scenario in the Christian apocalypse. The crucifixion scene in Matthew 27.51–54 can and should be
viewed as a proleptic judgment scene. The soldiers who brutalized,
humiliated and executed Jesus represent the very worst aspects of Roman
imperialism. Their terror and acknowledgement of defeat as they come to
understand the true identity of Jesus will be repeated by Rome and her
supporters on the day of judgment.

'THUS YOU WILL KNOW THEM BY THEIR FRUITS':[1]
THE ROMAN CHARACTERS OF THE GOSPEL OF MATTHEW

Dorothy Jean Weaver

6.1 *Introduction*

In the introduction to *Matthew and Empire: Initial Explorations* Warren Carter points to a 'simple observation' that he views as largely overlooked within Matthaean scholarship, namely 'that the Gospel [of Matthew] comes from and addresses a world dominated by the Roman Empire'. And Carter concludes: 'It seems difficult to imagine that this world left no mark on the Gospel as most interpretations seem to suggest by their sheer inattention to this context.'[2] Carter's observations are surely correct. While Matthaean scholars have always paid attention to the individual Roman characters or character groups of the Gospel of Matthew – and thus by implication to the Roman Empire which they represent and embody – Matthaean scholarship has focused its attention primarily on the theological issues at stake between Matthew's church and the wider Jewish community with whom it is in debate.

This narrative assessment of the Roman characters within Matthew's Gospel will focus explicit attention on what has until recently remained largely implicit and unexamined, namely the impact of the Roman Empire and, in particular, its human functionaries on Matthew's story of Jesus. And while it is in some respects unwarranted to focus on such ethnic distinctions,[3] the parameters of this study are for reasons of clarity and

---

1. Matt. 7.20. All biblical citations are taken from the New Revised Standard Version unless otherwise designated.

2. W. Carter, *Matthew and Empire: Initial Explorations* (Harrisburg, IL: Trinity Press International, 2001), 1.

3. That Matthew does not delineate his characters predominantly along the lines of 'Roman' and 'Jewish' becomes clear from several significant clues in his narrative. To begin with, the single most prominent face of the Roman occupation of Palestine is, for Matthew's Gospel, without question the ubiquitous 'tax collectors' (*telōnai*: 5.46; 9.9, 10, 11, 12, 13; 10.3; 11.19; 18.17; 21.31, 32; cf. 17.25–26; 22.15–22), Jewish functionaries who work at the

simplicity drawn to include only those characters within Matthew's story who can clearly be viewed as Romans: the centurion (*hekatontarchos*) who comes to Jesus on behalf of his sick servant (8.5–13); the emperor (*kaisar*: 22.15–22); Pilate, the governor (*hêgemôn*: 27.1–66; 28.11–15); Pilate's wife (*hê gynê autou*: 27.19); the soldiers (*stratiôtai*) of the governor, a cohort (*speira*) of troops (27.27–54);[4] the centurion (*hekatontarchos*) at Jesus's cross (27.51–54); and the guard (*koustôdia*) at Jesus's tomb (27.62–66; 28.11–15).[5]

This study will proceed in three stages. The first step will be to identify Matthaean evidence pointing to the normal activities and roles of each of the Roman characters or character groups and to paint a 'lower level'[6] portrait of Roman imperial power as it creates the sociopolitical backdrop to Matthew's narrative. But while Roman imperial power is the ultimate sociopolitical reality against which Matthew's narrative unfolds, this power stands necessarily and consistently in an ironic tension with the central reality of Matthew's story, namely, the 'kingdom of heaven'. And this 'kingdom' has 'come near' (4.17) in the person of Jesus of Nazareth, through his life, death and resurrection. Accordingly, the second step of this study will be to assess Matthew's treatment of each Roman character or character group within the

---

behest of their Roman overlords to collect the taxes assessed by Rome on their Jewish compatriots. Further, the Matthaean Jesus refers in the same breath (10.18) to 'governors and kings', a categorization which includes both Roman governors such as Pilate (27.1–66; 28.11–15) and local, part-Jewish client rulers such as 'Herod the king' (2.1–23) and 'Herod the tetrarch' (14.1–12). Most importantly, however, Matthew shapes his accounts of these three figures in such a way as to highlight the commonalities between them as political leaders, regardless of ethnic distinctions. On Matthew's parallel portrayals of these characters see my essay 'Power and Powerlessness: Matthew's Use of Irony in the Portrayal of Political Leaders' in D.R. Bauer and M.A. Powell (eds), *Treasures New and Old: Contributions to Matthaean Studies* (Atlanta, GA: Scholars Press, 1996), 179–96.

4. And while they are identified only obliquely, I likewise include the soldiers of Herod the Great (2.16, 20) and Herod the Tetrarch (14.3, 10) within Matthew's 'lower level' portrayal of Roman soldiers.

5. The verb *echete* (27.65) is grammatically ambiguous and could be construed either as imperative 'Take a [Roman] guard' or as indicative 'You have a [Jewish] guard.' But the fact that the Jewish authorities appeal to Pilate to 'command that the tomb be secured' (27.64) suggests that the guard (*koustôdia*) authorized to 'secure' the tomb (27.65) will be Roman and not Jewish. This conclusion is further supported by the concern of the Jewish authorities that word of the empty tomb and the failure of the guard (28.13) will 'be heard by the governor' and thereby get the guard itself into trouble (28.14). Cf. A.H. M'Neile, *The Gospel According to St Matthew* (New York: St Martin's Press, 1965), 428–9; R.H. Gundry, *Matthew: A Commentary on his Handbook for a Mixed Church under Persecution* (Grand Rapids, MI: Eerdmans, 2nd edn 1994), 584; L. Morris, *The Gospel According to Matthew* (Grand Rapids, MI: Eerdmans, 1992), 731–32.

6. Thus D.C. Muecke, *The Compass of Irony* (London: Methuen, 1969), 19–20, where he describes irony in terms of a 'double-layered or two-storey phenomenon' in which 'the lower level is the situation either as it appears to the victims of irony ... or as it is deceptively

ongoing plot of the narrative and to paint Matthew's own 'upper level' portrait of Roman imperial power as viewed through the lens of the 'kingdom of heaven' and ultimately as unmasked by that greater power.[7] The third step will be to reflect on Matthew's overall portrait of the Roman characters within his gospel and on the implications of this portrait for Matthaean theology.

6.2 *Matthew's Lower-Level Portrait: The Everyday Face of Roman Imperial Power Soldiers (*Stratiôtai*)*

Beyond the ever-present Jewish 'tax collectors' of Matthew's Gospel,[8] the most visible face of Roman imperial power for the characters of Matthew's narrative is surely that of the Roman 'soldiers' (*stratiôtai*) stationed in their land as the military force of the Roman occupation. These soldiers – organized into 'centuria' of 100,[9] 'cohorts' (*speirai*: 27.27) of 600,[10] and 'legions' (*legiônes*: 26.53) of 6,000[11] – form the broad base of a powerful and extensive military hierarchy reaching all the way from the foot-soldiers at the bottom (8.9; 22.7; 27.27–66; 28.11–15; cf. 2.16; 14.10) to the officers (8.5–13; 27.54), the client king (2.1–23; 14.1–12) or the governor (27.1–66; 28.11–15), and ultimately the emperor himself at the top (22.15–22; cf. 17.25–26; 20.25).

As the persons of lowest rank within this military hierarchy, the soldiers are subject to the commands of their superiors all the way up the line. They 'go' and 'come' at the command of their centurions (9.9). They perform the tasks that the client kings 'send' them to do (2.16; 14.10; cf. 14.3). They carry out the decisions of the Roman governor (27.26, 31–38;

---

presented by the ironist' and 'the upper level is the situation as it appears to the observer or the ironist'.

7.   See Weaver, 'Power and Powerlessness', 185–7, 188–91, 193–6. Cf. Carter's conclusion (*Matthew and Empire,* 1) that 'the Gospel resists Rome with a *social challenge* in offering a vastly different vision and experience of human community, and with a *theological challenge* in asserting that the world belongs to God not Rome, and that God's purposes run through Israel and Jesus, not Rome'.

8.   See n. 3 above.

9.   Thus U. Luz, *Matthew 8–20: A Commentary* (Minneapolis, MN: Augsburg Fortress, 2001), 10. While there is no specific mention of such 'centuria' in Matthew's narrative, the repeated references to the title 'centurion' (*hekatontarchos*: 8.5, 8, 13; 27.54) clearly imply their existence within the world of the story.

10.   Thus R.E. Brown, *The Death of the Messiah: From Gethsemane to the Grave,* 2 vols (New York: Doubleday, 1994), I, 248; Luz, *Matthew 8–20,* 10.

11.   Thus Brown, *The Death of the Messiah,* 248. While Matthew makes no mention of Roman legions within his narrative, Jesus's reference to 'twelve legions of angels' (26.53) clearly evokes the parallel image of these massive Roman forces.

cf. 27.62–66). And they ultimately serve as the 'troops' (*strateumata*) 'sent' by the emperor himself to do his bidding (22.7).[12]

But while the Roman soldiers of Matthew's Gospel have no authority over others within the Roman military establishment itself, they nevertheless wield genuine and fearsome power over the occupied populace. They have the authority to 'find' civilians (27.32) at will and compel them into 'forced' labour for stated tasks (27.32: carrying a cross for a condemned prisoner) and stated distances (5.41: one mile). They are the functionaries who carry out the official punishments decreed by the client king or the governor: arrest (14.3), binding (14.3), imprisonment (14.3), flogging (20.19; 27.26), beheading (14.10) and crucifixion (27.27–38, 51–54). Following executions they 'keep watch' over the executed criminal (27.36, 54), 'cast lots' for his clothing (27.35), and serve as a 'guard' at the tomb (27.65, 66; 28.11; cf. 28.4). In addition the soldiers likewise carry out special military operations against the occupied populace (2.16: 'killing all the [young] children' of Bethlehem; 22.7: 'destroying ... murderers' and 'burning their city').

In addition to the everyday violence demanded by their designated tasks as the troops of an occupying army, the soldiers of Matthew's narrative exhibit a brutality well beyond the call of duty. When Jesus, already subjected to a pre-execution flogging (27.26a), has been handed over to the soldiers for crucifixion (27.26b), they inflict their own crude mockery and physical abuse on him before carrying out the official sentence. Jesus has been tried and condemned as 'King of the Jews' (27.11, 37; cf. 27.17, 22). Accordingly, the soldiers surround him and set up a mock-royal court at his expense. Their tactics are evident from their actions. They seek to intimidate Jesus by their overwhelming numbers (27.27: 'the whole cohort') and to humiliate him with the public undressing (27.28, 31) and dressing (27.28, 31) to which they subject him. They ridicule him with mock-royal attire: a crimson robe (27.28), a

---

12. The 'king' in Jesus's parable of the wedding banquet (22.1–10) is a complex figure. Within Matthew's narrative Jesus tells the parable as an allegorical depiction of the course of salvation history and the bitter consequences for the Jewish people as a result of their role in that history. Central to the interpretation of Jesus's allegory is the identification of the 'king' with God and of 'his son' with Jesus himself. Accordingly, the death and destruction unleashed by the 'enraged king' are an ominous prophecy concerning the judgment of God about to fall on the Jewish people. From the vantage point of Matthew's church, however, the parable of Jesus has taken on a new layer of meaning. In their post-70 CE world, the language of the 'enraged king' who 'sends his troops' to 'destroy those murderers' and to 'burn their city' is a vivid allusion to the Roman 'king' (namely, the emperor) and the 'troops' which he sent to lay waste to Jerusalem (23.37–38; 24.1–2). Accordingly, the 'king' of Jesus's allegory is a complex and conflated image of God, whose judgment is falling on the Jewish people, and the Roman emperor, whose 'troops' are the agent of that judgment. Cf. the conclusion of M'Neile, *St Matthew*, 315: 'These verses refer to ... the sack of Jerusalem by the Roman armies, who, as God's instrument of punishment, are "His armies".'

'crown' of thorns (27.29), and a reed 'sceptre' (27.29). They 'mock' him (27.29, 31; cf. 20.19) with their genuflections and their cries of 'Hail, King of the Jews!' (27.29). And they abuse him physically as they 'spit' on him and 'strike' him with the reed (27.30).

For the Jewish characters of Matthew's narrative the Roman soldiers occupying their land are clearly a powerful and brutal force, widely recognized as those who are 'evil' (5.39). The everyday face of Roman occupation is one of compulsory labour, unrequited humiliations, cruel torture and bloody executions.

6.2.1 *Centurions (*Hekatontarchoi*)*

The centurions of Matthew's narrative are clearly people in the middle. As the leaders over centuria, detachments of one hundred soldiers, they have considerable power. Not only are they men of rank, 'having soldiers under [them]' (8.9; cf. 27.54), but they are also men of authority, issuing commands to soldiers and slaves alike and knowing that these commands will be carried out immediately. As one centurion explains (8.9): '... I say to one [soldier], "Go", and he goes, and to another, "Come", and he comes, and to my slave, "Do this", and the slave does it.'

At the same time, however, Roman centurions are likewise 'under authority' (8.9), receiving their own orders from higher up the military chain. The tasks that fall to them and their centuria are the routine tasks of military occupation: the crucifixion of condemned criminals (27.54; cf. 27.26–38), the posting of charges against those executed (27.37), and the subsequent vigil at the crucifixion site (27.36, 51–54).

Accordingly, centurions would appear to be people who inspire the same fear and hatred as their soldiers. As military leaders who issue commands to soldiers and civilians alike and expect immediate and unthinking obedience, centurions are clearly men whose word is to be feared. And as the captains of the Roman governor's torture and execution squads they are likewise conspicuous symbols of the oppressive Roman occupation.

6.2.2 *The Governor (*Hêgemôn*)*

Of all the Roman characters 'onstage' within Matthew's story[13] Pilate, the Roman governor (27.2–66; 28.11–15), is farthest up the military chain of command and accordingly, from a 'lower-level' perspective, the most powerful figure within the narrative. The predominant power of the Roman governor within the world of the story is clearly evident throughout Matthew's narrative rhetoric.[14]

13. 'Caesar', the Roman emperor (22.15–22; cf. 10.18; 17.25; 20.25), plays an unseen role in Matthew's narrative, as an 'offstage' character to whom the actors in the story make reference.

14. Thus Weaver, 'Power and Powerlessness', 191–2; Carter, *Matthew and Empire*, 163–4.

Matthew introduces the Roman ruler explicitly as 'Pilate *the governor*' (27.2) and then intersperses references to 'Pilate' (27.13, 17, 22, 24, 58 – twice, 62, 65) with parallel references to 'the governor' (27.11 – twice, 14, 15, 21, 27; 28.14),[15] 'thereby emphasizing his military and political power'.[16] The Jewish authorities address Pilate accordingly with the respectful title 'Sir' (27.63: *kyrie*), a title that carries with it the connotation of power and authority.

The power of the Roman governor also becomes visible in implicit fashion within Matthew's narrative, as the actions of the story flow toward him and appeals are addressed to him. The Roman governor is the one 'before whom' prisoners are 'dragged' (10.18), 'to whom' they are 'handed over' (27.2, 18; cf. 20.19), 'before whom' they 'stand' on trial (27.11), and 'before whom' community leaders 'gather' (27.62). He is likewise the one to whom people of position and power – family members (27.19), wealthy individuals (27.57–58), and Jewish authorities (27.62–66) – appeal for action on their behalf. And he is the one who inspires fear not only among the occupied populace but also among the soldiers under his command (28.14). As a 'tyrant' over his subjects (20.25b) and one who can 'lord it over' them (20.25a), the Roman governor has the ultimate power of 'command', a power both acknowledged by his supplicants (27.64) and confirmed by his own actions (27.58).

But it is in the depiction of his official duties that the power of the Roman governor is most clearly visible. While on duty in Jerusalem during the Passover, the governor has military command over a cohort (27.27b), a force of 600 men who together comprise 'the soldiers of the governor' (27.27a) and who assist him in the task of 'maintaining order'[17] among the crowds. And in this role the governor wields the awesome power of life and death over the occupied populace. Accordingly, he has the duty of holding prisoners (27.15–16), putting them on trial (27.11a), interrogating them (27.11b, 13–14), listening to the charges brought against them (27.12, 13), and sitting on the 'judgment seat' to determine their fate (27.19). Depending on the outcome of the trial, the governor then has the authority either to 'release' prisoners (27.15, 17, 21, 26; cf. 27.20) or to have them 'flogged' (27.26a)[18] and 'hand them over' (27.26b) to be 'crucified' (27.22, 23, 26, 31, 35, 38, 44; 28.6; cf. 27.20).

For the inhabitants of the land, the governor is hardly the most visible

15. Cf. Jesus's own references to 'governors and kings' (10.18), 'the rulers of the Gentiles' (20.25) and 'their great ones' (20.25).

16. F.J. Matera, *Passion Narratives and Gospel Theologies: Interpreting the Synoptics through their Passion Stories* (New York: Paulist Press, 1986), 104.

17. Morris, *Matthew*, 692.

18. While the text of 27.26 associates the governor himself with the act of 'flogging', this act of torture is without question delegated by the governor to soldiers who carry out the sentence.

face of the Roman occupation on a day-to-day basis. But within the occupied territory he is without question the most powerful human symbol of Roman Empire and domination.

6.2.3 *The Emperor (*Kaisar*)*

At the pinnacle of the Roman military hierarchy stands the emperor, the ultimate symbol (22.19–21) and the ultimate military power (22.7)[19] of the Roman imperial system. And while the emperor plays no 'onstage' role within the plot of Matthew's narrative, he is nevertheless a powerful 'offstage' character, whose impact is felt on the most mundane levels of existence as well as in the most profound human catastrophes. And it is no doubt the emperor above all others who inspires Jesus's words to his disciples about the 'rulers of the Gentiles' who 'lord it over' their subjects and 'their great ones' who are 'tyrants' over them (20.25).

The most obvious and widespread impact that the emperor has on the lives of his Jewish subjects within Matthew's narrative is the 'taxes' (*kênsos*: 17.25; 22.17, 19) and the 'toll' (*telê*: 17.25) that he levies on them through the agency of ubiquitous and universally despised Jewish 'tax collectors' (5.46; 9.9–13; 10.2–3; 11.19; 18.17; 21.31–32)[20] sitting at their 'tax booths'(9.9). This taxation of the Jewish people by their own compatriots, in obvious collaboration with the Roman occupiers, is the more galling (22.21a) and controversial (22.15–18) because the taxes are collected in the form of a Roman coin (22.19: *dênarion*) which bears both the 'head' (22.20: *eikôn*) and the 'title' (22.20: *epigraphê*) of the emperor himself.

But if taxes are the everyday face of the Roman emperor, violence, death and destruction are the catastrophic face of the Roman imperial system and its powerful 'king' (22.7).[21] In Jesus's allegorical parable of the wedding banquet, the outlines of a Roman emperor and his military campaign against Jerusalem (already history from the perspective of Matthew's church) are clearly visible in the image of the 'king' who 'sends his troops' to 'destroy those murderers' and to 'burn their city'. Shortly thereafter Jesus announces to 'Jerusalem' (23.38): 'See, your house is left to you desolate', an unmistakable allusion to the impending destruction of the Jewish temple. And as Jesus and his disciples then leave the temple, Jesus warns them (24.2) that 'not one stone will be left here upon another; all will be thrown down'. The devastation wrought by the military campaigns of

---

19. See n.12 above.

20. Within Matthew's narrative the term 'tax collectors' is coupled variously with the terms 'sinners' (5.46; 9.10, 11: 11.19), 'prostitutes' (21.31, 32) and 'Gentiles' (18.17). Tax collectors are associated derisively with the 'Son of Man', whose reputation is that of 'a glutton and a drunkard' (11.19). And Jesus identifies the tax collectors themselves as 'the sick' (9.12) and 'sinners' (9.13).

21. See n.12 above.

the Roman emperors is clearly massive and overwhelming, both to human life and to the physical infrastructure that sustains human community.

Accordingly, while the emperor himself is not an 'onstage' actor within Matthew's narrative, it is evident that his impact on the lives of the occupied populace extends both to the most mundane aspects of daily life and to the most terrifying of human catastrophes. Here is clearly the most powerful Roman of them all.

6.2.4 *Pilate's wife (*Hê Gynê Autou*)*

The final Roman character present within the world of Matthew's narrative is the wife of Pilate, the Roman governor. Her portrait differs significantly from that of the other Roman characters in that she is neither male nor military. Accordingly, within her first-century Hellenistic context she clearly has less power than they. Matthew's narrative offers no clues to the normal role of Pilate's wife. But the narrative nevertheless implies that as the wife of the Roman governor she is a woman of considerable authority. Her appeal to her husband '*while he [is] sitting on the judgment seat*' (27.19a, my emphasis), an action which interrupts him in the very course of his official duties, is one that could presumably be taken only by a person of such authority.

6.3 *Matthew's Upper-Level Portrait: Roman Imperial Power Unmasked*

With the exception of Pilate's wife, Matthew's 'lower-level' portrait of the Roman characters within his narrative is a monolithic portrayal of brutal and oppressive military might exercised by an occupying power against a subject people. But first appearances are notoriously deceptive within Matthew's narrative. Even as the Roman military hierarchy exercises overwhelming power against the occupied populace, Matthew paints an 'upper-level' portrait of these Roman characters which effectively unmasks their powerful façade and reveals the true state of affairs.

Unlike the 'lower-level' portrait, however, this 'upper-level' portrayal is far from monolithic. While Matthew uniformly unmasks Roman imperial power wherever he finds it, he does not, however, offer a uniformly 'damning' portrayal of the Roman characters within his story. Instead Matthew paints an astonishingly variegated portrait of these characters, mocking some of them with his narrative rhetoric and offering highest commendation to others.

6.3.1 *The centurion with the sick servant (8.5–13)*

The first Roman character to walk 'on stage' within Matthew's narrative is a figure who astonishes Jesus himself (8.10: *ethaumasen*). Matthew introduces this character with the powerful title, 'centurion' (8.5). And the centurion himself acknowledges this power with his references to the 'soldiers under [him]' (8.9a) and his authority to command them (8.9b). But ultimately Matthew's narrative rhetoric portrays this centurion revealing through his actions and confessing through his words his own effective powerlessness in the face of Jesus's genuine power.

The first indication of the true state of affairs lies in the reference to the centurion's servant (*pais*: 8.6, 8, 13; cf. 12.18; 14.2)[22] who is seriously ill. The urgency of the servant's condition is reflected in the corresponding urgency of the centurion's act in 'appealing' to Jesus (8.5: *parakalôn*)[23] and in his vivid description of the servant himself, who is 'lying at home paralysed, in terrible distress' (8.6). In spite of his authority over soldiers and civilians, the centurion is clearly overpowered by the illness of his servant. And in this respect he stands in the same position as all other supplicants who come, are brought, or appeal to Jesus for healing. The very fact that he appeals to Jesus indicates both that he himself has no power over human illness and, more importantly, that Jesus does have such power.

But not only is the centurion powerless *vis-à-vis* the illness of his servant, in pointed contrast to Jesus. He is also, in his own words, 'unworthy' (*ouk ... hikanos*) of the very presence of Jesus 'under [his] roof' (8.8a). And this self-acknowledged 'unworthiness' corresponds, in turn, to the centurion's reverential attitude towards Jesus himself. He addresses Jesus as 'Lord' (*Kyrie*: 8.6, 8): an honorific title normally accorded to those higher up in the Roman imperial hierarchy, namely the governor (27.63) or the emperor (cf. 20.25), but now used by the centurion to express his subordination to Jesus.[24] He likewise acknowledges the 'authoritative' position of Jesus,[25] a position parallel (8.9a) but clearly superior to his own, from which Jesus can 'heal' others (8.8c) simply by 'speaking the word' (8.8b; cf. 8.9b). And Jesus, conversely, acknowledges the 'faith' of the centurion (8.10: *pistin*; 8.13: *hôs episteusas*).

The overall impact of this narrative rhetoric is as 'amazing' for Matthew's readers as the centurion himself is to Jesus. Here Matthew portrays a demonstrably powerful Roman centurion who, with his own words and actions, reveals to the contrary his true powerlessness over the circumstances of his life and acknowledges his subordination to Jesus as one with 'authority' far beyond his own. And it is clear from Jesus's

---

22.   While *pais* could also refer to a 'child' (thus 2.16; 17.18; 21.15), the Lukan parallel to this story identifies the *pais* (7.7) unambiguously as a 'slave' (*doulos*: 7.3, 10).

23.   Cf. the urgency reflected in 8.31, 34; 14.36; 18.29, 32; 26.53.

24.   Cf. 8.2; 9.28; 14.28, 30; 15.22, 25, 27; 17.15; 20.30, 31, 33.

25.   According to the centurion, Jesus is, like himself, a 'man under authority' (8.9: *hypo exousian*), a phrase which clearly implies that Jesus's 'authority' (cf. 7.29; 9.6; 10.1) has come from a source beyond himself (cf. 9.8; 21.23, 24, 27; 28.18).

response to the centurion that Matthew in fact affirms this extraordinary self-assessment of Roman imperial power. Jesus offers the Roman (and thus Gentile) centurion the highest possible commendation ('Truly I tell you, in no one in Israel have I found such faith' [8.10]); and he offers him a space at the table 'with Abraham and Isaac and Jacob in the kingdom of heaven' (8.11) at the expense of the Jewish 'heirs of the kingdom' (8.12). Then he responds to the centurion's request, 'speaks the word' (8.13a; cf. 8.8b), and the 'servant is healed' (8.13; cf. 8.8c).

6.3.2 *Pilate the governor (27.1–2, 11–54, 57–66; 28.11–15)*

The next Roman character to appear in Matthew's narrative, Pilate the governor, does not fare as well, rhetorically speaking. While Matthew commends the centurion through his narrative rhetoric for recognizing Jesus's superior 'authority' (8.9) and placing his 'faith' in Jesus (8.10, 13), there is no such commendation for Pilate. To the contrary, Matthew portrays Pilate as a tragic figure, whose demonstrated powerlessness is compounded and made culpable by his failure to act on that which he knows to be true and to do that which he knows to be right.

Throughout the trial scene, and even beyond, Matthew persistently unmasks the true powerlessness of this most powerful of all characters 'onstage' in his narrative.[26] Ultimately, Pilate's powerlessness is visible *vis-à-vis* every other character or character group present on the scene: Jesus; the Jewish crowd; the Jewish leaders; Pilate's wife; Pilate's soldiers; and Pilate himself.

Early in the trial scene Pilate is unable to get his prisoner to speak in his own defence (27.12–14).[27] In spite of the governor's best efforts (27.13), Jesus instead asserts the one freedom left to a 'bound' prisoner (27.2) and maintains a complete silence when facing the charges brought against him by the Jewish leaders (27.12, 14). And in the end Pilate is capable only of 'great amazement' (cf. 27.14).

As the trial scene progresses, Pilate's powerlessness is further highlighted as he intentionally places himself at the mercy of the crowd. He already has a dangerously flawed judicial policy in place for the Passover festival, namely, 'to release a prisoner for the crowd, *anyone whom they wanted*' (27.15, my emphasis). And in the midst of the trial Pilate invokes this policy and repeatedly abdicates his authority to the wishes of the crowd (27.17, 21), thus leaving himself powerless to adjudicate the trial according to his own best judgment and the dictates of justice (cf. 27.18, 19, 23). Instead he is forced into indecorous public debate with the crowd

---

26. Cf. Weaver, 'Power and Powerlessness', 191–5.

27. Cf. Carter's observation (*Matthew and Empire*, 164) that '(Pilate) has not been able to intimidate Jesus into lying, begging, or recanting in order to save his life.'

(27.17, 21–23), an escalating shouting match that Pilate eventually loses when it turns into a full-scale 'riot' (27.24b). And in the end Pilate is forced by his own self-imposed policy to grant the crowd their wishes rather than to enact the justice incumbent upon him.

Pilate is equally ineffective in his dealings with the Jewish leaders, the power bloc behind the crowd (27.20). These leaders, headed by the high priest Caiaphas (26.3, 51, 57, 58, 62, 63, 65) and widely identified as 'the chief priests and the elders (of the people)' (26.3, 47; 27.1, 3, 20; 28.11/12)[28] have already been prominently involved in the events leading up to Jesus's trial before Pilate.[29] And throughout the trial itself it is these Jewish leaders, rather than Pilate, who succeed in setting the agenda (27.11–14, 17, 22; cf. 26.63, 65–68),[30] organizing public opinion (*against* the apparent views of Pilate: 27.20; cf. 27.15–18, 19, 21–23)[31] and manipulating the judicial system itself in order to accomplish their predetermined strategy for destroying Jesus (27.24–26, cf. 26.3–4, 59, 65–66; 27.1, 20).

After Jesus's death these Jewish leaders continue to orchestrate events by insisting that Pilate give them a 'guard' for the tomb of Jesus (27.62–66). And two days later, faced with the double challenge of an empty tomb (28.11) and the dangerous implications of their own cover-up conspiracy (28.12–13), the Jewish leaders promise Pilate's soldiers that they will manipulate Pilate himself on the soldiers' behalf (28.14): 'If this comes to the governor's ears, we will satisfy him and keep you out of trouble.' As Matthew's narrative demonstrates, Pilate the powerful governor shows himself to be effectively and ironically powerless not only in relation to the Jewish leaders but also as far as his soldiers are concerned.

28. But see also the variant references in 26.14, 57, 59; 27.6, 41, 62.

29. They have 'conspired to arrest Jesus by stealth and kill him' (26.4) and paid money to an informant who will 'hand him over' (26.15, 16). They have come to Gethsemane 'with swords and clubs' (26.47), 'laid hands' on Jesus (26.50), and 'arrested' him (26.48, 50, 57). They have put him on trial at the home of Caiaphas (26.57–64) and condemned him to death on the charge of 'blasphemy' (26.65–66; cf. 27.1). Finally they have mocked and physically abused him (26.67–68) before 'binding him', 'leading him away' and 'handing him over' to Pilate (27.2).

30. Pilate's question about Jesus's identity as 'King of the Jews' (27.11), his questions about 'Jesus who is called Messiah' (27.17, 22) and the charge which he posts above the cross (27.37: 'This is Jesus, the King of the Jews') correspond directly to the 'messianic' charges ('Messiah': 26.63, 68; 'Son of God': 26.63) on which Jesus is condemned in his trial before Caiaphas the high priest.

31. That Pilate, *contra* Carter (*Matthew and Empire*, 165–7), does not view Jesus's identity itself as cause for execution is evident from the fact that it is only *after* the crowd repeatedly calls for Jesus's crucifixion (27.22, 23; cf. 27.20) that Pilate concludes that he is *ineffective* in his efforts (27.24) to arrive at a *different* course of action than that demanded by the crowd. This conclusion is further confirmed by the prominent evidence to which Pilate has access that points to Jesus's innocence rather than his guilt. He is a 'righteous man' (27.19) who has 'done no evil' (cf. 27.23). And he has been framed by his enemies 'out of jealousy' (27.18).

But it is in contrast to the moral courage shown by his wife that Pilate's powerlessness comes into focus most prominently. Right in the midst of Pilate's futile shouting-match with the crowd (27.19; cf. 27.17–18, 20–24a), Pilate's wife takes the clearly unusual step of interrupting her husband in the course of his official duties to give him an urgent warning (27.19): 'Have nothing to do with that righteous man, for I have suffered many things today in a dream because of him' (my translation). The urgency of her warning and its moral clarity stand in stark contrast to the feeble actions of Pilate *vis-à-vis* the crowd. Not only does Pilate have a policy already in place for abdicating his responsibility as the arbiter of justice (27.15), but by the time he receives the message from his wife, he has likewise committed himself to that expedient course of action (27.17). Accordingly, the outcome of Pilate's public debate with the crowd is never in doubt. Even as his wife exhibits the extraordinary courage to speak truth to power (27.19; cf. 14.3–4), Pilate is in the very process of abdicating that power to the wishes of the crowd and neglecting all corresponding questions of truth and justice.

And it is Pilate himself who makes the ultimate acknowledgement of his own powerlessness. Faced with the outbreak of an angry 'riot' (27.24b) Pilate finally recognizes what Matthew's readers have been able to observe throughout the entire scene, namely that he '[can] do nothing' (27.24a: *ouden ôphelei*, my translation).[32] And in the end Pilate is trapped by his own policies (27.15) and his own fears (27.24b) into disregarding everything that he knows to be true: the ulterior motives of those who accuse Jesus 'out of jealousy' (27.18); the urgent, dream-inspired warning of his wife that Jesus is a 'righteous man' (*dikaios*: 27.19); and his own internal conviction that Jesus has 'done no evil' (cf. 27.23). And he is accordingly obliged to take the expedient and face-saving action of 'wash[ing] his hands' in front of the crowd (27.24c) and proclaiming his own 'innocence' (27.24d) in an obvious but futile attempt to rid himself of guilt for the manifest injustice that he is about to perpetrate.[33]

---

32.   Or 'was achieving [or benefiting] nothing'. Cf. Carter, *Matthew and Empire*, 166. But, *contra* Carter, the implications of either translation are the same: Pilate is incapable of doing what he hopes to do.

33.   *Contra* Carter (*Matthew and Empire*, 165), who argues that, from Pilate's perspective, because Jesus does not contest the title 'King of the Jews' he is not 'innocent' but rather 'guilty of rebellion and sedition'. In fact the entire trial scene is structured rhetorically to highlight the moral dilemma of Pilate, who is fully aware that he is faced with the condemnation of a 'righteous man' (27.19) who has 'done no evil' (cf. 27.23) but has been framed by his enemies 'out of jealousy' (27.18). The evident innocence of this 'righteous man' is rhetorically confirmed by the fact that his counterpart in the trial scene is depicted as a 'notorious prisoner' (27.16). If Matthew intended to portray Pilate as believing his prisoner to be 'guilty', there would be no need for the elaborate and self-serving scene in which Pilate seeks to establish his own 'innocence' (27.24) *vis-à-vis* the (apparently culpable) act that he is about to carry out (27.26).

But if Pilate is ultimately shown to be powerless, he is not by the same token rendered 'innocent', his own protestations notwithstanding. Pilate appears to believe that he has absolved his guilt by 'washing his hands' (27.24c), proclaiming his own 'innocence' (27.24d) and deflecting the responsibility for Jesus's death onto the crowd (27.24d). And for their part 'the people as a whole' (27.25a: *pas ho laos*) willingly accept the responsibility that Pilate has handed over to them: 'His blood be on us and on our children!' (27.25b).

But the narrative rhetoric of Matthew's story does not absolve Pilate of his guilt. Instead Pilate's own words and actions portray him unmistakably as the character ultimately responsible for the death of Jesus. It is Pilate who 'hands (Jesus) over to be crucified' (27.26b), the last link in a significant chain of characters who participate, each in their turn, in 'handing Jesus over' to death.[34] It is Pilate who establishes the 'charge' against Jesus that is subsequently posted over his head on the cross: 'This is Jesus, the King of the Jews' (27.38; cf. 27.11). It is Pilate at whose 'command' (27.58) the body of Jesus is given to a disciple for burial (27.57–59) and at whose further 'command' (27.64–65) the stone is then 'sealed' (27.66) and the tomb thereby 'secured' against theft (27.64, 65, 66). And, in the ultimate and ongoing irony of Matthew's narrative rhetoric, it is Pilate who must, in a future out beyond the end of the story, be 'satisfied' (28.14: *peisomen*) in the matter of the empty tomb.

In the rhetoric of Matthew's narrative there is in the end no commendation for Pilate. To be sure, Matthew portrays Pilate as one who recognizes both truth (27.18, 19) and justice (27.23). But this awareness serves only to confirm Pilate's guilt. Ultimately Matthew's narrative rhetoric portrays Pilate as culpable for neglecting his own better judgment, abdicating his authority to the wishes of the crowd, intentionally perpetrating injustice and failing in his attempt to absolve himself of the guilt for his actions.

6.3.3 *Pilate's wife (27.19)*

Of all the Roman characters in Matthew's narrative, Pilate's wife stands in a category by herself. She is the single non-military figure among the Roman characters. And she is likewise, *and apparently by the same token*, the sole Roman character whose power is not ironically unmasked before she receives commendation through the rhetoric of Matthew's narrative. The actions and the words of this woman mark her only for the highest approbation.

---

34. Thus Judas (10.4; 17.22; 20.18; 26.2, 15, 16, 21, 23, 24, 25, 45, 46, 48; 27.3, 4); the chief priests and scribes/elders of the people (20.19; cf. 20.18; 27.2; cf. 27.1); the crowd (27.18; cf. 27.15); and finally Pilate himself (27.26).

That Pilate's wife takes the extraordinary step of interrupting her husband in the course of his official duties points implicitly to the urgency of her cause and the corresponding courage required for this act of advocacy. But her words themselves are an explicit pointer to the significance and the truth of her cause.

On the one hand Pilate's wife indicates that she has had a 'dream'. And in the world of Matthew's narrative, 'dreams' are important messages from 'the angel of the Lord' (1.20, 24; 2.13, 19; cf. 2.12, 22). These messages call people to courageous action in the face of adverse public opinion (1.20), civil disobedience in the face of the powers that be (2.12) and timely response in the face of impending danger or its resolution (2.13, 19–20, 22). Accordingly, the 'dream' of Pilate's wife is likewise to be trusted as a divine message and one that calls her to courageous action.[35]

Pilate's wife does not reveal the specifics of her dream concerning Jesus. But she indicates that in this dream she has 'suffered many things ... because of him' (*polla ... epathon ... di' auton*). And while she does not explain this cryptic statement, Matthew's readers can hear in her words the overtones of Jesus's words to his disciples that they will be hated 'because of my name' (10.22; 24.9: *dia to onoma mou)* and persecuted 'on my account' (5.11: *heneken emou*).[36] Pilate's wife, while not formally identified as one of Jesus's 'disciples', nevertheless 'suffers', just as they will, 'because of him'.

Most significantly, however, Pilate's wife has become convinced – whether before, during, or after her dream – that Jesus is a 'righteous man' (*tô dikaiô*) and accordingly not deserving of the death-penalty which her husband is even at that moment 'sitting on the judgment seat' to deliver. And in this confession Matthew's readers recognize a true word spoken about Jesus, who begins his ministry with an act carried out 'to fulfil all righteousness' (3.15) and who proclaims 'righteousness' as the hallmark of the kingdom of heaven (5.20; 6.33).[37]

But Pilate's wife is commended by Matthew not simply for her divinely inspired confession that Jesus is a 'righteous man' and her corresponding 'suffering' on his behalf. Ultimately she is commended for the action that she takes in response to her dream. Like Joseph the 'righteous man' (1.19) and the 'wise men from the East' (2.1), who took action 'as the angel of the Lord commanded' (1.24; cf. 2.12, 14, 21, 22), Pilate's wife also responds immediately and faithfully to the dream that she has had.[38] And

---

35. Cf. J.P. Heil, *The Death and Resurrection of Jesus: A Narrative-Critical Reading of Matthew 26–28* (Minneapolis, MN: Augsburg Fortress, 1991), 74.

36. Cf. 5.10.

37. Cf. Donald Senior, *The Passion of Jesus in the Gospel of Matthew* (Wilmington, DE: Glazier, 1985), 114.

38. Cf. Matera, *Passion Narratives*, 108.

this prompt and faithful response sets the actions of Pilate's wife in sharp and positive contrast to those of her husband, who neglects the divine warning and instead takes action to save himself rather than his 'righteous' prisoner.[39] In the end Matthew has only the highest commendation for this extraordinary Roman woman.

6.3.4 *The centurion and 'those with him' (27.54; cf. 27.27–53)*

When Pilate, who does not heed the warning of his wife (27.19), finally succumbs to the expedient and 'hands [Jesus] over to be crucified' (27.26), it is 'the centurion and those with him' (27.54), namely 'the soldiers of the governor' (27.27), who enter the narrative and take over the action. And it is these soldiers and their centurion, of all the Roman characters in Matthew's narrative, who exhibit the most radical shift in their actions and their perspectives from the beginning of the scene to the end.

As those who 'flog' Jesus (27.26), 'mock' him (27.31; cf. 27.27–29), physically abuse him (27.30) and finally 'crucify' him (27.31, 35), these characters exhibit all the power and brutality expected of an occupying army, which can do what it will to the occupied populace. But this arrogance and apparent omnipotence are brought to a sudden and dramatic halt by the cosmic disruptions which accompany the death of Jesus: the 'tearing' of the temple curtain 'from top to bottom' (27.51); the 'shaking' of the earth (27.51); the 'splitting' of the rocks (27.51); the 'opening' of the tombs (27.52); and the 'raising' of the bodies of many 'saints' (27.52).

In the face of this massive display of divine power (27.54: 'the earthquake and what took place'), the centurion and his soldiers recognize instantaneously that they are witnessing events far beyond their control and encountering power far greater than their own. And in this same instant their arrogance is transformed into abject 'terror' (27.54: *ephobêthêsan sphodra*, 'they were terrified') and their 'mockery' (27.31) into confession of the highest order (27.54): 'Truly this man was God's Son!'

The profound significance and the corresponding irony of this transformation are immediately evident to Matthew's readers. The 'terror' of these Roman soldiers not only serves negatively to subvert their status as powerful occupiers but also serves positively to identify these soldiers with the followers of Jesus who are likewise 'terrified' (17.6, *ephobêthêsan sphodra*; cf. 14.27, 30; 17.7; 28.5, 8, 10) at the visible evidence of God's power. And with their confession of Jesus as 'God's Son' this Roman centurion and his soldiers give human voice, along with Jesus's disciples (14.33), Peter (16.16) and Jesus himself (26.63–64; cf. 27.43;

---

39. Cf. Matera, *Passion Narratives*, 108.

21.37, 38; 22.2), to the central truth of Matthew's narrative, confirmed by none other than the voice of God (3.17//17.5; cf. 2.15): 'This is my Son, the Beloved, with whom I am well pleased.'[40]

In a profoundly ironic move Matthew's narrative rhetoric offers the highest commendation to these Roman characters, *whose place in the narrative exists simply because they mock, torture and crucify Jesus*. At the climactic moment of the narrative it is these Roman soldiers with their officer who proclaim the true identity of Jesus for all to hear. And in so doing they join a growing chorus of Gentile witnesses within Matthew's narrative who recognize Jesus's true identity (2.2; 8.6, 8; 15.22, 25, 27), place their 'faith' in him (8.10, 13; 15.28) and 'worship' him (2.2, 11), even as many of Jesus's Jewish compatriots fail to do so[41] and accordingly forfeit their position of privilege within the kingdom of heaven.[42]

6.3.5 *The guard at the tomb (27.62–66; 28.2–4, 11–15)*

The final Roman characters to show up 'on stage' in Matthew's narrative are the soldiers of the 'guard' (27.65, 66: 28.11: *koustôdia*; cf. 28.4: *hoi têrountes*), requested by the chief priests and Pharisees (27.62–64) and authorized by 'command' of Pilate (27.65; cf. 26.64). These Roman soldiers, whose commission and actions are inextricably linked to the strategic concerns of the Jewish authorities (27.63–64; 28.12–13), receive no commendation from Matthew's narrative rhetoric. To the contrary, they are the victims of intense mockery within Matthew's narrative, as they demonstrate their inability to carry out their assigned task and face the ongoing consequences, both humiliating and dangerous, of this failure.

The first clue to Matthew's ironic treatment of the guard is that Pilate places these soldiers under the oversight of the Jewish leaders themselves, thus in effect subordinating the authority of the army of occupation to those whose land they occupy. Not only are the Jewish authorities, for their part, instructed to 'take' (27.65: *echete*)[43] the guard and employ them to 'secure' (26.65: *asphalisasthê*; cf. 27.64, 66) the tomb, but the soldiers of the guard themselves implicitly acknowledge their subordination to the Jewish authorities by going to them rather than to Pilate with their story of 'everything that had happened' at the tomb (28.11).

But with this turn of events Matthew's unmasking of the power of the guard has only begun. The task of this guard is to 'secure' a tomb (27.64, 65, 66) whose door has been closed with a 'great stone' (27.60) and then 'sealed' (27.66). The goals are to prevent the theft of a dead body from the

---

40.   Cf. Heil, *Death and Resurrection*, 87–8. See also 4.3, 6; 8.29; 27.40, 43.
41.   Thus, for example, 21.32, 37–39; 22.2–3; 23.37; 27.20–23, 24–25.
42.   Thus, for example, 8.11–12; 21.31, 43. Cf. Heil, *Death and Resurrection*, 87.
43.   See n. 5 above.

tomb (27.64; cf. 28.13), and to forestall the spread of a rumour ('the last deception') that the one buried 'has been raised from the dead' (27.64). But the 'great earthshaking event' (28.2a, *seismos ... megas*, my translation) instigated by the 'angel of the Lord, descending from heaven' (28.2b) demonstrates that the soldiers on guard are powerless to carry out their task.

The guard is first outmanoeuvred by the angel of the Lord, who 'rolls back the stone' (28.2b: *apekylisen ton lithon*) which has been 'rolled to' (27.60: *proskylisas*) the entrance of the tomb and 'sits' on it (28.2b), thus effectively undoing the 'seal' (27.66) and dismantling all 'security' measures (cf. 27.64, 65, 66). The guard is then overwhelmed by the sight of this divine messenger, whose 'appearance' is 'like lightning' and whose 'clothing' is 'white as snow' (28.3).[44] And in a note of biting irony Matthew delivers the *coup de grâce* (28.4): 'For fear of him the guards shook (*eseisthêsan*) and became like dead men (*hôs nekroi*).'

Matthew's unmasking of the power of the Roman guard has now reached its climax, if not its conclusion. The military detail commissioned to 'secure' a tomb instead witnesses all their 'security' measures dismantled by a divine power that dwarfs their own human efforts. The soldiers employed to guard a dead man are instead 'shaken' by the 'earth-shaking' power of God and temporarily transformed by their own 'fear' into 'dead men' themselves. And the guards charged to prevent a corpse from being 'stolen' will shortly discover[45] that in spite of their best efforts the body has undeniably disappeared from the tomb (cf. 28.11–15).

But this is not yet the end of their humiliation. Following the announcement by the angel (28.5–7) and the women's departure (28.8–10), 'some of the guard' set off for Jerusalem to inform the chief priests about 'everything that had happened' at the tomb (28.11). That they are not in fact aware of 'everything that had happened' and have only an incomplete story to relate to the Jewish authorities is merely the first of their problems.

Once the chief priests have 'assembled with the elders' and 'devised a plan' (28.12a), the situation of the soldiers becomes both more humiliating and more dangerous. To begin with, the soldiers are bought off by the chief priests and elders with a 'large sum of money' (28.12; cf. 28.15), a bribe intended to suppress the story about the angel and any possible rumours about Jesus's resurrection (28.13; cf. 27.63–64). The tenuous situation into which this secret alliance places the soldiers is heightened

---

44. Cf. Matthew's similar depiction of the 'transfigured' Jesus (17.2), whose face 'shone like the sun' and whose clothes 'became dazzling white'.

45. The dead faint (28.4: *hôs nekroi*) into which the guards have fallen would appear to prevent them from overhearing the words of the angel (28.5–7). Note the pointed indication that the angel speaks 'to the women' (28.5a).

still further by the false story that they are obliged to repeat, a fabrication not only humiliating but also dangerously incriminating (28.13): 'His disciples came by night and stole him away while we were asleep.' That the Jewish authorities recognize the grave danger that this cover-up conspiracy poses to this Roman guard, ultimately answerable to Pilate himself, is evident from the contingency plans with which they reassure the soldiers (28.14): 'If this comes to the governor's ears, we will satisfy him *and keep you out of trouble*' (my emphasis).

Accordingly, the soldiers of this Roman guard have, by their own deliberate actions, put themselves under the power and at the mercy of the Jewish authorities for all time to come. The bribe that they have accepted from the chief priests and elders ensures that they will be obliged to keep on repeating the humiliating story of their own failure and the corresponding 'success' of Jesus's disciples. And the real danger to which this story exposes them *vis-à-vis* the governor ensures that these Roman soldiers are at the ongoing mercy of the Jewish leaders for their own physical safety.

Faced with this dangerous dilemma the Roman soldiers guarding the tomb take the expedient step of 'do[ing] as they are directed' (28.15a), thereby becoming the mindless and powerless puppets of the Jewish religious establishment. And Matthew notes the ironic success of their expedient response in terms of its ongoing afterlife within the Jewish community (28.15b): 'And this story is still told among the Jews to this day.'

Clearly Matthew's narrative rhetoric offers no commendation for this Roman guard, whose story is intimately intertwined with that of the Jewish authorities. Instead there is only unrelenting mockery of these powerful Roman occupiers who have chained themselves forever to the will and the word of their Jewish subjects.

6.3.6 *The emperor (4.1–11; 20.20–28; 22.15–22; 28.16–20)*

The Roman emperor, the single most powerful human figure on the 'lower level' of Matthew's narrative, does not play an 'onstage' role. However, his policies and actions nevertheless ensure his presence in the narrative as a powerful 'offstage' character, whose name and reputation are invoked by the characters 'on stage'. Yet Matthew treats the emperor just as he does every other Roman military figure, subverting the power of the emperor through his narrative rhetoric and demonstrating the indisputable subordination of the emperor to the authority of God and God's Son, Jesus. Matthew's narrative offers three strategic indicators of the Roman emperor's true status in the cosmic scheme of reality.

The third and climactic temptation to which the devil subjects Jesus in the wilderness is the offer of 'all the kingdoms of the world' in exchange for Jesus's 'worship' (4.8–9). Implicit in this offer is the stunning revelation that 'all the kingdoms of the world', *including the Roman imperial power* (8.5–13 *et al.*), in fact belong to Satan and are therefore at his disposal. Accordingly, just as Jesus is about to claim his messianic ministry as Son of God (3.17; cf. 4.3, 6) on behalf of the 'kingdom of heaven' (4.17 *et al.*), Matthew's narrative rhetoric implicitly depicts the Roman Empire, *and by the same token its emperor*, as the ultimate and 'satanic' opposition to Jesus's own mission.[46] But the subsequent indications that Jesus rejects Satan's ultimate temptation (4.10a: 'Away with you, Satan!') and forces Satan himself off the scene (4.11a: 'Then the devil left him') confirm that neither the devil nor his 'satanic' empire *with its emperor* are a match for Jesus, Son of God.

Jesus later makes explicit to the Pharisees that which the temptation scene communicates implicitly: the emperor's definitive subordination to the authority of God. Presented with the legal tender used for paying Roman taxes, a coin bearing the 'head' and the 'title' of the emperor (22.19–21a), Jesus offers an enigmatic, debate-stopping response to the Pharisees' query about taxes (22.21b): 'Give therefore to the emperor the things that are the emperor's, and to God the things that are God's.' As Warren Carter cogently observes: 'Whatever else this cryptic comment may mean, it cannot in the Gospel's point of view mean that God and Caesar are the same, or equal, or unrelated, or that God is subordinate to Caesar.'[47]

And ultimately the risen Jesus subverts the hegemonic claims of Satan altogether, *and by the same token those of the Roman emperor on Satan's behalf*, when he announces (28.18b): 'All authority in heaven *and on earth* has been given to me' (emphasis mine), and sends his disciples out to carry on the mission of the kingdom of heaven in his authority and with his presence (28.19–20). As Carter concludes: 'The center of the divine purposes is not Rome but the community that acknowledges God's reign. This community and its claims exist within the very heart of the Roman Empire in an ambivalent relationship to it. The emperor cannot be ignored, but he does not define ultimate reality. Caesar has power but God is sovereign.'[48]

7.1 Conclusions: Matthew's Overall Portrayal of Roman Characters

The world of Matthew's narrative is deeply polarized, with sharp divisions between the 'good' and the 'evil' (5.45a; 7.17–18; 12.35), the 'righteous' and the 'unrighteous' (5.45b), the 'blessed' and the 'accursed' (5.1–12; cf.

46. Cf. Carter, *Matthew and Empire*, 62–3.
47. Carter, *Matthew and Empire*, 63.
48. Carter, *Matthew and Empire*, 63–4.

23.13–36; 25.31–46), the 'faithful' (9.2, 22, 29; 15.28) and the 'unbelieving' (21.25, 32; 27.42). But while other major characters or character groups consistently reflect either good[49] or evil traits,[50] Matthew paints an astonishingly complex portrait of the Roman characters within his narrative.

On the one hand they are powerful people. These Roman characters, with the single exception of Pilate's wife, comprise the military hierarchy that is the face of Roman imperial power for the people of occupied Palestine. And collectively they have powers ranging from the massive to the mundane. They can undertake military campaigns against rebellious cities (22.7); tax the occupied population (22.15–22); imprison, try, torture and execute criminals (27.1–2, 11–54); perform guard duty following executions (27.62–66; 28.11–15); and compel civilians at will into forced labour on their behalf (5.41).

But even as Matthew invests these characters with power on the 'lower level' of the narrative, he consistently subverts that same power through his own 'upper-level' narrative rhetoric. These demonstrably powerful Roman occupiers, from the foot-soldiers all the way up to the emperor himself, are in the end portrayed as powerless *vis-à-vis* an entire range of challenges, natural and supernatural: physical illness (8.6), political riots (27.24), cosmic disruptions (27.51–54) and divine appearances (28.2–4). From the least of these Romans to the greatest, Matthew unmasks their military might and demonstrates their subordination to the far greater power of God (22.21b) and the authority that God has granted to Jesus, his 'Beloved Son' (28.18b; cf. 3.17b; 17.5b).

But while Matthew consistently subverts the military might of the Roman imperial power, he does not offer a monolithic condemnation of the Roman characters themselves. Instead Matthew evaluates these characters individually, according to their varied responses to Jesus. For those Romans who fail to do what they know to be right (27.24–26; cf. 27.18, 19, 23) or to say what they know to be true (28.11–15; cf. 28.2–4), Matthew has nothing but unrelenting mockery. But for those Romans who acknowledge the power of Jesus (8.8–9), place their faith in him (8.10, 13) and confess his true identity as 'Lord' (8.6, 8), 'righteous man' (27.19) and 'Son of God' (27.54), Matthew has only the highest commendation. These Romans are ultimately counted among the 'many' who 'will come from east and west and will eat with Abraham and Isaac and Jacob in the kingdom of heaven' (8.11).

In the end Matthew's overall portrait of the Roman characters within

---

49. Thus the supplicants who appeal to Jesus for healing. Cf. 8.1–4; 9.2–8, 27–31; 14.34–36; 15.21–28, 29–31; 17.14–20; 21.14.

50. Thus the Jewish authorities, who consistently challenge Jesus's actions. Cf. 9.2–8, 9–13, 32–34; 12.9–14, 22–32, 38–42; 15.1–9; 16.1–4; 21.23–27; 22.15–22, 23–33, 34–40.

his narrative is 'round' and realistic rather than 'flat' and ideologically driven. In this respect it closely resembles the group portrait of Jesus's disciples themselves. The Romans of Matthew's narrative are complex characters, capable, just as Jesus's own disciples, of extraordinary faith, tragic moral failure and profound experiences of conversion. They are portrayed, in short, as real human beings, for whom Jesus's maxim holds true (7.20): 'Thus you will know them by their fruits.'

Matthew's Missionary Strategy in Colonial Perspective

John Riches

Matthew's Gospel concludes with an extraordinary passage in which Jesus claims that 'all authority in heaven and earth has been given' to him and *therefore* charges his disciples to go and make disciples of all the nations, baptizing them and teaching them to observe all that he has commanded them. This clearly breaks the ban which Jesus had placed on mission to the Gentiles (Matt. 10.5, 6, cf. especially: 'Go nowhere among the Gentiles') and also represents the transcendence/clarification of the titles which Jesus was given at the beginning of the gospel: son of David, son of Abraham. The Davidic messiah will rule, not just over his own people, the people of Israel, but over all nations (the whole world, including Jews and Gentiles). The manner of his rule will be through the teaching of his commandments and his disciples' obedience to them.

These final verses contain other important references back to earlier passages in the text: Jesus's promise to be with his disciples recalls the fulfilment citation in 1.23: 'Look, the virgin shall conceive and bear a son, and they shall name him Emmanuel', which means, 'God is with us', which in turn is linked to the giving of the name Jesus/Joshua: 'She will bear a son, and you are to name him Jesus, for he "will save his people from their sins"' (1.21). Jesus's appellation 'God with us' again links to the key passages where he is referred to as Son of God: by the divine voice at his baptism by John, (3.17); at the Temptation where Satan offers him all the kingdoms of the world; at the exorcism of the two demons, (8.29); at the stilling of the storm, (14.33); at Peter's confession at Caesarea Philippi, 16.16; at the Transfiguration, 17.5; at the trial before the High Priest, (26.63–64); at the mocking on the cross, (27.40); and again at the cross where the centurion and his troop together confess Jesus as truly the Son of God (27.54, diff. Mark, who has the centurion alone).

The story of the centurion and his troop at the cross relates to the story of another centurion whose faith Jesus praised in 8.10 'Truly I tell you, in no one in Israel have I found such faith.' Similarly there are links between the breaking of the ban on mission to 'the lost sheep of the house of Israel'

(10.6) and Jesus's encounter with the Canaanite woman in 15.21–28, where she challenges and persuades him to reverse the ban, at least temporarily.

All of this is of course well known. Our interest here is twofold. First, to consider what the possible contemporary reading contexts of these and related passages might have been. How would they have sounded to those whose primary interests were in the future of the Jewish people and their worship of God? How might they have sounded to those, both Jews and non-Jews, who harboured resentment or even fostered resistance against the might of imperial Rome? Second, assuming that, to some at least, these texts will have resonated with their feelings of resentment against Rome, to consider what sort of strategies, what 'arts of resistance'[1] may be deployed here, how the various themes enunciated – teaching authority, political power, territorial expansion – interact with the theme of Jesus's divine status, which is conferred on him from the outset of his ministry by the voice at his baptism.

I think it is important to make the initial point that our texts are patient of being read in very different modes. For those who wish to hear them within a predominantly Jewish context, then there are plenty of cues to take the reading in this direction. The opening claim that Jesus is the 'son of David, the son of Abraham' quite clearly locates Jesus among Jewish authority figures and leads the reader to expect an unpacking of those claims. Huge amounts of scholarly activity have been expended on showing how those claims are developed within a Jewish context, most recently exploring the ways in which they are made over against the other more powerful Jewish groupings of the time. I think there is no doubt whatsoever that the cues which take the readings in such a direction are clear and direct. This is not, however, to say that there may not be other, perhaps more subtle, cues embedded within the text, or that some of the cues may not be differently read. The more specifically Jewish claims may well be given a wider context. Thus claims that Jesus is the messianic son of David, son of Abraham, need to be linked to further motifs about the Gentiles coming to Zion to bring gifts and to witness the glory of the Lord (the magi from the east, 2.1–12; cf. Isa. 60.6) as well as to the gathering of peoples from the east and from the west to sit down with Abraham and Isaac and Jacob in the kingdom of heaven (8.11; cf. Ps. 107.3; Isa. 43.5; Bar. 4.37), though the clearest references here are to the return of the scattered peoples of Israel.

More significantly for our purposes, the introduction of Roman figures into the narrative, not least of the centurion in Chapter 8 and the intensification of the narrative of the centurion's confession in 27, give strong signals that this is a story not only for Jews but certainly also about and maybe even for Romans. Carter and others[2] have already shown how

---

1. J.C. Scott, *Dominance and the Arts of Resistance: Hidden Transcripts* (New Haven, CT: Yale University Press, 1992).

much of Matthew's material can be read from a Roman perspective. Alongside showing the kinds of connections which can be made between Matthew and the world of imperial Rome, it is also interesting to consider what kinds of rhetorical strategies may be in play here. As the Jews well knew, tolerance of resistance was not one of Rome's virtues; articulation of dissent, therefore, needed to be subtle and hidden.

James C. Scott has argued that in societies where there is a strong dominant force exercising hegemony over its subaltern people, one must be aware of the different modes of discourse which are adopted by rulers and subalterns alike.[3] A nice example taken from the novelist Nadine Gordimer is quoted by Jean Comaroff:

> Every household in the fine suburb had several black servants – trusted cooks who were allowed to invite their grandchildren to spend their holidays in the backyard, faithful gardeners from whom the family watchdog was inseparable, a shifting population of pretty young housemaids whose long red nails and pertness not only asserted the indignity of being undiscovered or out-of-work fashion models but kept hoisted a cocky guerrilla pride against servitude to whites: *there are many forms of resistance not recognized in orthodox revolutionary strategy.*

Publicly, officially, both the rulers and the ruled adopt a mode of discourse which expresses the accepted, official view about the relations between the two sides. Thus, in the South African situation described, there is an official account of the relations between blacks and whites being played out, where the black servants are treated as if trusted members of the family and they accept this role. What is said by both sides when neither is present, or what is said in veiled and oblique ways, may however be very different. The servants' painted fingernails are a signal 'hoisted' to give notice of a different view of a different reality and intention/hope. The servants' masters may talk rather differently when they are not talking 'in front of the servants'. Thus a visiting white South African in London in the 1960s on seeing my mother's dishwasher remarked: 'But I have a pair of black hands to do my washing up.' There is a nice irony in the contrast between this remark and the 'cocky guerrilla pride' and 'long red nails and pertness' of Nadine Gordimer's servant-girls.

Similarly, the subalterns under the Roman Principate sacrifice to the ruler's image, and express allegiance to Rome; the imperial cult spreads

---

2. W. Carter, *Matthew and the Margins: A Sociopolitical and Religious Reading* (Maryknoll, NY: Orbis, 2000); W. Carter, *Matthew and Empire: Initial Exploration* (Harrisburg, IL: Trinity Press International, 2001);. P. Oakes (ed.), *Rome in the Bible and the Early Church* (Grand Rapids, MI: Baker Academic, 2002).

3. Jean Comaroff, *Body of Power, Spirit of Resistance: The Culture and Resistance of a South African People* (Chicago, IL: University of Chicago Press, 1985), vi. The quotation is from Nadine Gordimer, *Something Out There*, emphasis added by Jean Comaroff.

freely throughout the cities in Asia Minor. The rulers in turn define the terms of the cult (carefully ensuring that not too much power is attributed to the ruling families), and proclaim (as do their biographers) the benefits which they bring to their world: peace, prosperity and well-being, as well as conferring benefits on their people by their public works and benefactions and the support of their clients. The style of such claim is well brought out by an inscription from Halicarnassus:

> Since the eternal and immortal nature of the universe, out of overflowing kindness, has bestowed on human beings the greatest of all goods by bringing forth Caesar Augustus, the father who gives us a happy life and father of his own native goddess Roma, the native Zeus and saviour of the human race. Providence not only granted all his wishes, but went far beyond them, for land and sea live in peace, cities are resplendent with the order of law, in harmony and abundance; now is the favourable zenith for all good things – good hopes for the future, solid courage for the present state of human beings, who with feasts, statues, sacrifices and songs ...[4]

Such was the official discourse. But when rulers and subalterns were among themselves (when, as it were, the servants had withdrawn, or when they were back in the servants' quarters), different modes of discourse will have begun to emerge: the language of unashamed class and cultural superiority, of exploitation; jokes, a coded language of resistance, dreams and visions of overthrow and destruction. The pent-up frustrations and anger of the suppressed/oppressed may break out in diverse and sometimes very violent ways. The coded apocalyptic visions of 2 Baruch and 4 Ezra, which Philip Esler has discussed, constitute one form of resistance; so too, perhaps, does Josephus's account of the Jewish war, if, as James McLaren suggests, we pay attention to his criticisms of Roman administration and even of the conduct of the campaign, coupled as is such criticism with an insistence that the final outcome was predetermined by Israel's God.

Such 'hidden transcripts' through which the resistance is expressed often draw on local traditions and adapt them to current need. The more localized and the more modified and adapted the better, from the point of view of difficulty of detection by outsiders. The outsiders and their spies simply don't get the joke, the half-allusion; even if they do, it is harder to prove sedition on this basis. Apocalyptic literature provides good examples of such coded resistance using local, esoteric traditions. Where does Matthew fit in such a scheme?

Matthew operates at different levels. Much of his story is narrative, much of it taken over and adapted from Mark, another collection of

---

4. See the text in H.-J. Klauck, *The Religious Context of Early Christianity: A Guide to Graeco-Roman Religion* (SNTW, Edinburgh: T&T Clark, 2000), 296 and the wider discussion of the cult of rulers and emperors, 250–330.

inner-Jewish, inner-Jesus-movement material. In some cases, the stories are more or less retold; in others they have undergone subtle transform-ations. As we have already noticed, Matthew has the whole troop of soldiers who execute Jesus confess him as Son of God (not just the centurion alone). On the other hand, he greatly shortens Mark's account of the exorcism of the Gadarene demoniac, omitting his very suggestive name, *Legion*, retaining the demons' recognition of Jesus as Son of God, but so avoiding any possible connection between the demoniacs and Roman power. Is this deliberate? I certainly think that there is quite a strong case to be made for Mark's having conceived this narrative in political terms.[5] It also seems prima facie unlikely that Matthew would have overlooked the political overtones of Mark's naming of the demoniac as 'Legion'. It would, however, have stood in flagrant contrast to his narrative, in the same chapter, of the centurion's faith and receptivity to Jesus. To symbolize the occupying power through the depiction of an uncontrollable maniac would be quite inconsistent with the presentation of the Roman soldier, with his great power and authority, nevertheless recognizing unreservedly Jesus's 'alternative' power to heal his servant. In this context, Jesus's exorcism of the two demoniacs set in the Gentile territory of the Decapolis is a further demonstration of this unlimited, alternative power.[6] Any links between the demonic powers and Rome remain indirect. As Carter has argued, the

5.   See, e.g. C. Myers, *Binding the Strong Man: A Political Reading of Mark's Story of Jesus* (Maryknoll, NY: Orbis, 1988), 190–94. Cf. G. Theissen, *The Miracle Stories of the Early Christian Tradition* (SNTW; Edinburgh: T&T Clark, 1983), 256–7:

> Miracle stories involving exorcism can be understood as symbolic actions which break the demonic spell of all-pervading dependence … The miracle stories show that their social setting is the tension between different cultures and peoples, and it is perhaps therefore less important to attribute them to a particular socio-cultural environment and to show their dependence on Jewish Christianity, Gentile Christianity or Hellenised Jewish Christianity. What is more important is the fact that they bear witness to a dynamism which pushes beyond these socio-cultural boundaries.

6.   Theissen, *The Miracle Stories*, 257:

> The fact that charismatic miracle workers of the 1st century AD were invariably from the east which was firmly under Roman domination invites the hypothesis that belief in charismatic miracle-workers can be treated as a reaction of subjugated Hellenistic and eastern peoples: the politically inferior proclaims and propagates his superiority on the level of miraculous activity.

Cf. on the healing of the centurion's servant and of the Syro-Phoenician woman's daughter:

> The miracles stories themselves show that they are reaching out beyond socio-cultural boundaries, but they also articulate a clearly perceived awareness of the boundaries, a tension between different cultures. Gentiles appear in them in an ambivalent position, now worthless (Mk 7.27; Mt 8.10; Lk 17.11ff.), now close, now far off (Mk 5.19f.). Overall the dynamic between the different ethnic groups tends to be expansive and missionary, (254).

fact that Satan at the Temptation can offer Jesus all the kingdoms of the world does indeed imply that they are all in his gift, and therefore in his power.

It is, however, not only in the introduction of Roman characters into the narrative that Matthew begins to open up the links between his story and Roman *imperium*. Matthew, as we shall see in a little more detail, makes use of the language of Jewish apocalyptic. Specifically he cites Daniel 7.13f. at the trial scene, and alludes to it again in the concluding passage.

Matthew's apocalyptic eschatology, like pretty much every other apocalyptic text, draws on two forms of mythology: a cosmic dualist one and a forensic one.[7] In the first, the human predicament is attributed to a satanic invasion of the world, by which men and women are held in thrall and from which they can be rescued only by divine intervention, most notably in some final battle. In the second, the source of the human predicament lies in human disobedience, archetypally in Adam's fall, and the remedy for this is the giving of the law, by which men and women may learn to obey and so prepare themselves for judgment, when God will finally rid the world of those who remain disobedient.

Different apocalyptic texts give different emphases to these two broad cosmological perspectives. In my view Matthew's eschatology is *principally* forensic; nevertheless, at crucial points (notably in 13.36–43) Matthew introduces elements of a cosmic dualistic schema which stand in striking contrast to the forensic view which shapes most of the material in his gospel. These passages are clearly Matthaean insertions; as such they introduce a new and strikingly discordant note into Matthew's cosmology, which qualifies his predominantly forensic mode of thinking.

The point is that whereas Matthew's portrayal of Jesus as the great teacher who teaches the perfect form of the Law and sends his disciples out to teach all nations to obey 'all that he has commanded' (28.20) implies that human beings are faced with an essential choice: whether or not to accept the authority of the Son of Man and to do what he commands; the parable of the tares simply does not leave any room for human choice at all. Either you are a tare or you are wheat; the one cannot change into the other. You are either born of God or of the devil (1 John 3). The language of moral choice, which dominates the discourse of the gospel, is here challenged by a darker view of the world: one where people are in bondage to dark powers in such a way that they cannot of

---

7.   I have argued this in greater detail in my *Conflicting Mythologies: Identity Formation in the Gospels of Mark and Matthew* (SNTW; Edinburgh: T&T Clark, 2000); for a different view, see D.C. Sim, *Apocalyptic Eschatology in the Gospel of Matthew* (SNTSMS 88; Cambridge: Cambridge University Press, 1996) and my discussion of his views in my *Mythologies*, 264–9.

their own volition escape. I find this an extremely illuminating moment in the gospel, where the forensic schema is qualified, where there is a recognition that not everything lies within the power of human willing, where, if you like, we come rather closer to the Paul of Galatians 1.4 and 4.3 than we seem to be most of the time.

Two things flow from this for the purposes of our discussions. First, I am inclined to think that apocalyptic thought is considerably more fragmentary, more tensive and less systematic than many other forms of thought.[8] This should not surprise us: a lot of what is said is communicated through dreams and visions, and we should be very cautious about giving too great a measure of coherence to this kind of communication. Things are hinted at, alluded to, sometimes explained (but then often there is more than one explanation). Thus I would be cautious about assuming that Matthew has a tightly worked-out vision of the events of the End, leading up to some final battle. Moreover, even if Matthew had such a vision, culminating in a battle with the forces of darkness and a final judgment of all, one would need to be aware that there was still a tension between his vision of some final cosmic battle between opposed cosmic, spiritual forces and his rather different vision of a world to be won over by the missionary activity of the Son of Man's disciples. It is *possible* to fit such pictures together, but the danger is that it will lead to distortion of one or other or both.

Second, however tensive Matthew's vision of the end may be, his use of apocalyptic language and imagery is a strong indicator that here we are entering the world of a community which sees itself as deeply at odds with the dominant political powers. The visions of Daniel were widely interpreted in terms of various political kingdoms and their rise and fall, their persecution of Israel and its final vindication. As the subsequent literature shows, such visions lend themselves to a variety of interpretation (4 Ezra;[9] Revelation;[10] and, as we are arguing, Matthew), but there is no

---

8.   This is generally true of non-philosophical, pre-scientific forms of religious thinking. This general idea is given interesting expression both in the work of Clifford Geertz, 'Religion as a Cultural System' in C. Geertz, *The Interpretation of Cultures* (London: Fontana, 1993), 98 (who speaks of religious symbols as formulating, 'however obliquely, inarticulately, or unsystematically, general ideas of order'), and of Claude Lévi-Strauss, who has argued that myths are fundamentally oppositional, that they express and seek to mediate between different patterns of social organization and different ways of viewing the world: see e.g. his account of the Oedipus legend in: Lévi-Strauss, 'The Structural Study of Myth', *Journal of American Folklore*, 68 (1955), 428–43.

9.   The text of 4 Ezra 12.10–39 interprets Ezra's eagle vision (4 Ezra 11) as a version of Daniel's fourth kingdom (4 Ezra 12.11) but identifies it not with the Greek or Macedonian, but with the Roman empire: see Philip Esler's discussion in this volume.

10.   The vision of the beast in Revelation 13 is a 'composite of the four beasts and "little horn" of Daniel 7', which is now taken to refer to the Roman Empire: cf. J. Sweet, *Revelation* (TPINTC; London: SCM Press 1979), 206–9.

mistaking the political dimension of the dreams which they inspire. And in the aftermath of the Jewish war, we can safely assume that echoes of the Danielic texts, such as we have in Matthew, will have served to create a field of expectations which would be readily discernible to Jewish readers, if not to those outside. Such allusions would awake longings for some ultimate vindication of God's people and their liberation from oppressive world empires.

Nevertheless, we should not lose sight of the fact that what we have are indeed echoes of Daniel rather than the fully-fledged reworkings of the Danielic visions which we find in 4 Ezra and Revelation. This too should make us a little cautious about attempting to reconstruct Matthew's own visions of the end (if indeed he had such things) in any great detail. If there are traces of the language of some final cosmic battle, as David Sim has intriguingly argued,[11] then we may see here evidence of deep resentments within the Matthaean community which would be fuelled by such allusions to a final destruction of the Roman forces.

Let me then turn to a brief discussion of the main themes enunciated in the final section of the gospel: teaching authority, political power and territorial expansion.

7.1 *Teaching Authority*

The gospel makes it clear that Jesus is first and foremost a teacher. Almost immediately after their call, the disciples are taken up (with the crowds) onto the mountain to be taught. As Dale Allison has persuasively argued, Matthew, through the birth narratives and his arrangement of Jesus's teaching into blocks, has made a deliberate comparison of Jesus with Moses.[12] Jesus, who comes to fulfil the Law and the prophets, is the one who assumes the authority of Moses. Matthew takes Mark's comment from the short *Sammelbericht*, 1.21–22 – for 'they were astounded at his teaching for he taught them as one having authority, and not as the scribes' – which immediately follows his call narrative and places it as final editorial comment at the end of the Sermon on the Mount (7.28–29). In this sense, its focus is clear: Jesus's authority is greater than that of any one else in Israel.

So far we might say the discourse is easily accommodated within the rhetoric of inner-Jewish debate/polemic. But just as the restrictions on Jesus's and the disciples' mission (10.6; 15.24) are eventually lifted in 28.16–20, so too the claims about the nature of Jesus's authority are equally clearly extended. In the first place, Jesus's teaching is given an

---

11. Sim, *Apocalyptic Eschatology*, 73–177, esp. 99–108.
12. D. Allison, *The New Moses: A Matthean Typology* (Minneapolis, MN: Fortress, 1993).

eschatological extension, in the remarkable passage Matthew 11.25–30, where Jesus praises God for imparting through him a hidden wisdom to babes. In words strikingly reminiscent of the final verses of the gospel, Jesus claims that 'all things have been given to him by the Father' and that he will reveal the Father to whom he chooses. This claim to complete authority, and the concomitant freedom to reveal the truth of God to whomsoever he wills, extends Jesus's authority beyond that of Moses, whose authority, like that of the prophets, is limited to the words which have been revealed to him and is specifically commissioned to lead a particular people.

It is interesting to consider this passage in the light of a wider mode of cultural discourse of the time which Martin Hengel has referred to as 'higher wisdom through revelation'.[13] Hengel sees this as having its roots in a quest for closer personal ties 'of the individual to particular deities': ties which were grounded in 'personal supernatural experiences, dreams, epiphanies, healings, direct instructions from God, etc.', all elements which can be identified readily enough in Matthew's Gospel. This quest for wisdom focuses in many cases on the 'mysterious, age-old wisdom of barbarian peoples, especially in the East … including the Indian Brahmins, the Persian "Magi", the Babylonian "Chaldaeans" and the Egyptian priests.' Hengel links this to Jewish apocalyptic, which too 'stands in a wider cultural context as a counter-movement to "Greek alienation"' and in this sense owed a debt to the Hellenistic period. He cites a hermetic text in which Asclepius appears to the Egyptian king Ammon and forbids him to make 'any translation of the wisdom communicated to him "so that these mysteries would not reach the Greeks and the arrogant, impotent and elaborate talk of the Greeks would not destroy the honourable, terse and powerful expression of the words"'.[14] This is essentially an argument among the elite against Greek philosophy and language, but Greek is nevertheless the language of the powerful and the 'arrogant' and what is advocated is a secret counter-cultural language for the initiates.

With apocalyptic, this counter-cultural language also becomes the language of the disempowered and the subaltern, opposed to the language of the rulers.[15] That we are here moving in the world of cultural resistance

---

13. M. Hengel, *Judaism and Hellenism* (London: SCM, 1974), 210–18.

14. Hengel, *Judaism and Hellenism*, 210–12.

15. This is not to deny that apocalyptic is also the language of cultural elites within Judaism, as is clearly evidenced by its presence in literary texts like Jubilees and in the writings of Qumran. But its occurrence in works of *Kleinliteratur*, like the Gospels and in the traditions which are collected in the Gospels, makes it clear that it is *also* the language of the disempowered. For a defence of the view of the Gospels as *Kleinliteratur*, see my 'Introduction' in K.L. Schmidt, *The Place of the Gospels in the General History of Literature* (Columbia, SC: University of South Carolina Press, 2002), vii–xxviii.

can be seen from the visions in Daniel which are echoed in Matthew 28.16–20 and which are given different references in their reception in apocalyptic literature. If in Daniel the fourth beast represented the Greek rulers, in 4 Ezra the fourth beast is identified as an eagle and linked to the Roman Empire (4 Ezra 12.12–30). Similarly in Revelation 12–13, the Danielic imagery is taken up into Revelation's polemic against Rome. This is certainly a coded, hidden wisdom for the subalterns and it is the language which, as it were, lurks below the surface of Matthew's overtly inner-Jewish polemic.

What is being claimed here, in this extension of the claim that Jesus has teaching authority unlike that of the scribes? It is, as G. Theissen has argued,[16] that the wisdom and virtues which 'belong' to the ruling elite are in fact to be appropriated by the 'little people', the marginalized and oppressed, 'the babes' (Matt. 11.25), and that they will be empowered, once Jesus's true authority is recognized and confirmed, to preserve and transmit his teaching throughout the world. It is a truly revolutionary claim, linked as it is to the language of authority and judgment from Daniel 7 and tied into the vision of judgment in 25.31–46.[17] At the same time, this claim to teach the whole world clearly represents a universalization of an ethos which until now has been the preserve of a particular people.[18]

7.2 Political Claims

The introduction of Daniel 7 into the discussion raises the question of the extent to which Matthew's ending and his account of the mission of the disciples is to be seen as overtly or covertly political.

The evidence for a close relationship between the two texts (Dan. 7.13f.

16. G. Theissen, *A Theory of Primitive Christian Religion* (London: SCM, 1999), 100–7; see too G. Theissen, 'Jesusbewegung als charismatische Wertrevolution', NTS 35 (1989), 243–60.

17. With again its echoes of Daniel 7.13f. in 25.31: 'When the son of Man comes in his glory, and all the angels with him, then he will sit on the throne of his glory.'

18. Theissen, *Primitive Christian Religion*, 81–2:

> The primitive Christian ethic consists first of all in the universalization of values and norms which had hitherto been attached to a particular *ethnos*, the people chosen by God. They also become accessible to others (here this universalization corresponded to Jewish expectation and hopes). In this way election and promise, law and wisdom, being a child of Abraham and an heir, are universalized. When at the end of the Gospel of Matthew the exalted Jesus says, 'Go and make disciples of all nations ... and teach them to observe all that I have commanded you' (Matt. 28.19f.), the disciples are being commanded to make the Jewish ethic as presented by Jesus accessible to all peoples. This process of the universalization of Jewish values and norms is bound up with a 'counter-current', a partial exchange between Judaism and the pagan world.

and Matt. 28.16–20) seems overwhelming.[19] Daniel 7.13f. is a text which Matthew has already cited in the trial scene with the High Priest; there are strong verbal agreements between Daniel 7LXX and Matthew 28. Moreover, there are close thematic links between the Daniel passage and the gospel: judgment (19.25); thrones (in the plural, 19.28); angels/ heavenly court (25); the coming of the Son of Man (10.23; 24.27); the clouds of heaven (24.30; 26.64). We are, that is to say, in the world of revolutionary apocalyptic rhetoric, where the *parousia* of the Son of Man/ Son of God with his heavenly retinue and court is contrasted with the advent[20] of the *divi filius*[21] emperor. Here resistance and counter-culture are buoyed up by hopes of a final dramatic divine intervention in which all those who have become disciples and have obeyed the commandments of the Son of God, 'the sons of the Kingdom', will be vindicated and those who rejected his disciples' teaching will be condemned.

Further support for this anti-imperial reading of the Danielic allusions can be garnered from formal considerations of the conclusion of the gospel. A number of scholars have argued that the conclusion is couched in the enthronement genre, which follows a pattern of presentation– proclamation–acclamation and is found exemplified in Daniel 7.13–14 and Philippians 2.9–11; others have argued that we have here a commissioning narrative (cf. Deut. 31.14–15,23; Josh 1.1–9).[22] In practice it looks as if we have something of a hybrid, but the enthronement rhetoric is hard to overhear, once one has begun to listen for the political overtones. Jesus is being proclaimed as the true ruler of the world, the one who – alone – can call himself 'Son of God'.

Moreover, once these cues are discerned, then retrospectively other pointers become apparent: the dreams and astrological portents of the birth narratives find their parallel in the literature of imperial biography.[23]

19. For a convincing summary of the evidence, see W.D. Davies and D.C. Allison, *Matthew III* (ICC; Edinburgh: T&T Clark, 1997), 682–3.

20. Cf. the hymn transmitted by Duris of Samos celebrating the arrival (*parousia*) in Athens of Demetrius Poliorketes as a god, together with Demeter:

> The greatest among the gods have drawn close to our city and shown us the greatest favour ... Hail to you, O son of mighty god Poseidon and of Aphrodite. The other gods dwell so far away, or else they have no ears, or they do not exist, or do not care at all about us. We see you in our midst, not a wooden or stone presence, but bodily. And so we pray to you.

In Klauck, *Religious Context*, 257.

21. The title was given to Octavian, as the adopted son of Julius Caesar, once Caesar was deified; cf. Klauck, *Religious Context*, 293.

22. See Davies and Allison, Matthew, III, 676–7 for a review of scholarly views. While Davies and Allison see the narrative as principally a commissioning narrative, they also recognize the sense in which Jesus is established as *pantokrator*. 'Mt 28.16–20 preserves a primitive enthronement Christology', 683.

23. For legends relating to Alexander's and Augustus's birth see Klauck, *Religious Context*, 268–70, 300–1.

The political and not just the healing aspects of the 'son of David' title come into focus, and the centurion's confession of Jesus as Son of God gains political, alongside its theological, connotations. Not only do Roman soldiers acknowledge the healing power of Jesus and show deep faith in Jesus's ability to perform amazing miracles; precisely at the point where Jesus is exposed to the military might of Rome, in his crucifixion, the agents of imperial power recognize in him a new and different kind of authority and power, as they confess him as the (true) Son of God.[24]

There are important distinctions to be made between the Danielic literature with its visions of a final battle between the imperial powers and the saints of the most high and Matthew's vision of Jesus' reign. The one who is enthroned and given all authority over heaven and earth in Matthew's story is the one who reveals his wisdom only to babes, he whose yoke is easy and light and who is himself meek and lowly in heart (cf. 21.5). His authority is exercised not through military or quasi-military might[25] (certainly there is no reference to such power in this final section) but through his teaching and commissioning of his disciples to teach *all the nations* what he has commanded them. Ultimately, his authority will be exercised at the final judgment; for the present, it is known and acknowledged only by his disciples, who already include Roman centurions.

---

24. I would therefore find it difficult to see this principally as a proleptic form of judgment.

25. Sim has argued that 24.15–28 'refers to nothing less that the full-scale attack upon the righteous by the forces of evil as the final event of history'. He finds evidence of this final attack in the reference to the 'gates of Hades' in 16.18, which, following J. Jeremias and Davies and Allison (1991, 630–44), he reads as 'refer[ring] to the final attack upon the righteous by the powers of evil who will gather in and advance from the underworld' (Apocalyptic Eschatology, 100). Intriguingly, Sim finds further evidence for such a final military conflict in Matthew's references to the 'angelic army and military paraphernalia' (101). Specifically, he is referring here to the 'sign (*sémeion*) of the Son of Man' in 24.30 and the sending out of his angels with 'a loud trumpet call' in 24.31 (104–5). I think that Sim is probably right to see military imagery in these verses and to regard 24.15–28 as referring to some final crisis in Judaea. Precisely how the references to the 'abomination of desolation' or to the vultures/eagles gathered round the corpse are to be understood is much more open to argument. For some the 'abomination of desolation' would undoubtedly recall the Roman desecration of the Temple, and the reference to the eagles would easily be taken as a reference to Roman armies. But precisely how any reader might imagine the end on the basis of these elusive and somewhat fragmentary predictions is much harder to say. In the first place, they would have been reading this *after* the destruction of Jerusalem and therefore would be puzzled by the reference to the holy place. Were they to suppose that the Temple would first be restored in order to be desecrated again? Second, while the references to the sign of the Son of Man and the sending out of the angels with a loud trumpet call might well have evoked military images to some, what the text says is not that they ride out to do battle with the Romans and/or with satanic forces, but that they go out 'to gather in the elect from the four winds' (24.31). What this suggests quite strongly is not that the elect have come together for one last stand against the forces of evil in Judaea, but that they are where, according to 28.19–20, they should be: scattered across the world preaching the Gospel and teaching all

7.3 *Territorial Expansion*

Jesus's commission in Matthew 28.16–20 lifts the prohibition on 'going to the Gentiles' from Matthew 10.5. What was until now a purely inner-Jewish affair suddenly becomes something with unlimited territorial pretensions. The disciples are to embark on a universal mission to bring all nations to obey the commandments of the one on whom all authority has been conferred. What is intriguing about this is not simply that Jesus claims authority over all. The Isaianic vision of the return of the exiles to Mount Zion also looked to the day when all would come to see and acknowledge the glory of the Lord in Zion; what is striking here is the movement out from Jerusalem to embrace all the nations.

This has its immediate 'cause' in the events surrounding Jesus's death, which is portrayed by Mark and Matthew as a moment of eschatological significance. For Mark, the rending of the veil of the Temple forms an *inclusio* with the rending of the heavens at Jesus's baptism. For Matthew (who misses Mark's touch here), the eschatological nature of the event is marked by the earthquakes and the appearances of the saints, which anticipates Jesus's own resurrection. Rather than the apocalyptic climax of this story of restoration and fulfilment being the return of the glory of the Lord to Mount Zion, it is by contrast the rending of the veil of the Temple and the centurion's recognition of God's presence in the crucified Christ. *His* presence, however, as 28.20 makes clear, will be no longer located in the cult in Jerusalem but wherever his disciples are at work: making disciples, baptizing and teaching all nations to keep all that he has commanded them.

It is interesting to consider the nature of this territorial expansionism a little further. I have argued[26] that it is indeed this which we encounter in Matthew, the expansion of sacred space to include no longer only the land but the whole world, *in so far as Jesus's authority is acknowledged in it*. This contrasts with the views of W.D. Davies, who argued that 'In sum, for the holiness of space, Christianity has fundamentally, though not

---

nations to obey Jesus commandments. This is interestingly also affirmed in 24.14, which in context seems to be intended to discourage readers from developing too precise a scenario of the end, particularly one which would spell it out in terms of wars and rumours of wars (24.6). This would hardly, I suspect, deter readers from allowing such a text to feed their longing for the breaking of Rome's military might; but there is, equally, a discernible sense in which Chapter 24 is designed to encourage the believers to remain true to their task of bringing the Gospel to all nations, to resist all those who might encourage them to take up military struggle against Rome (are there echoes here of Jewish messianic movements post 70?) and to discourage them, even in the case of some actual uprising from taking part. As Sim (*Apocalyptic Eschatology*, 102–3) rightly points out, there is a great difference between Matthew's treatment of these matters and that of the Qumran War Scroll.

26.   Riches, *Mythologies*, esp. 229–61.

consistently, substituted the holiness of the Person: it has Christified holy place.'[27]

These are fine, but important, distinctions: Jesus is *cosmocrator,* even if his rule is recognized as yet only by the few who are his disciples and if his presence is assured only among them (18.20; 28.20). Nevertheless, this is a very different claim from saying that Jesus reigns in his followers' hearts only: his reign over the whole world is assured and will be revealed at the parousia of the Son of Man, when all will see him seated at the right hand of power and coming on the clouds of heaven (Matt. 26.64). Then indeed his rule will be established over the whole world. Byzantium and Rome will both in their own ways understand this very well. It is only at the Reformation, with Luther's doctrine of the two kingdoms, that Christ's reign will be spiritualized.

This universalization of sacred space is brought out clearly in the interpretation of the parable of the wheat and the tares. The parable starts by announcing that the householder sows seed 'in his field'. The enemy attacks him by sowing tares, but his work will be undone at the harvest when the tares will be burnt. What the interpretation makes abundantly clear is that the field, the Son of Man's territory, is the *world* and that those who he 'sows' are the children of the kingdom. They are those who will shine like the sun in the kingdom of their Father. There is no room here for accommodation with hostile political powers; Jesus's reign demands acknowledgement. Its claims to authority mirror those of the political powers to whom it is opposed.

7.4 Conclusion

The conclusion of Matthew's Gospel may been seen as the assertion of the Matthaean community's claim to be the true heirs of the Jewish tradition, to be the followers of the new Moses who fulfils God's law and will carry this to all nations. But there is at another level a different thrust to this passage, one which sends us back to the gospel to pick up further cues. Here Jesus asserts his authority over all the world: an authority which resides in his 'higher wisdom' which is proclaimed not to the wise and the learned (the powerful and mighty) but to the babes. The gospel here adopts a counter-cultural idiom which finds its expression both in the cults which came into the Hellenistic world from the east in the third/second centuries BCE and in Jewish apocalyptic with its polemical edge against the Greek and Roman political powers. This is borne out further by Matthew's own use of Daniel 7.13f., a text which had wide currency in these circles. Here a claim is staked to an alternative mode of power and

27. Davies, *Gospel and Land,* 368.

governance, which will be effected through the dissemination of Jesus' teaching and the judgment which he will execute at his parousia, when his rule will be revealed to all.

Finally, I suggested that these counter-cultural claims are further developed in the territorial claims made in these verses and which are rooted in the events at Jesus' death, when the veil of the Temple is rent and the presence of God is manifested in the crucified and risen Christ. There is here alongside the more overt inner-Jewish language, which recent scholarship has been at pains to elaborate, a more covert but still, for those who have ears to hear, clearly discernible anti-Roman polemic, which has its roots in the traditions of Jewish apocalyptic.

MATTHAEAN CHRISTOLOGY IN ROMAN IMPERIAL KEY: MATTHEW 1.1

Warren Carter

The gospel's opening verse employs five markers to identify its central character: 'the book of the origins'; 'Jesus'; 'Christ'; 'son of David'; and 'son of Abraham'. I will interpret the significance of these identifiers by attending somewhat to the intratextuality between titles and narrative, but more so to the intertextuality[1] that exists between the Jewish traditions that they evoke and the experience and 'knowledge' of the Roman imperial world assumed of Matthew's audience, who were likely located in Antioch on the Orontes, the capital of the Roman province of Syria.[2] My argument is that Matthew's christological claims, elaborated by both the subsequent gospel narrative and Jewish traditions, intersect with the gospel's (frequently neglected) Roman imperial context to present Jesus as the agent of God's saving purposes, who contests and relativizes Rome's claim to sovereignty and divine agency and who offers a vision for a different social experience that enacts God's purposes. The discussion of these five key christological claims from 1.1 demonstrates both the necessity and usefulness of hearing this gospel in its Roman imperial context.

The method to be employed – a focus on titles elaborated by both the narrative and by (predominantly) Jewish traditions, in the context of the Roman imperial world – builds on strengths of previous christological work, as well as redressing the serious neglect of the Roman imperial world in contemporary Matthaean scholarship.

---

1.   J. Kristeva ('The Bounded Text') in L.S. Roudiez [ed.], *Desire in Language: A Semiotic Approach to Literature and Art* [New York: Columbia University Press, 1980], 36–63, esp. 36–7) defines intertextuality as locating 'different textual arrangements ... within the general text (culture) of which they are a part and which is in turn, part of them'.

2.   For support, W. Carter, *Matthew and the Margins: A Sociopolitical and Religious Reading* (Maryknoll, NY: Orbis, 2000), 14–17, 17–29, 36–43; W. Carter, *Matthew and Empire: Initial Explorations* (Harrisburg, IL: Trinity Press International, 2001), 9–53. None of the following analysis, though, depends on an Antiochene location.

8.1 *Titles, Narratives and Contexts*

A focus on the titles that the gospels employ for Jesus has often comprised the standard approach to New Testament and Matthaean christology.[3] Initial history-of-religions work on the origin and meaning of titles focused on various religious expressions in the Graeco-Roman world.[4] While some minimal attention to the Graeco-Roman world in relation to particular titles (Kyrios, Son of God, the Word) has continued,[5] most have not found attention to Hellenistic mystery cults persuasive,[6]

---

3. Interestingly, Matthew has played a relatively minor role in efforts to make titles central to understanding the christological developments of the early Christian movement. For example, cf. W. Bousset, *Kyrios Christos* (Nashville, TN: Abingdon, 1970), esp. Chapter 2. Bousset emphasizes interaction with the Hellenistic world, especially with mystery religions. F. Hahn, *Christologische Hoheitstitel: Ihre Geschichte im Frühen Christentum* (FRLANT 83; Göttingen: Vandenhoeck & Ruprecht, 1963); O. Cullmann, *The Christology of the New Testament* (London: SCM, 1963); J.D.G. Dunn, *Christology in the Making: A New Testament Inquiry into the Origins of the Doctrine of the Incarnation* (Grand Rapids, MI: Eerdmans, 1989).

4. For example, Bousset, *Kyrios Christos*, 11–23, esp. 19, argued for the influence of 'broad intellectual connections' with Hellenistic–Oriental (syncretistic) mystical piety, especially pre-Christian Gnosticism evidenced by the Hermetic literature. Bousset, *Kyrios Christos*, 138–47, 310–17, and others, such as A. Deissmann, *Light from the Ancient East* (New York: Hodder & Stoughton, 1910), 347–84, also appealed to the influence of – or at least parallels with – ruler cults such as worship of the Roman emperor. However, the discussions did not recognize the imperial cult's central political role in constituting imperial relations and pervading socio-economic life. cf. S. Price, *Rituals and Power: The Roman Imperial Cult in Asia Minor* (Cambridge: Cambridge University Press, 1984).

5. For example, Cullmann, *Christology*, 195–9, 239–40, 251–4, 271–2; Dunn, *Christology*. W.J. Cotter, 'Greco-Roman Apotheosis Traditions and the Resurrection Appearances in Matthew' in D.E. Aune (ed.), *The Gospel of Matthew in Current Study* (Grand Rapids, MI: Eerdmans, 2001), 127–53, engages Graeco-Roman and Jewish traditions of apotheosis of heroes in interpreting Matthew 28.16–20.

6. Factors include the post-first-century dating of claimed source material; the realization that 'Judaism' and 'Hellenism' were not isolated cultures and that 'Judaism' was not monolithic; renewed attention on pre-Pauline and Pauline material, the discovery of the Dead Sea Scrolls and renewed attention to diverse Jewish traditions; and attention to the piety and practices of the earliest Christian communities. See B.M. Metzger, 'Methodology on the Study of the Mystery Religions and Early Christianity' in R. Berkey and S. Edwards (eds), *Historical and Literary Studies: Pagan, Jewish, and Christian* (Grand Rapids, MI: Eerdmans, 1968), 1–24; L.W. Hurtado, 'Introduction' in his *One God One Lord: Early Christian Devotion and Ancient Jewish Monotheism* (Philadelphia, PA: Fortress, 1988); T. Schmeller, 'The Greco-Roman Background of New Testament Christology' in R. Berkey and S. Edwards (eds), *Christology in Dialogue* (Cleveland, OH: Pilgrim Press, 1993), 54–65; also N. Dahl, 'Sources of Christological Language' in D. Juel (ed.), *Jesus the Christ: The Historical Origins of Christological Doctrine* (Minneapolis, MN: Fortress, 1991), 113–36.

preferring to find the origin and meaning of the titles in (some combination of) Jesus's own ministry,[7] Palestinian and Diaspora/ Hellenistic Judaisms, and/or early Christian practices and piety.[8] Beyond influence on the obvious titles (Messiah, Son of Man, Son of David, etc.), Matthaean scholars have also identified the importance of other Jewish traditions – Moses,[9] wisdom[10] – for Matthaean christology.

Extensive redaction studies in the 1960s–70s sought to identify Matthew's most important or central title/s. While various titles had their advocates (Son of David and Lord,[11] Lord,[12] Son of Man,[13] Son of God),[14] no argument carried the day because the approach was methodologically inadequate and the question was unhelpfully restrictive.

In a very important 1986 article, Leander Keck offered a strong critique of this titular approach, emphasizing its linguistic, conceptual and synthesizing limitations:[15] (1) Title-dominated approaches fail to understand that meaning does not reside in isolated words but in words connected in and by sentences. (2) Title-dominated approaches do not adequately embrace non-titular material, the plurality of titles, or insights in a passage not expressed in that passage's title/s. The claim that titles interpret Jesus, Keck argues, ignores the rest of the 'christological hermeneutic' that 'the Jesus-event interprets the titles'. A focus on titles cannot adequately engage the relationship of Jesus to the Old Testament. (3) A title-dominated approach, especially the quest for the most important title, engages christology in a piecemeal way but cannot synthesize the material. Central to Keck's proposal for a way ahead was a

---

7. E.g. C.F.D. Moule, *The Origin of Christology* (Cambridge: Cambridge University Press, 1977); Dunn, *Christology*, 22–33.

8. M. Hengel, *Between Jesus and Paul* (Philadelphia, PA: Fortress, 1983); Hurtado, *One God*.

9. D.C. Allison, *The New Moses: A Matthean Typology* (Minneapolis, MN: Fortress, 1993).

10. C. Deutsch, *Lady Wisdom, Jesus, and the Sages: Metaphor and Social Context in Matthew's Gospel* (Valley Forge: Trinity Press International, 1996); F.T. Gench, *Wisdom in the Christology of Matthew* (Lanham: University Press of America, 1997); also Carter, 'Take my Yoke, not Rome's: Matthew 11.28–30' in *Matthew and Empire*, 108–29.

11. G. Strecker, *Der Weg der Gerechtigkeit* (FRLANT 82; Göttingen: Vandenhoeck & Ruprecht, 1962), 118–20, 123–6.

12. W. Trilling, *Das Wahre Israel* (Munich: Kösel, 1964), 21–51; H. Frankemölle, *Jahwebund und Kirche Christi* (NTAbh 10; Münster: Aschendorff, 1974).

13. E.P. Blair, *Jesus in the Gospel of Matthew* (Nashville, TN: Abingdon, 1960), 83; R.H. Fuller, 'Christology in Matthew and Luke', in R.H. Fuller and P. Perkins (eds), *Who is this Christ? Gospel Christology and Contemporary Faith* (Philadelphia, PA: Fortress, 1983), 86.

14. J.D. Kingsbury, *Matthew: Structure, Christology, Kingdom* (Philadelphia, PA: Fortress, 1975), 40–127. For critique, D. Hill, 'Son and Servant: An Essay on Matthaean Christology', *JSNT* 6 (1980), 2–16.

15. L. Keck, 'Toward the Renewal of New Testament Christology', *NTS* 32 (1986), 362–77, esp. 368–75.

focus on New Testament texts in pursuit not of the origin of the material but of understanding 'the overall construal of Jesus' identity and significance in the text'. For Keck, such a construal elucidates the relation of Jesus to 'God, world, and the human condition'.[16]

Keck's call for a move away from fragmentary approaches and his emphasis on attention to 'texts as they actually exist' resonated with developing narrative approaches in 1980s gospel studies.[17] This approach focused on the finished form of the text (not its sources) and engaged a unified narrative in a sequential rather than comparative fashion. Influenced also by reader-response criticism,[18] scholars employed categories of 'implied readers' or 'authorial audiences' to actualize the text by utilizing its various generic and narrative conventions, supplying its grammatical, intertextual, extra-textual (cultural and historical) gaps, and connecting its disparate elements into a coherent understanding. Categories of plot and characterization ('building character' from traits), for example, framed discussions of 'Matthew's Understanding of Jesus'.[19] In this approach, christological titles were seen to contribute to Jesus's characterization as part of the larger narrative of his actions, sayings, interactions with other characters, settings and intertextual echoes and extra-textual information, as well as by posing questions of meaning that could only be answered from the larger narrative.[20]

Attention to the active, synthesizing work of readers or audiences involved attention to the knowledge and experience that an audience brings to the interpretive task. Identifying the extra-textual material (information and experience) that an audience supplies to the interpretive

---

16. Keck, 'New Testament Christology', 372–3.

17. E.g. J.D. Kingsbury, *Matthew as Story* (Philadelphia, PA: Fortress, 1986); M.A. Powell, *What is Narrative Criticism?* (Minneapolis, MN: Fortress, 1990); W. Carter, *Matthew: Storyteller, Evangelist, Interpreter* (Peabody: Hendrickson, 1996); for discussion, S. Moore, *Literary Criticism and the Gospels: The Theoretical Challenge* (New Haven, CT: Yale University Press, 1989).

18. E.g. S. Fish, *Is there a Text in this Class?: The Authority of Interpretive Communities* (Cambridge, MA.: Harvard University Press, 1980); P.J. Rabinowitz, 'Whirl Without End: Audience-Oriented Criticism' in G.D. Atkins and L. Morrow (eds), *Contemporary Literary Theory* (Amherst, MA: University of Massachusetts Press, 1989), 81–100.

19. E.g. Kingsbury, *Matthew as Story*, 9–27; Carter, *Matthew*, 189–256.

20. E.g. E. Richard, *Jesus. One and Many: The Christological Concept of New Testament Authors* (Wilmington, DE: Glazier, 1988), 145–56; R. Schnackenburg, *Jesus in the Gospels* (Louisville, KY: Westminster John Knox, 1995), 74–130; B. Gerhardsson, 'The Christology of Matthew' in M.A. Powell and D.R. Bauer (eds), *Who Do you Say that I Am? Essays on Christology* (Louisville, KY: Westminster John Knox, 1999), 14–32; F. Matera, *New Testament Christology* (Louisville, KY: Westminster John Knox, 1999), 26–47; M. Müller, 'The Theological Interpretation of the Figure of Jesus in the Gospel of Matthew: Some Principal Features in Matthaean Christology', *NTS* 45 (1999), 157–73; C. Tuckett, *Christology and the New Testament: Jesus and his Earliest Followers* (Louisville, KY: Westminster John Knox, 2001), 119–32.

task has been a regular part of recent scholarly enquiry. But consistently, such exploration has been restricted in Matthaean scholarship to two areas.

One area comprises intellectual and religious traditions, to the neglect of political and socioeconomic spheres.[21] The early social-scientific work emerging in the late 1970s and 1980s protested the 'methodological docetism' from which studies of the theology of the New Testament suffered, 'as if believers had minds and spirits unconnected with their individual and corporate bodies'.[22] These 'disembodied' souls, comprised only of minds concerned with religious matters, seemed not to be concerned with or participate in societal practices and daily social realities. This protest is certainly true of christological discussions and it has not yet been redressed. This is not to say that intellectual and religious traditions are not crucial cultural forces at work in the formulation of either Matthaean christology in particular or New Testament christology in general, nor is it to overlook attention to social dimensions such as the role of a dispute with(in) a synagogue, but it is to recognize that hitherto the discussion has been partial at best.

Second, Matthaean scholars have restricted investigation of extra-textual material to Jewish traditions, institutions and texts. Debates about 'Matthew and the Gentiles', for example, commonly frame the issue on a microlevel as to whether individual Gentiles might belong to the Matthaean community and if so, how.[23] But patently evident is the failure to engage any macrolevel or systemic considerations, notably the relationship between Matthew's story of Jesus and the Roman imperial world.[24] Attention to this interaction with the Roman imperial world is instantly justifiable on at least two grounds: the gospel's plot centres on the execution of the main character by the distinctly Roman means of crucifixion, and the gospel's late-first-century audience cannot but help bring its daily experiences of life in the Roman imperial world to its hearing of the gospel and understanding of Jesus. To be clear, I am not

---

21. I. Gradel, *Emperor Worship and Roman Religion* (Oxford: Clarendon Press, 2002), 1–32.

22. R. Scroggs, 'The Sociological Interpretation of the New Testament: The Present State of Research', *NTS* 26 (1980), 164–79, esp. 165–6; W. Meeks, 'A Hermeneutics of Social Embodiment' in G. Nickelsburg and G. MacRae (eds), *Christians among Jews and Gentiles* (Philadelphia, PA: Fortress, 1986), 176–86.

23. W. Carter, 'Matthew and the Gentiles: Individual Conversion and/or Systemic Transformation?', *JSNT* 26 (2004), 259–82.

24. The questions are (1) much more systemic than the usual individualistic framing of considerations of Matthew and the Gentiles; (2) much more comprehensive than previous discussions of 'Lord/Son of God in the Imperial Cult' recognize; and (3) much more nuanced than discussions about whether Jesus was a revolutionary, in which 'revolutionary' is often naïvely equated with violence. See E. Bammel, 'The Revolution Theory from Reimarus to Brandon' in E. Bammel and C.F.D. Moule (eds), *Jesus and the Politics of his Day* (Cambridge: Cambridge University Press, 1984), 11–68.

contesting the formative importance of Jewish traditions nor of a dispute with a synagogue community, nor am I arguing for the Roman imperial world as the definitive or exclusive source of Matthaean christology. Rather, informed by recent work on the active role audiences play in interpretation, I am approaching the matter from the perspective of the gospel's late-first-century audience, located in Antioch (the capital city of the Roman province of Syria), and an exploring the question of how the gospel might be heard when it interacts with the cultural knowledge and experience of Roman imperialism that was the lot of first-century audiences. Matthaean scholars, often acquainted neither with sociological models of empire,[25] nor with studies of aspects of the Roman imperial world, have not taken this context seriously.

Some previous work indicates the value of the exploration of Matthaean christology in relation to the Roman imperial world. This discussion of the christological claims of Matthew 1.1 assumes and builds on a previous essay on Matthew's christology in which I observed significant parallels between four themes that are central to Roman imperial ideology/theology, well-known and widely attested in the first century, and to the presentation of Jesus in Matthew's Gospel:[26]

Roman imperial theology	Matthew's Gospel
Rome and its emperor exercise the sovereignty of the gods over human history and society.	God exercises his sovereignty over his world through Israel and Jesus.
Rome and its emperor manifest the will and presence of the gods.	Jesus is the agent of God's will and presence.
Rome and its emperor are the chosen agents of the gods.	Jesus is God's chosen agent.
Rome and its emperor ensure the well-being of the world.	God through Jesus blesses the world now and in the yet-future final establishment of God's empire or reign. Rome's imperial order is precisely the world from which people need saving.

I argued that since the gospel's late-first-century audience brings its knowledge and daily experience of Roman imperialism to its interaction with Matthew's text, these parallelisms are not an irrelevant or benign coincidence. Rather, Matthew's audience hears the gospel's claims about Jesus as contesting the claims of the Roman *imperium* and as offering an alternative worldview and social experience. Of course, whether and how many consent to such a contesting and how daily living might be impacted are questions that are unanswerable.

8.2 *What Does Matthew's Audience Know and Experience?*

Basic to this approach is identifying the knowledge and experience of imperial realities assumed of the gospel's audience. At the distance of two millennia, there is much we cannot know and the temptation to construct a monolithic or idealized audience must be resisted. But given the extensive and diverse resources that exist from the Roman world,[27] and with the help of studies of ancient Roman cities[28] and a sociological model of agrarian empires,[29] we can reconstruct, at least with broad brushstrokes, some of the significant experiences of life in a late-first-century provincial city like Antioch on the Orontes.[30] Such efforts at reconstruction are no more unlikely than the assembly of copious Jewish materials that Matthaean scholars commonly claim to be influential for the gospel's author and audience. In fact, attention to the Roman imperial context corrects some mistaken impressions created by Matthaean scholarship: that Matthew's author and/or audience know only Jewish traditions; that they engage the gospel only intellectually and religiously; that they have no interest in or awareness of any 'non-religious' matters (to impose a very false distinction); that they have no societal experience other than a ('religious') fight with a synagogue; that they have no concern with power, rule, or socio-economic realities; and that they are isolated from all such concerns and leave their daily experience of the Roman imperial world behind when they engage Matthew's 'religious' text.[31] Such an imagined author and/or

---

27. E.g. J. Huskinson, *Experiencing Rome: Culture, Identity and Power in the Roman Empire* (London: Routledge, 2000); K. Wengst, *Pax Romana and the Peace of Jesus Christ* (Philadelphia, PA: Fortress, 1987).

28. E.g. J. Rich and A. Wallace-Hadrill (eds), *City and Country in the Ancient World* (New York: Routledge, 1991).

29. Lenski, *Power and Privilege*, 189–296.

30. For some synthesis, discussion and bibliography, see Carter, *Matthew and the Margins*, 17–29, 36–43, 609–36; Carter, *Matthew and Empire*, 9–53, 221–41.

31. For instance, a (white, Western, male) reviewer ('Review', *The Princeton Seminary Bulletin* 23 [2002] 384–5) of my *Matthew and the Margins* complains that my attention to matters of sociopolitical power distorts the text. He asks, incredibly and rhetorically: 'Was Matthew's implied audience really so sensitive to, indeed so completely consumed by, the issues of power as Carter supposes?' Interestingly, reviews from readers in the so-called two-thirds world find no such problem.

audience (created in 'our' image) says much about comfortable (and prosperous) contemporary individualism that conceives of religion as a private matter isolated from sociopolitical matters; much about scholarly specialization that has often concentrated on and valued intellectual traditions but ignored socioeconomic realities; and much about the neglect of the Roman imperial world by New Testament scholars – but little about the complexities of the late-first-century world.

Those who heard Matthew's gospel in this late-first-century imperial world experienced a world marked, for example, by:

- vast societal inequalities, economic exploitation and political oppression. The ruling class and its retainers, comprising Roman and allied provincial elites – no more than 5 per cent of the population – controlled power and resources for wealth. A huge socioeconomic gap separated this group from the rest comprising traders, urban artisans and rural peasants. Few notions or opportunities for social improvement existed.[32]
- tensions between rich (wealth is acquired for conspicuous consumption) and poor, Roman and provincial (including among ethnic groups), propertied and non-propertied, male and female, rural and urban.[33] The status system generally honoured wealthy, powerful, Roman and provincial males, and despised those of little power, wealth and status.
- pervasive displays of Roman power and control, including military presence (and deterrence),[34] and taxation that typically claimed somewhere between 37 per cent of productivity. By this means, about 5 per cent of the population consumed over 50 per cent of agrarian production, ensuring that most lived at subsistence levels.[35]
- no separation of religious institutions and personnel from socioeconomic and political commitments. The 'religious leaders' with whom Jesus conflicts are allies of Roman rule and representatives of a particular socioeconomic vision that benefits themselves. Synagogue leaders similarly require power, wealth and status to perform their leadership duties.[36]
- imperial theology or propaganda, proclaimed by imperial personnel, buildings, statues and gates, coins, temples, rituals and festivals, announced Rome and its emperor as chosen by the gods to manifest the blessing of *Pax Romana*, the vertical, Roman-controlled, sociopolitical order.

---

32.   Carter, *Matthew and Empire*, 9–53, for support.

33.   E.g. R. MacMullen, *Roman Social Relations. 50 BC to AD 284* (New Haven, CT: Yale University Press, 1974). For Martial's hierarchical social vision and attitudes, J.P. Sullivan, *Martial: The Unexpected Classic. A Literary and Historical Study* (Cambridge: Cambridge University Press, 1991), 159–70.

34.   E.g. J. Rich and G. Shipley (eds), *War and Society in the Roman World* (London: Routledge, 1993); S. Mattern, *Rome and the Enemy: Imperial Strategy in the Principate* (Berkeley, CA: University of California Press, 1999).

35.   Lenski, *Power and Privilege*, 267–8; see my 'Paying the Tax to Rome as Subversive Praxis: Matt. 17.24–27', *JSNT* 76 (1999), 3–31; also in *Matthew and Empire*, 130–44.

36.   D. Binder, *Into the Temple Courts: The Place of the Synagogues in the Second Temple Period* (Atlanta, GA: SBL, 1999), 343–71.

- obvious signs, sounds and smells of the destructive impact of the imperial sociopolitical order structured for the elite's benefit: poverty, poor sanitation, disease, malnutrition, overwork, natural disasters (fire and flooding) and social instability.[37]

Rodney Stark observes that

> Any accurate picture of Antioch...must depict a city filled with misery, danger, fear, despair, and hatred. Antioch was a city where the average family lived in filthy and cramped quarters, where at least half of the children died at birth or during infancy...The city was filled with hatred and fear rooted in intense ethnic antagonisms and exacerbated by a constant stream of strangers (competing, we might add, for very limited economic resources and opportunities)...Crime flourished and the streets were dangerous at night...And perhaps, above all, Antioch was repeatedly smashed by cataclysmic catastrophes.[38]

In such a context, how might an audience hear the gospel's opening verse: 'The book of the origin of Jesus the Christ, son of David, son of Abraham?'

I do not claim an exhaustive discussion but wish to point to the interaction between some of the gospel claims about Jesus shaped by Jewish traditions and elaborated in the narrative, and the Roman imperial world in which the gospel's audience lives and in relation to which it interprets the gospel. Because of space limitations, I will focus more on the intertextual dimensions than on intratextual elaborations. I should also note that the argument is informed throughout by J.M. Foley's work demonstrating that in texts deriving from oral cultures, phrases function metonymically to evoke not isolated entities but larger narratives from a cultural repertoire assumed of and shared by the audience.[39] The argument also assumes M. Perry's attention to 'the primacy effect'; whereby material located at the outset of a work functions to shape an audience's expectations and understandings of the subsequent narrative.[40]

---

37. E.g. R. Garland, *The Eye of the Beholder: Deformity and Disability in the Graeco-Roman World* (Ithaca, NY: Cornell University Press, 1995), 18–44; P.D.A. Garnsey, *Famine and Food Supply in the Graeco-Roman World* (Cambridge: Cambridge University Press, 1988).

38. R. Stark, 'Urban Chaos and Crisis' in *The Rise of Christianity* (Princeton, NJ: Princeton University Press, 1996), 160–61.

39. J.M Foley, *Immanent Art: From Structure to Meaning in Traditional Oral Epic* (Bloomington, IN: Indiana University Press, 1991). I employ Foley's work in 'Evoking Isaiah: Matthaean Soteriology and an Intertextual Reading of Isaiah 7–9 in Matthew 1.23 and 4.15–16', *JBL* 119 (2000), 503–20.

40. M. Perry, 'Literary Dynamics: How the Order of a Text Creates its Meaning', *Poetics Today* 1 (1979–80), 35–64.

8.3 *The Book of the Origin (*biblos geneseôs*)*

How should the noun *geneseôs* be translated: 'genealogy'? 'origin'? 'birth'? 'history'? 'genesis'? It is used elsewhere with a range of meanings, and the choice of an appropriate translation here is complicated by deciding whether verse 1 functions as a title for the whole gospel, or as the introduction to the birth narrative of Chapters 1–2, or as the introduction only to the genealogy of Matthew 1.1–17. My choice of 'origin' reflects its double use in 1.1 at the outset of the genealogy and in 1.18 for the narration of Jesus's conception. The term attempts to recognize with one English word a polyvalent reading that embraces a literary function (introducing the genealogy [1.1–17] and conception/birth [Chs 1–2]), and a thematic focus for the gospel on a divine act of creation that expresses God's purposes. It is this last claim that I want to elaborate on here.

For Matthew's scripturally literate audience, the phrase *biblos geneseôs* evokes the name of the first book in the biblical collection, Genesis.[41] The phrase itself appears twice in the opening five chapters of Genesis at strategic locations. Its first appearance (2.4) ends one account of origins and divine activity (the story of the creation of the heavens and the earth) and begins another, the story of the creation of man and woman. Its second appearance (5.1) again emphasizes origins and divine activity in recalling the creation of Adam and Eve and introducing the generations from Adam to Noah. Employing Foley's argument, it is fair to claim that the term *geneseôs* evokes, then, this larger narrative of God's creation of the world and of humans. It recalls the assertion of Israel's traditions that God is creator of and therefore sovereign over his world. It recalls the vision of human beings in Genesis 1–2 created by God to live according to God's purposes, yet departed from that purpose. Later, in Matthew 19.3, Jesus will evoke these creation accounts as exhibiting God's will and purposes for human existence.[42] Moreover, the phrase recalls, with the listing of generations to Noah, human faithlessness, God's judgment and God's willingness to start again.

Such intertextual echoes at the start of the gospel story are not inconsequential. They provide crucial perspectives, locating Jesus from the outset in relation to assertions of the creator's sovereignty over the world, to human fickleness and to new beginnings in God's purposes. They provide foundational framing for the story of Jesus.

At least two experiences of Matthew's audience interact with such claims. One was the daily experience of a Roman imperial world that so often did not seem to reflect God's sovereignty and life-giving purposes.

---

41. Both Philo (*Poster C*, 127; *Abr.* 1; *Aet. mund.* 19) and Justin (*Dial.* 20.1) know the first biblical book by this name.
42. For other new creation echoes, Carter, *Matthew and the Margins*, 55–6.

Stark's description of tough socioeconomic living conditions for many (noted above) presents a world under Roman control, the world of *Pax Romana* that was very different from the blessed paradise of Genesis 1–2. And second, the ever-present Roman sovereignty over the world had been freshly exhibited in the recent siege and destruction of Jerusalem (70 CE). Antioch had been a source of troops in the unsuccessful initial campaign in 66 CE by Cestius Gallus, the Roman governor of Syria, against the Jewish rebels. Based in Antioch, Cestius Gallus sustained significant losses as his troops retreated northward from Jerusalem (Josephus, *War*, 2.499–500, 540–55). Antioch was an initial staging ground for troops under Vespasian in 67 (*War*, 3.8, 29; 7.46). Syrian grain and corn supplied Roman troops during the war (*War*, 5.520). Riots against Jews in Antioch broke out (*War*, 7.47–62), and when the victorious Titus visited Antioch in 70–71 on his way to his triumph in Rome, he refused demands to have Jewish rights rescinded (*War*, 7.100–11), though he did display troops and booty from Jerusalem (Malalas, *Chron.*, 260–61).

Such actions demonstrated the imperial ideology – constantly announced by the presence of Roman personnel (governor, staff, troops), buildings, statues, festivals, temples and coins – that Jupiter reigned over the earth, and that Rome was the chosen agent of the gods. The destruction of the Jerusalem temple, God's house, signified Jupiter's victory over the powerless God of Israel.[43] The assertion of Roman sovereignty and peace was but an expression of the will and blessing of the gods, especially Jupiter. In fact, Augustan propaganda evidenced for instance in Virgil and Horace,[44] and in the post-70 CE decades by Flavian propagandists Statius and Martial, had announced previously the

---

43. Note both Josephus, *War*, 6.299–300, 'we [i.e. heavenly beings] are departing hence', and Tacitus, *Histories*, 5.13, 'the gods were departing', indicate divine abandonment of the Jerusalem Temple in the face of Roman power. Josephus says as much explicitly: 'My belief, therefore, is that the Deity has fled from the holy places and taken His stand on the side of those with whom you are now at war' (*War*, 5.412). Subsequently the gospel will reframe the fall of Jerusalem as an act of divine judgment (22.7). Rome, like previous imperial powers (Assyria, Babylon, the Seleucids), is the agent of God's purposes in punishing the people, especially the elite, for their sins. Jesus is commissioned to save from sins (1.21) by various means, but ultimately by defeating Roman power through resurrection and parousia (24.27–31). Carter, *Matthew and the Margins*, 435–6; Carter, '"To Save his People from their Sins" (Matthew 1.21): Rome's Empire and Matthew's Salvation as Sovereignty' in *Matthew and Empire*, 75–90; Carter, 'Evoking Isaiah', 503–20; Carter, 'Are there Imperial Texts in the Class? Intertextual Eagles and Matthean Eschatology as "Lights Out" Time for Imperial Rome (Matt. 24.27–31)', *JBL* 122 (2003), 467–87.

44. Virgil, 'Fourth Eclogue'; *Aeneid*, 1.257–96; 6.791–807; Horace, *Carmen saeculare*, 29–68, praises plenty, virtues and peace through conquest and ongoing labour. For literary expressions under Augustus, H.P. L'Orange, 'The Floral Zone of the Ara Pacis' in H.P. L'Orange, *Art Forms and Civic Life* (New York: Rizzoli, 1985), 211–30; for visual-monumental expressions, D. Castriota, *The Ara Pacis Augustae and the Imagery of*

dawning of the golden age of fertility and material abundance through agricultural labour and the emperor's rule.[45]

In the face of such displays of Roman sovereignty and claims of realized eschatology, namely the gods' sanction for a golden age realized in and through Roman rule, Matthew's evoking the Genesis 'golden age' account[46] in the post-70 context is a bold gesture. In the midst of Rome's claims, the evoked Genesis creation narrative makes present God's claim over the world as its creator, suggesting (as the subsequent narrative will confirm, e.g. 4.17) that God is, in association with Jesus, reasserting his claim and purposes. Moreover, the narrative depicts a different vision of the world as God created it to be: a world not ruled by a small Roman and provincial elite for its own benefit but one in which the creator's purposes for all the world are realized. The evoked narrative thereby collides with Roman claims, casting a negative verdict on them, contesting them and refusing to accept them as supreme and final. James Scott notes that resistance among oppressed and relatively powerless groups seldom takes the form of direct, armed confrontation with an overwhelmingly superior power.[47] Such groups prefer gestures of protest and subversion that are calculated, veiled and self-protective, such as this subtle evoking of 'insider' traditions announcing God's sovereignty.[48]

Further, Jewish apocalyptic traditions unveiled God's intent to end this

---

Abundance in Later Greek and Early Imperial Art (Princeton, NJ: Princeton University Press, 1995); T. Woodman and D. West, *Poetry and Politics in the Age of Augustus* (Cambridge: Cambridge University Press, 1984); A. Wallace-Hadrill, 'The Golden Age and Sin in Augustan Ideology', *Past and Present* 95 (1982), 19–36; K. Garlinsky, *Augustan Culture: An Interpretive Introduction* (Princeton, NJ: Princeton University Press, 1996), 90–128.

45.   Statius, *Silvae*, 1.6.39–42, abundant food for all; Martial, *Epig.*, 5.19.1–6; on Flavian propaganda, K. Scott, 'Statius' Adulation of Domitian', *American Journal of Philology* 54 (1933), 247–59, esp. 255 (founder of a new golden age); K. Scott, *The Imperial Cult under the Flavians* (Stuttgart: Kohlhammer, 1936), 25–39, notes links between Vespasian and Augustus attested by coins and buildings. See J. Ferguson, *Utopias in the Classical World* (Ithaca. NY: Cornell University Press, 1975), 154–74. That such perspectives were known outside Rome in eastern provincial centres is attested by (1) the decrees issued by the *koinon* of Asia in 9 BCE proposing a new calendar to honour Augustus's birthday as equal to 'the beginning of all things' and restoring all that had 'become imperfect' (texts in V. Ehrenberg and A.H.M. Jones, *Documents Illustrating the Reigns of Augustus and Tiberius* [Oxford: Clarendon Press, 2nd edn 1955], 81–84); and (2) Philo, *Leg. Ad Gaium*, 8–13, who refers to Gaius's initial reign as a 'plenitude ... of good fortune ... indeed, the life under Saturn pictured by the poets no longer appeared to be a fabled story so great was the prosperity and well being, the freedom from grief and fear...'

46.   The phrase comes from Ferguson, *Utopias*, 146–7.

47.   J.C. Scott, *Weapons of the Weak: Everyday Forms of Peasant Resistance* (New Haven, CT: Yale University Press, 1985).

48.   W. Carter, 'Vulnerable Power: The Roman Empire Challenged by the Early Christians' in A.J. Blasi, J. Duhaime and P.-A. Turcotte (eds), *Handbook of Early Christianity* (Walnut Creek: Alta Mira Press, 2002), 453–88.

sinful and oppressive world by starting over with a new world where, as with the initial creation, God's purposes would be established.[49] Several post-70 Jewish texts contemporary with Matthew depict God's new world as resembling the fertility and abundance of the Garden of Eden (2 Bar. 29–30; for the renewal of the earth, 32.6; 44.11–12; 57.2), a return to 'as it was at the first beginnings' (4 Ezra 7.30). Also from the first century, 1 Enoch 37–71 depicts the creation of a new heaven and earth free of sin and marked by peace (45.3–6; cf. 72.1) following the Son of Man's punishment of 'the kings, governors, high officials and landlords' (1 En. 62) who greedily oppress the righteous (1 En. 46, 48). In these three texts, a Messiah plays some role in the events surrounding this new creation, anticipating God's rule (4 Ezra 7.28) and executing judgment (1 En. 46–48.10; 2 Bar. 39–40). Matthew shares such expectations, referring to 'the renewal of all things' (19.28), to a new heaven and earth (5.18; 24.35), to judgment on Rome by the returning Son of Man (24.27–31),[50] and to God's purposes for wholeness and abundance in the healing and feeding miracles (11.2–6; 14.13–21).[51]

Fundamental to such visions of God's new creative act and world is radical dis-ease with the world of *Pax Romana*. The longing for God to intervene to establish a different social order and experience of life expresses a negative commentary on the status quo, and presents a fundamental challenge to Roman sovereignty, judging it to be both contrary to (sinful) and subject to God's purposes. In 1.1, then, Matthew locates the origin of Jesus in relation to the initial creation to evoke this previous enactment of God's purposes and to anticipate the re-establishment in a new creation. The Jewish creation traditions evoked by this opening phrase collide with Roman imperial claims to begin the process of defining Jesus's significance.

8.4 *Of Jesus (*Iêsou*)*

Numerous interpreters have remarked on the frequency with which Matthew uses Jesus's name, even introducing it where Mark or Q do not use it.[52] The opening chapter (1.21–23) clearly states the meaning of the name Jesus ('he will save his people from their sins') and further defines it by the term Immanuel ('God with us'), cited from Isaiah 7.14. What this

49.   E. Käsemann, 'On the Subject of Primitive Christian Apocalyptic' in *New Testament Questions of Today* (Philadelphia, PA: Fortress, 1969), 108–37, esp. 135, observes that the central question addressed by apocalyptic traditions is 'To whom does the sovereignty of the world belong?'

50.   Carter, 'Are there Imperial Texts?'

51.   Carter, *Matthew and the Margins*, 123–27; 250–51, 305–8.

52.   E.g. Matthew 8.4 par., 13 (Q), 14 par., 18 (Q); 9.9 par.

saving presence looks like and how Jesus carries out this divinely given task is elaborated partly in the intertextual links with Isaiah 7–8, as well as by the subsequent narrative.[53] It embraces Jesus's words, actions like healings and exorcisms, feedings and meals, his death, resurrection and return when he overcomes Roman rule and all that resists God's purposes (24.27–31).[54]

But while the use of the name in 1.1 identifies the main character and anticipates the subsequent elaboration, it also contributes to the process of defining Jesus's significance. Partly this happens by association with the matter of 'origin' noted above: the reassertion of God's sovereignty over and purposes for God's world takes place in Jesus. But it also happens through the name itself. 'Jesus' (*Iēsous*) is the Greek form of the name 'Joshua', which means 'God saves'. For a second time, 1.1 recalls the title of a scriptural writing, recounting the exploits of Joshua/Jesus in leading the Israelites into Canaan and distributing the land to the tribes.[55]

By attending to the name's metonymic function at the beginning of the narrative, the audience gains some rich possibilities for understanding the significance of Jesus, possibilities that will have to be assessed in the light of the following narrative. For instance, Joshua/Jesus is divinely chosen for his task (Num. 27.12–23; Deut. 3.23–28; Josh. 1.1–9), a claim for Jesus already emerging in the opening phrase *biblos geneseōs* and made explicit by the following *christou*. Joshua/Jesus with Moses 'went up into the mountain of the Lord' (*anabēsan eis to oros*) to receive the revelation of God's will at Sinai (Exod. 24.13; 32.15–18) just as Jesus, the revealer of God's will, 'went up on the mountain' (*anebē eis to oros*) in 5.1. Joshua/Jesus with Caleb are the only spies who trust that God can, despite the apparent odds, give the people victory over the Canaanites and their land as promised (Num. 13–14). Joshua/Jesus faithfully carries out his commission and, after the victory and possession of land (cf. Josh. 1.2–5; 23),[56] leads the assembled Israelites in renewing the covenant with God (Josh. 24). Jesus will conduct his mission in life and death while similarly trusting God's purposes (16.21; 26.36–46).

The name 'Jesus', then, evokes one of the giants of Israel's traditions: a man who faithfully carries out his divinely assigned task to defeat the

---

53. Carter, 'Evoking Isaiah'.

54. For elaboration, Carter, *Matthew and Empire*; Carter, 'Are there Imperial Texts?'

55. Assessing how much the name evokes raises an interesting question. Three others with the name Joshua appear in scriptural writings (1 Sam. 6.14; 2 Kings 23.8; Hag 1.1). I have limited my observations here to the successor of Moses partly because the name evokes a scriptural writing for the second time in 1.1, and partly because this Joshua is such a dominant figure in the traditions.

56. Matthew's subsequent narrative will indicate that violent or military opposition is not part of Jesus's mission (5.38–48); see Carter, *Matthew and the Margins*, 150–57, though qualified by 24.27–31, 'Are there Imperial Texts?'

Canaanites and occupy their land, thus completing God's promises to save the people from Egyptian rule and establish them in the land. Just what Matthew's Jesus is to do, how he is to do it, and whether he will do it, awaits elaboration in the narrative. But the evoking of Joshua in 1.1 suggests that God's new creative act and establishment of sovereignty in the post-70 era at least involves a task comparable to that of Joshua. The land promised to God's people is again occupied by another power, this time Rome. Again it needs deliverance. Again God has commissioned an agent of his saving purposes. And there is reassurance. Just as God's purposes, despite all appearances to the contrary, overcame the power of the Canaanites through Joshua/Jesus, so too will God overcome Rome through Jesus. The evoking of Joshua/Jesus thus draws a parallel with the circumstances of Matthew's audience and invites them to understand the significance of Jesus, the nature of their own circumstances, and the purposes of God in analogous terms, while finding elaboration and nuancing (especially of the means of deliverance) in the subsequent narrative.

Matthaean scholars, shaped by the contemporary separation of 'religion' and 'politics' and by their location in a long 'spiritualizing' (and confessional) tradition of reading Matthew, have avoided 'political' interpretations of Jesus's mission to save from sins, preferring 'spiritualized' interpretations.[57] There is no denying that inner transformation matters, but contemporary attempts to separate the religious and the secular (political, socioeconomic) should not anachronistically control the exegesis. If this gospel, along with numerous post-70 texts, views Rome's destruction of Jerusalem in 70 as punishment for sins (especially elite sins) (as most interpret 22.7), sins and politics are very intertwined and require a similar sort of salvation. The Joshua/Jesus echoes in 1.1 begin the process of framing the sort of salvation Jesus will effect, the deliverance of this world from Rome's sinful control and the establishment of God's empire (*basileia*) over all.

8.5 *Christ* (christou)

Basic to the meaning of the term 'Christ' (the Greek translation of the Hebrew word 'messiah') is the notion of commissioning for God's service. Such commissioning is enacted by anointing (pouring or rubbing oil on) the person, rendering them an 'anointed' ('christed', so Isa. 61.1) or commissioned agent for God's work. Various figures are anointed for particular acts of divine service: priests to offer sacrifices (Lev. 4.3, 5);

57. E.g. W.D. Davies and D.C. Allison, *A Critical and Exegetical Commentary on the Gospel According to Saint Matthew* (ICC; 3 vols; Edinburgh: T&T Clark, 1988, 1991, 1997), I, 210.

kings to rule (Ps. 2.2); prophets to proclaim God's word (1 Kings 19.16); and the Persian/Gentile ruler Cyrus to free the people from Babylonian exile (Isa. 44.28–45.1). During the first century CE, some figures claim to be anointed by God to deliver the people from Roman rule, but Roman retaliation is swift and fatal.[58]

In some writings, an expectation emerges for a figure that God will anoint to play a special role in his purposes for a new world. These expectations are not widespread in existing texts and are by no means uniform in their content.[59] For example, in the first-century BCE Psalms of Solomon, several of the eighteen Psalms beseech God to restore an anointed king from the line of David (17.21, polemic against the non-Davidic Hasmonean rulers) whose task will be to remove the Romans from Jerusalem not by military means but 'by the word of his mouth' (17.24), to purify Jerusalem and to establish God's just reign (17.26–46). The Qumran scrolls attest expectation for several messianic figures, the dominant one being a high priest from the line of Aaron, along with a king from the line of David (1QS 9.11; 4QFlor. 11–12). But in 1 Enoch 37–71, the messiah/Christ is a heavenly judge who conducts the final judgment, condemning the wicked kings, officials, and landowners, while vindicating the righteous (48.10; 52.4). In 4 Ezra 7.26–44, the messiah overcomes Roman rule and evil, rules for 400 years and then dies. After seven days of silence, God creates the new world.

Given such diverse expectations, how does the term 'Christ' function in 1.1? First, it affirms that Jesus is God's agent, commissioned or anointed by God for service. But second, since all Jews were not looking for 'the messiah' to carry out a fixed and standard agenda, the term also poses a question: what is Jesus anointed to do and how will he do it? A partial answer is emerging from this verse, and more will be added in the subsequent narrative. Third, and here I generalize with caution, the messiah/Christ traditions that were prominent in the first century seem often to focus on functions of judgment over the status quo and on the establishment of God's rule. While the traditions envisage these functions happening in different ways by different figures, the visions of transformation are very sociopolitical and do not offer good news for those, like Rome, who hold power. In various ways they signal the end of the status

58.   R.A. Horsley and J. Hanson, *Bandits, Prophets, and Messiahs. Popular Movements at the Time of Jesus* (Minneapolis, MN: Winston, 1985), 88–134.

59.   M. de Jonge, 'Messiah' in D.N. Freedman (ed.), *Anchor Bible Dictionary. Volume 4* (New York: Doubleday, 1992), 777–88. Also J. Neusner, W. Green and E. Frerichs (eds), *Judaisms and their Messiahs at the Turn of the Christian Era* (Cambridge: Cambridge University Press, 1987); J.H. Charlesworth (ed.), *The Messiah: Developments in Earliest Judaism and Christianity* (Minneapolis, MN: Fortress, 1992); J.J. Collins, *The Scepter and the Star: The Messiahs of the Dead Sea Scrolls and Other Ancient Literature* (New York: Doubleday, 1995).

quo and the establishment of God's very different world. This verse, then, suggests that in such transformation Jesus will have a central role. Evoking Jewish messianic traditions in 1.1 challenges Roman imperial claims and enables the audience to formulate the further significance of Jesus.

8.6 *Son of David* (huiou Dauid)

The 'son of' construction, often expressive of claims of belonging,[60] appears twice in verse 1. This construction is commonly used to link emperors favourably to gods and to previous and deified (*divi filius*) emperors in order to claim legitimate succession and glory-by-association.[61] Inscription and coins, for example, link Vespasian, descended neither by birth nor adoption from a divinized emperor, with Augustus.[62] The same means identify both Titus and, more commonly, Domitian as *Augusti filius* as well as *theou Ouespasianou huios*.[63]

Here, the construction associates Jesus with David, evoking the extensive traditions about this major political–religious figure in Israel's history. The subsequent designation of Joseph as the son of David who names Jesus (1.20) fleshes out the link, with Joseph claiming paternity when the narrative has made it very clear that Jesus has no human father (1.18c, d, 20e, 25a). Two traditions about David will be important through the gospel, one concerning kingship and rule (21.9, 15), the other concerning healing and exorcisms: five of the gospel's nine uses of 'son of

---

60. For example, 'Son of Man' can indicate one belonging to the group of humanity. Hence the phrase in Ezekiel 2.1 is translated in the NRSV as 'mortal'.

61. R.L. Mowery, 'Son of God in Roman Imperial Titles and Matthew', *Biblica* 83 (2002), 100–10, esp. 103–4, collects data from inscriptions and coins, especially from the East, concerning Vespasian, Titus (*theou huios* and *theou Ouespasianou huios*), and Domitian (*theou huios* and *theou Ouespasianou huios*). For language and conceptual considerations, see S. Price, 'Gods and Emperors: The Greek Language of the Roman Imperial Cult', *Journal of Hellenic Studies* 104 (1984), 79–95.

62. For coins in Syria claiming Vespasian's continuation of Augustus's rule by celebrating virtues such as peace, well-being, etc., see A. Burnett, M. Amandry, P.P. Ripollès, *Roman Provincial Coinage Vol. 2. From Vespasian to Domitian AD 69–96* (London: British Museum Press, 1999), 1924 (*Pax Augusti*), 1925, 1929 (*Victoria Augusti*), 1926 (*Virtus Augusti*), 1927 (*Concordia Augusti*).

63. For Domitian as *Augusti filius* on coins issued by Vespasian from 73–79 CE, see H.C. Mattingly, *Coins of the Roman Empire in the British Museum Volume 2: Vespasian to Domitian* (London: British Museum Press, 1966), Plate 3 nos 14–18; Plate 4 nos 15–18; Plate 6 nos 1–3; Plate 7 nos 5–9; Plate 8 nos 3–8, some of which appear in Syria (Burnett *et al.*, *Roman Provincial Coinage*, 2001, 2005). For the less common identification of Titus as this, see Burnett *et al.*, *Roman Provincial Coinage*, nos 310, 836, 1604. The title *Divi Vespasiani filius* is used for both Titus (Burnett *et al.*, *Roman Provincial Coinage*, nos 501–3, 507, 2045) and Domitian (nos 526–33, 543).

David' appear in such accounts (9.27; 12.23; 15.22; 20.30, 31). Interpreters have often been puzzled about how, if at all, the audience might be able to connect these two traditions.

The Davidic traditions emphasize that God chooses the shepherd David to be king at Saul's expense (1 Sam. 16–2; Sam. 5). God also makes a threefold promise to David that there will be future kings from the line of David, that each will enjoy a father–son relationship with God and that the Davidic line will enjoy eternal reign on the throne of the kingdom of Israel (2 Sam. 7.11–16; also Ps. 89.4–5, 27–30). D.C. Duling traces the growth of these promises through to the first century CE.[64] While the title son of David is unusual, a cluster of metaphors (e.g. 'shoot') keeps the promise tradition alive, as do prophetic (Mic. 5.1–3; Jer. 23.1–6; Ezek. 34.23–24) and psalmic (e.g. Ps. 72) visions of a future ideal time in which a Davidic ruler enacts the divine rule marked by peace, abundance, justice and the absence of oppression. Psalms of Solomon 17, from the first century BCE, employs the term 'son of David' (17.21) for a king who will remove Rome, purify Jerusalem, redistribute land and establish God's just, peaceful and compassionate rule over Israel and the nations (17.21–46). In 4 Ezra 11–12, the Davidic messiah establishes God's victory and reign over Rome.

Evoking such traditions begins to define Jesus as a Davidic king who represents and enacts God's rule and just purposes. In this regard he contrasts with most of the kings named in the following genealogy (1.6b–11), who did not faithfully live out their commission. He is identified as a king in 2.1 who threatens King Herod (2.3), and in 2.6 as one who will 'shepherd/govern my people Israel' in contrast to the false rulers/ shepherds who cannot recognize or enact, but instead resist, God's purposes (2.4–5; 12.1–14; 15.13; 21.45; 22.15; cf. Ezek. 34). In 4.17, kingship frames his message at the start of his public ministry as he proclaims God's empire, 'the kingdom/empire of the heavens'. In 21.9, 15, as a 'meek' king, one of the righteous poor oppressed by the elite but who trusts God to end violent war and establish peace, Jesus enters Jerusalem in accord with the similar vision of Zechariah 9.9.[65]

But such traditions and definition do not exist in a vacuum. Another king ruled the world, the Roman emperor, also identified as a *basileus* (Josephus, *War*, 3.351; 4.596; 5.58, 563). Evoking the Davidic visions of just kingly rule that enacts God's purposes provides a means of comparison with and evaluation of the empire's rule in terms of God's

---

64. D.C. Duling, 'The Promises to David and their Entrance into Christianity – Nailing down a Likely Hypothesis', *NTS* 19 (1973), 55–77.
65. Carter, *Matthew and the Margins*, 132–3, 413–18.

purposes.[66] The vision of Psalm 72, for instance, of a king ruling compassionately with justice, protecting the poor from oppressors and ensuring abundant food, is a far cry from daily life under the Flavian emperors. The identification of Jesus as the one who will 'shepherd my people Israel' (2 Sam. 5.2; Matt. 2.6) continues the Davidic link and evokes the condemnation of bad 'shepherds' or rulers in Ezekiel 34. Like them, Rome's emperors and their imperial practices deprive the sheep of food, shelter and protection, in contrast to good shepherds who enact God's rule. In the light of such traditions, the emperor is clearly seen not to be God's anointed despite Roman propaganda claims to rule at Jupiter's election and on Jupiter's behalf. It is precisely from such a rule that the world needs saving. Jesus is not a military saviour but he is a very political one.

The Davidic promises collide in another way. Imperial claims presented Rome as the eternal city (*urbs aeterna*: Tibullus, 2.5.23; Ovid, *Fasti*, 3.72; *urbs in aeternum condita*: Livy, 4.4.4; 28.28.11), entrusted by Jupiter with an 'empire without end' (*imperium sine fine*: Virgil, *Aeneid*, 1.279). Augustus (through his adopted son Tiberius) and, later, Vespasian (through Titus and Domitian), ensured successors and thereby the *aeternitas* of Rome and its emperors.[67] The Davidic tradition promises that the line of David, representing God's rule, will reign forever. The prophetic and psalmic visions, including that of Psalms of Solomon 17, depict the triumph of the Davidic king to whom the nations submit. Yet Jesus, the king anointed by God, had suffered the same fate as other kingly pretenders in the Roman sphere, where only puppet-kings like Herod were permitted to rule. Roman power did seem invincible. Yet over against this appearance of invincibility, the traditions maintain God's promise of a different reign in which his blessing lasts forever, and visions of a very different world. For those who chose to believe the traditions, Rome's claims were relativized, and hopes for God's intervention sustained. The return of Jesus presented the definitive opportunity to establish God's purposes (cf. 24.27–31). Jewish traditions collide with imperial claims to interpret the subversive significance of Jesus.

In this context, the second 'son of David' tradition evoked by 1.1 and

---

66. For philosophical traditions about ideal Hellenistic kingship (often far removed from the realities of imperial rule), see F.W. Walbank, 'Monarchies and Monarchic Ideas' in *The Cambridge Ancient History*, Vol. 7, 1 (Cambridge: Cambridge University Press, 1982), 62–100. The ideal ruler provides peace and justice for the ruled; see *Letter of Aristeas*, 187–300, esp. 290–1. For some Roman discussion that is indebted to this tradition, see Seneca, *On Mercy*; Dio Chrysostom, *Four Orations on Kingship*. J. Moles, 'The Date and Purpose of the Fourth Kingship Oration of Dio Chrysostom', *Classical Antiquity* 2 (1983), 251–78, argues that Dio criticizes Trajan's imperialist ambitions.

67. M.P. Charlesworth, 'Providentia and Aeternitas', *HTR* 29 (1936), 107–32; Josephus, *War*, 4.596.

elaborated in the gospel's healing and exorcism scenes makes much sense. The Septuagint refers to a number of sons of David, but most commonly Solomon is identified as David's son.[68] Numerous traditions depict David's son Solomon as a miracle-worker and exorcist with control over demonic activity.[69] It is in the context of healings and exorcisms of disease-causing demons that Matthew's Jesus is most often identified as 'son of David' by the poor and desperate (9.27; 12.23; 15.22; 20.30, 31). Jesus' healings/exorcisms are presented as demonstrations of God's reign, the in-breaking of God's rule over all that resists God's purposes – in this instance Satan (12.22–32). Significantly, the gospel identifies Satan as the one who controls 'all the empires (*basileias*) of the world' (4.8). For the gospel, Rome's empire is diabolical, controlled by the devil and not God, sickening and destructive in its impact. In this context, Jesus manifests God's empire (*basileia*: 4.17) in his teaching and healings (4.23), overcoming Satan's rule and setting people free from the debilitating cost of living in an oppressive empire.

Interestingly, prophetic and apocalyptic visions of life according to God's reign – that is, free from all that is contrary to God's life-giving purposes including empires – picture physical transformation from sickness to health as one of the visible signs of God's reign. Jubilees 23.29 depicts a world of wholeness and healing. T. Zebulon 9.7–8 envisions God healing the 'sickness and tribulation' brought on by the spirits of deceit. 1 Enoch 96.3 envisions healing for those with pain inflicted by the sinful powerful who carry out 'oppression, deceit, blasphemy' and 'coerce the righteous'. 4 Ezra unveils a paradise of 'abundance and healing' (7.123) from which 'illness is banished' (8.53). 2 Baruch knows a world in which there will be abundant food and 'the dew of health' (29.7). When the messiah establishes his reign in peace and joy, 'health will descend in dew, and illness will vanish, and fear and tribulation and lamentation will pass away...' (73.2). Accordingly, the gospel cites Isaiah 35.5 in 11.2–6 to interpret Jesus's identity as the one commissioned to bring wholeness and healing (cf. Isa. 29.17–21; 61.1–2). Ironically, Roman imperial propaganda uses the metaphor of a sick world 'healed' by Rome to depict the benefits of Roman rule.[70] For Matthew, it is precisely from Rome's sickness that Jesus, son of David, must heal the

---

68.　E.g. 1 Kings 1.13; 2.1; 3.6; 5.5, 21; 2 Kings 21.7; 1 Chronicles 22.5, 17; 23.1; 28.20; 29.1, 22; 2 Chronicles 1.1; 2.11; 30.26; 33.7; 35.3; Proverbs 1.1.

69.　Wisdom of Solomon 7.17–22; Josephus, *Ant.*, 8.45–49; esp. Testament of Solomon. See D.C. Duling, 'Solomon, Exorcism, and the Son of David', *HTR* 68 (1975), 235–52; Duling, 'The Therapeutic Son of David: An Element of Matthew's Christological Apologetic', *NTS* 24 (1978), 392–410.

70.　Josephus identifies revolts against Rome as an 'inflammation' and 'contagion' in Rome's healthy world: *War*, 2.264; 7.260; cf. Aristides, *Roman Oration*, 97: Rome has brought a 'sick world' to 'a state of health'.

world. Again, Jewish traditions evoked by the gospel collide with the daily realities of the imperial world, providing perspective on those realities, hope for a transformed world in God's purposes and understanding of the significance of Jesus.

8.7 *Son of Abraham (*huiou Abraam*)*

The final element of verse 1 evokes another major figure in Israel's history, another recipient of significant promises and another set of extensive and expanding traditions. In the limited space here, it will suffice to note that the extensive traditions about Abraham often struggle to interpret the promises to Abraham in Genesis 12.1–3 that he would be the father of many nations and that through him all nations will be blessed.[71] In some texts, the promise is reinterpreted more exclusively to emphasize Israel's privileged particularity,[72] while in other texts that exhibit much more openness to Hellenism Abraham is an international figure of significance for Jews and Gentiles.[73] Matthew joins the latter tradition. Abraham points to the inclusion of Jew and Gentile in God's purposes.[74] The subsequent genealogy locates Jesus in continuity with Israel's participation in God's purposes but recognizes, with the inclusion of some Gentile women (and adoration by the magi in Chapter 2), that God's purposes are not ethnically restricted.[75] This point is reiterated in 3.7–10 with John's attack on the presumption of claiming descent from Abraham. Children of Abraham are God's work whose identity is evidenced by repentance and good works, and not constituted by ethnicity, as 8.5–13 confirms.[76]

But for a gospel audience that inhabits the Roman imperial world, the insistence on the inclusion of all people in the sphere of God's blessing has further dimensions. MacMullen has demonstrated the abundant preju-

71. K.-J. Kuschel, *Abraham: Sign of Hope for Jews, Christians and Muslims* (New York: Continuum, 1995), 3–68; J. Siker, *Disinheriting the Jews: Abraham in Early Christian Controversy* (Louisville, KY: Westminster John Knox, 1991).

72. For example, Sirach 44.19–21: Abraham the faithful keeper of Torah; 1 Maccabees 2.51–52, 64–68: the faithful Abraham loyal to Torah invoked to resist Hellenism; Jubilees 15.25–32: Abraham, the champion of monotheism, opponent of idolatry, faithful observer of sacrifices and advocate of circumcision as a mark of Israel's exclusive election; Apocalypse of Abraham 29.17, with similar themes but a focus now on the righteous remnant within Israel as the seed of Abraham, namely those who will be vindicated over Rome.

73. Philo, for example, presents Abraham as a foreigner who uses nature and reason to quest for God (*On the Virtues*, 211–19; cf. Kuschel, *Abraham*, 40–44). Josephus presents Abraham as the father of many nations (*Ant.*, 1.235), the bearer of culture who teaches Egyptians and Greeks astronomy and arithmetic (*Ant.*, 1.168). cf. Kuschel, *Abraham*, 44–8.

74. Matthew has seven references to Abraham: 1.1, 2, 17; 3.9 (twice), 8.11; 22.32. cf. Kuschel, *Abraham*, 93–7; Siker, *Disinheriting*, 77–86.

75. Carter, *Matthew and the Margins*, 58–61.

76. Carter, *Matthew and the Margins*, 200–4.

dices and divisions that marked Roman social relations, namely Roman/
non-Roman, elite/non-elite, urban Rome/provincial, country elite/urban
poor, etc. His 'lexicon of snobbery' indicates plenty of verbal options for
expressions of derision and scorn.[77] A similar lexicon for acts of physical
scorn could easily be compiled. While MacMullen's dividing-lines cut
across various categories, groups such as the rural–urban poor in a
provincial city like Antioch never fare well. Nor are such divisions 'only' a
matter of social attitudes and verbal abuse. They also reflect and reinforce
the vast socioeconomic and political divisions of the imperial world in
which no more than 5 per cent comprise the elite that controls for its own
advantage political power, access to resources and wealth. Such a
sociopolitical structure is enmeshed in and secured by military and
religious sanction. The gods have chosen Rome to rule and to manifest
their blessings through *Pax Romana*.

But while such well-being may have been evident to Roman and
provincial elites, it was not so for many living in and around the diseased,
poverty-stricken, overcrowded and volatile city of Antioch, where life did
not seem especially blessed. The evoking of the promises to Abraham
points to a different sort of divinely blessed life known through Jesus.
Subsequently, Jesus will elaborate the blessings of God's empire that
reverse such societal injustice. The desperately poor and the powerless
who lack options, resources and hope will be saved from the present
unjust order to know God's just and merciful reign (5.3–4) in which they
will have access to adequate resources and land to sustain a satisfying life
marked by justice (5.5–6). This future reversal is assured, but it is also
anticipated in the present by carrying out actions of mercy, seeking and
doing God's will, making peace that expresses the justice of God's
purposes and not the militarily sustained domination of the Roman order,
and faithfully enduring the inevitable backlash that comes from a status
quo challenged by different social practices and vision (5.7–12).[78] The
eschatological scenarios of Jesus's blessings provide a cosmic framework
in which Rome's demise is certain. The formation of a community of
followers of Jesus offers a different social experience in the present and
provides, as Stark has argued, some relief from the harshness of daily
imperial life.

8.8 *Conclusion*

Michael Mann has argued that the Roman failure to provide a social
experience that matched its theological/ideological claims meant that the

---

77. MacMullen, *Roman Social Relations*.
78. Carter, *Matthew and the Margins*, 130–37.

empire forged no deep hold on the loyalties of those living in its sway.[79] The empire was thus vulnerable to those, like Matthew, who offered different social visions and experience.[80] In the gospel's opening verse, the Jewish traditions of promises to Abraham as well as traditions and aspirations associated with David, the Christ, Jesus/Joshua, and (new) creation evoked in relation to Jesus collide with and contest Roman imperial claims. The verse functions to dispute the truthfulness of the imperial claims, suggesting Rome's demise, offering some present relief and proclaiming an alternative and just social vision under way now but yet to be fully realized in the future new creation through Jesus Christ son of David, son of Abraham.

79. M. Mann, *The Sources of Power, Volume 1. A History of Power from the Beginning to AD 1760* (Cambridge: Cambridge University Press, 1986), 327–8.
80. I develop this thesis in 'Vulnerable Power', 453–88.

CONCLUSIONS

David C. Sim

In the Conclusions to this volume I wish to draw together some of the implications of the preceding contributions, and also highlight some areas of conflict that future research may care to ponder. The essay by Dennis Duling sets out the various models and theories used by social scientists and historians to describe the workings of the Roman imperial system and to analyse modes of ideological control and resistance. Despite differences between these models and theories, it is nonetheless agreed that the Roman Empire provided both advantages and disadvantages for its subjects. On the positive side, it ensured good communications and a considerable measure of security and peace. Yet these benefits must be weighed against the fact that the Roman Empire, like other ancient imperial systems, served the real interests of only a small minority, while causing much economic hardship and personal misery for the majority of those within its borders. As Philip Esler highlights, Roman imperial conquest and occupation was achieved courtesy of Rome's highly efficient and equally brutal military machine. The reality of Roman domination and oppression was well known to the author of Matthew's Gospel. David Sim emphasizes how large Rome loomed in Antioch on the Orontes, the most plausible location for the gospel, while Dorothy Jean Weaver spells out how the evangelist's story of Jesus presumes in many ways the Roman occupation of the traditional Jewish homeland. In the light of these considerations, we should expect that Matthew had particular views about Roman imperialism as well as the ultimate fate of this empire.

These issues were certainly topical in both Christian and Jewish circles in the late first century. At that time Christians had little reason to admire or support the Roman Empire. Whatever they might have believed regarding Jewish involvement in the death of Jesus, it was still an indisputable fact that their messiah was ultimately condemned by the Roman governor of Judea and executed by Roman soldiers under his command. A generation later the Christians in Rome had come to the attention of the emperor Nero. These Christians suffered a localized but horrific persecution as Nero, in an attempt to counter rumours that he had caused the great fire that destroyed much of Rome, blamed them for this disaster. A further generation later, at the time when the Book of Revelation was written, we find more widespread Roman persecutions of Christians, at least in Asia Minor.

The discussion of Peter Oakes provides a necessarily brief but rather useful summary of early Christian attitudes to Roman imperialism. Oakes finds a tension in many of the Christian texts that refer to Rome, in that each of them contains a positive depiction of Rome (awe in the face of its power and/or an appreciation of the peace it provided) alongside a negative assessment of the empire (including resentment, contempt, denial of ultimate authority and expectation of its overthrow). The universal belief in or hope for Rome's eventual demise, whether expressed implicitly as in 1 Thessalonians, or explicitly as in Revelation, is an important reminder that the early Christians viewed the Roman Empire as a system that was contrary to the purposes of God. For the reign of God to become a reality, the rule of Rome must be swept away.

An even more negative view of the Roman Empire was understandably held by those Jewish authors who wrote in the aftermath of the Jewish revolt. The essay of Philip Esler well describes the Roman destruction of the Jewish homeland, including Jerusalem and the Temple, and its wholesale slaughter or enslavement of its Jewish subjects. Esler also relates the excesses of the Romans in celebrating this triumph and their corresponding humiliation of the Jews. In delineating the Jewish responses to these calamitous events, Esler singles out a number of contemporary apocalyptic texts, notably 4 Ezra and 2 Baruch, which specify clearly that Rome will inevitably be punished by the messiah for its crimes against the people of Israel. While these texts thus look forward to an eschatological struggle in which Rome will meet with defeat, they encourage in the meantime a generally quietist attitude towards the empire. A similar viewpoint is found in the works of Josephus. James McLaren presents a convincing case that Josephus, who owed his life and his patronage to the victorious Flavians, was nonetheless a veiled critic of his Roman masters and their imperial system. Josephus tolerated Roman rule by seeing it as an instrument of God's will, but he held the general Jewish view that in the future God would bring about the downfall of Rome and restore his elect people.

That Matthew largely shared these anti-Roman perspectives in Jewish and Christian circles is argued in the essays by Warren Carter and David Sim. The evangelist's complete renunciation of Rome and its divine pretensions is suggested by Carter, who builds upon his earlier work in this area. In his detailed analysis of the very first verse of the gospel, Carter maintains that the christological references contained therein establish not merely who Jesus is and the role he is to play in the divine plan, but offer as well a clear critique of Roman imperial claims.

Matthew's hope for the destruction and punishment of Rome is emphasized in Sim's contribution. According to Sim, the evangelist's eschatological views are similar to those in contemporary apocalyptic texts, especially the Christian Apocalypse. Like the author of Revelation, Matthew affirms that the Roman Empire is an ally of Satan, and that this unholy coalition will meet with defeat when Jesus returns with his angelic army: an event that will usher in the final judgment and eternal punishment for the wicked. Sim argues that the scene at the cross, where the Roman executioners of Jesus come to the realization that he is the Son of God, acts as a proleptic judgment on the Roman Empire.

John Riches sees things rather differently in his discussion of the evangelist's missionary strategy. Riches is not convinced that Matthew links together Satan and Rome, nor does he find in the gospel more than fragmentary references to a final war between the forces of good and their evil counterparts. Taking his cue from the final pericope of the gospel, Riches presents a case that for Matthew the world will be won over and Rome defeated by the missionary activity of the Son of Man's disciples. The universal authority given to the risen Christ in this passage does indeed provide a subtle critique of Roman imperial pretensions, but the evangelist has no intention of condemning all Romans to eternal punishment. On the contrary, a number of Roman soldiers in the narrative, in particular the centurion of Capernaum and the soldiers who confess Jesus as the Son of God, become disciples of Jesus.

Dorothy Jean Weaver's essay on the Roman characters in the gospel lends support to the last point made by Riches. She argues that Matthew shows no consistency in his presentation of these figures. There are Romans who are depicted in rather negative terms (Pilate and the soldiers who guard the tomb of Jesus), but these are contrasted with other Romans who express faith in Jesus (the centurion of Capernaum), who acknowledge that Jesus is righteous (Pilate's wife) and who make the Christian confession of faith (the soldiers at the foot of the cross). Though Weaver does not make the connection, Matthew's treatment of his Roman characters finds a significant contemporary parallel in Acts. In his analysis of the Romans in Acts, Peter Oakes notes a similar tendency on the part of Luke.

These different conclusions regarding Matthew's view of the Roman Empire perhaps point the way for future research. Of particular interest is the manner in which the evangelist has been influenced by contemporary apocalyptic traditions. Did he, in the tradition of Revelation, 4 Ezra and other texts, condemn Rome outright and hope for its eschatological destruction and punishment or, as John Riches would argue, was his use of apocalyptic themes more nuanced and subtle than this? Did Matthew consider the demise of Rome not in terms of its defeat at the eschaton, but more in terms of its conversion to the Christian Gospel? This possibility is intriguing, given that the Roman Empire did embrace the Gospel less than three centuries later. The same kind of tensive attitude to Rome is identified in other Christian texts by Peter Oakes, and in the rabbinic writings by Philip Esler.

Another important topic is the evangelist's characterization of the Romans in his narrative. While there is some difference between the contributors over the status of the soldiers who exclaim that Jesus is the Son of God, they all agree that Matthew's Roman characters are a mixture of good and bad. At the very minimum, the centurion of Capernaum and the wife of Pilate are positive figures in the Matthean narrative. But what requires more attention is the significance of Matthew's portrayal of his Roman characters. Why did he depict the Romans in such an inconsistent way? Do any Roman characters represent the Roman Empire as a whole? What precisely did the evangelist expect his readers to infer when they encountered positive Roman figures in his story?

It might be the case, as Riches argues, that the good Romans, such as the centurion of Capernaum and (possibly) the soldiers who acknowledge Jesus as the Son of God, are intended to be depicted as disciples. But if this is correct, then what point is Matthew making to his readers? Are these models of Roman faith meant to convince his community members that even the agents of Roman imperialism and occupation are capable of conversion? Is Matthew perhaps encouraging his community to take the Gospel to local Roman soldiers? None of this is implausible. The command of the risen Christ to evangelize all the nations must include the nation of Rome and its imperial agents. On the other hand, if it is true that Matthew fervently believes that Rome is allied with Satan and is therefore destined for destruction and punishment, then how can the positive Romans in the gospel be explained? Are they perhaps exceptions rather than the rule? Is the evangelist informing his readers that, while individual Romans may come to faith in Jesus and so escape the judgment, the majority of them will not? If this interpretation is valid, then what are the consequences for the mission of the Matthean community? This discussion raises extremely interesting and important questions about the signals and codes used by Matthew and other contemporary texts in relation to Rome. How do we identify and decode these cues? Where do we find the 'strategies of resistance' against the superior power of Rome?

Whatever the future holds in terms of these and other relevant questions, one thing is certain: the empire is definitely back in fashion (as Dennis Duling makes clear at the beginning of his essay). Future Matthean studies will need to take into account the imperial setting of the gospel just as much as past studies have highlighted its Jewish and Christian settings. It is hoped that this volume, following on from the pioneering work of Warren Carter, can make its own contribution to this new direction.

BIBLIOGRAPHY

Adam, I. and H. Tiffin (eds), *Past the Last Post: Theorizing Post-Colonialism and Post-Modernism* (Hemel Hempstead: Harvester Wheatsheaf, 1991)

Alföldy, G., *The Social History of Rome* (Totowa: Barnes & Noble, 1985)

Allison, D.C., *The New Moses: A Matthean Typology* (Minneapolis, MN: Fortress, 1993)

Anderson, J.C., 'Life on the Mississippi: New Currents in Matthean Scholarship 1983–1993', *Currents in Research: Biblical Studies* 3 (1995), 169–218

Bammel, E., 'Ein Beitrag zur paulinischen Staatsanschauung', *ThLZ* 85 (1960), 837–40

Bammel, E., 'The Revolution Theory from Reimarus to Brandon' in E. Bammel and C.F.D. Moule (eds), *Jesus and the Politics of his Day* (Cambridge: Cambridge University Press, 1984), 11–68

Barclay, J.M.G., *Jews in the Mediterranean Diaspora: From Alexander to Trajan (323 BCE to 117 CE)* (Edinburgh: T&T Clark, 1996)

Beard, M., 'The Triumph of Flavius Josephus' in A.J. Boyle and W.J. Dominik (eds), *Flavian Rome* (Leiden: Brill, 2003), 543–58

Berquist, J.L., *Judaism in Persia's Shadow: A Social and Historical Approach* (Minneapolis, MN: Fortress, 1995)

Berquist, J.L., 'Postcolonialism and Imperial Motives for Canonization' in L.E. Donaldson (ed.), *Semeia 75. Postcolonialism and Scriptural Reading* (Atlanta, GA: Scholars Press, 1996), 15–35

Bhabha, H.K., *The Location of Culture* (London: Routledge, 1994)

Bilde, P., *Flavius Josephus between Jerusalem and Rome: His Life, his Works and their Importance* (Sheffield: JSOT, 1988)

Bilde, P., 'Josephus and Jewish Apocalypticism' in S. Mason (ed.), *Understanding Josephus: Seven Perspectives* (Sheffield: Sheffield Academic Press, 1998), 35–61

Binder, D., *Into the Temple Courts: The Place of the Synagogues in the Second Temple Period* (Atlanta, GA: SBL, 1999)

Blair, E.P., *Jesus in the Gospel of Matthew* (Nashville, TN: Abingdon, 1960)

Bousset, W., *Kyrios Christos* (Nashville, TN: Abingdon, 1970)

Braund, D.C., *Rome and the Friendly King: The Character of Client Kingship* (New York: St Martin's Press, 1984)

Brocke, C. vom, *Thessaloniki – Stadt der Kassander und Gemeinde des Paulus* (WUNT 2/125; Tübingen: Mohr Siebeck, 2001)

Brown, R.E., *The Death of the Messiah: From Gethsemane to the Grave*, 2 vols; (New York: Doubleday, 1994)

Brunt, P.A., 'The Romanization of the Local Ruling Class in the Roman Empire' in P.A. Brunt, *Roman Imperial Themes* (Oxford: Clarendon Press, 1990), 267–81

Burke, P., *History and Social Theory* (Ithaca, NY: Cornell University Press, 2nd edn 1993)

Burnett, A., M. Amandry and P.P. Ripollès, *Roman Provincial Coinage: Volume 2. From Vespasian to Domitian AD 69–96* (London: British Museum Press, 1999)

Burnett, F.W., 'Historiography' in A.K.M. Adam (ed.), *Handbook of Postmodern Biblical Interpretation* (St Louis: Chalice Press, 2000), 106–12

Burridge, K., *New Heaven, New Earth: A Study of Millennarian Activities* (Oxford: Basil Blackwell, 1969)

Bushnell, T., Translation of *Res Gestae Divi Augusti* (*http://classics.mit.edu/Augustus/deeds.html*)

Byrne, B., 'The Messiah in Whose Name "The Gentiles Will Hope": Gentile Inclusion as an Essential Element of Matthew's Christology', *ABR* 50 (2002), 55–73

Carney, T.F., *The Shape of the Past. Models and Antiquity* (Lawrence: Coronado Press, 1975)

Carter, W., *Matthew: Storyteller, Evangelist, Interpreter* (Peabody: Hendrickson, 1996)

Carter, W., 'Paying the Tax to Rome as Subversive Praxis: Matt. 17.24–27', *JSNT* 76 (1999), 3–31

Carter, W., 'Evoking Isaiah: Matthean Soteriology and an Intertextual Reading of Isaiah 7–9 in Matthew 1.23 and 4.15–16', *JBL* 119 (2000), 503–20

Carter, W., *Matthew and the Margins: A Sociopolitical and Religious Reading* (Maryknoll, NY: Orbis, 2000)

Carter, W., *Matthew and Empire: Initial Explorations* (Harrisburg, IL: Trinity Press International, 2001)

Carter, W., 'Vulnerable Power: The Roman Empire Challenged by the Early Christians' in A.J. Blasi, J. Duhaime and P.-A. Turcotte (eds), *Handbook of Early Christianity* (Walnut Creek: Alta Mira Press, 2002), 453–88

Carter, W., 'Are there Imperial Texts in the Class? Intertextual Eagles and Matthean Eschatology as "Lights Out" Time for Imperial Rome (Matthew 24.27–31)', *JBL* 122 (2003), 467–87

Carter, W., *Pontius Pilate. Portraits of a Roman Governor* (Collegeville: Liturgical Press, 2003)

Carter, W., 'Matthew and the Gentiles: Individual Conversion and/or Systemic Transformation?', *JSNT* 26 (2004), 259–82

Cassidy, R.J., *Paul in Chains: Roman Imprisonment and the Letters of St Paul* (New York: Crossroad, 2001)

Castriota, D., *The Ara Pacis Augustae and the Imagery of Abundance in Later Greek and Early Imperial Art* (Princeton, NJ: Princeton University Press, 1995)

Chaney, M., 'Systemic Study of the Israelite Monarchy' in J.H. Elliott (ed.), *Semeia 35. Social-Scientific Criticism of the New Testament and its Social World* (Decatur: Scholars Press, 1986), 53–76

Charlesworth, J.H. (ed.), *The Old Testament Pseudepigrapha. Volume 1. Apocalyptic Literature and Testaments* (London: Darton, Longman & Todd, 1983)

Charlesworth, J.H. (ed.), *The Old Testament Pseudepigrapha. Volume 2. Expansions of the 'Old Testament' and Legends, Wisdom and Philosophical Literature, Prayers, Psalms and Odes, Fragments of Lost Judeo-HellenisticWorks* (London: Darton, Longman & Todd, 1985)

Charlesworth, J.H. (ed.), *The Messiah: Developments in Earliest Judaism and Christianity* (Minneapolis, MN: Fortress, 1992)

Charlesworth, M.P., 'Providentia and Aeternitas', *HTR* 29 (1936), 107–32

Childs, P., and R.J.P. Williams, *An Introduction to Post-Colonial Theory* (London: Prentice Hall, 1997)

Cohen, S.J.D., *Josephus in Galilee and Rome: His Vita and Development as a Historian* (Leiden: Brill, 1979)

Cohen, S.J.D., 'Masada: Literary Tradition, Archaeological Remains, and the Credibility of Josephus', *JJS* 33 (1982), 385–405

Collins, J.J., 'Sibylline Oracles (Seventh Century BC – Seventh Century AD)' in J.H. Charlesworth (ed.), *The Old Testament Pseudepigrapha. Volume 1. Apocalyptic Literature and Testaments* (London: Darton, Longman & Todd, 1983), 317–472

Collins, J.J., *The Apocalyptic Imagination: An Introduction to the Jewish Matrix of Christianity* (New York: Crossroad, 1987)

Collins, J.J., *The Scepter and the Star: The Messiahs of the Dead Sea Scrolls and Other Ancient Literature* (New York: Doubleday, 1995)

Comaroff, J., *Body of Power, Spirit of Resistance: The Culture and Resistance of a South African People* (Chicago, IL: University of Chicago Press, 1985)

Cotter, W.J., 'Greco-Roman Apotheosis Traditions and the Resurrection Appearances in Matthew' in D.E. Aune (ed.), *The Gospel of Matthew in Current Study* (Grand Rapids, MI: Eerdmans, 2001), 127–53

Crossan, J.D., *The Birth of Christianity* (San Francisco, CA: Harper, 1998)

Cullmann, O., *The State in the New Testament* (London: SCM, 1957)

Cullmann, O., *The Christology of the New Testament* (London: SCM, 1963)

Dahl, N., 'Sources of Christological Language' in D. Juel (ed.), *Jesus the Christ: The Historical Origins of Christological Doctrine* (Minneapolis, MN: Fortress, 1991), 113–36

Davies, W.D., *The Gospel and the Land: Early Christianity and Jewish Territorial Doctrine* (Sheffield: JSOT, 1994)

Davies, W.D., and D.C. Allison, *A Critical and Exegetical Commentary on the Gospel According to Saint Matthew* (ICC; 3 vols; Edinburgh: T&T Clark, 1988, 1991, 1997)

Deissmann, A., *Light from the Ancient East* (New York: Hodder & Stoughton, 1910)

Deutsch, C., *Lady Wisdom, Jesus, and the Sages: Metaphor and Social Context in Matthew's Gospel* (Valley Forge: Trinity Press International, 1996)

Donaldson, L.E., 'Postcolonialism and Biblical Reading: An Introduction' in L.E. Donaldson (ed.), *Semeia 75. Postcolonialism and Scriptural Reading* (Atlanta, GA: Scholars Press, 1996), 1–14

Donfried, K., 'The Cults of Thessalonica', *NTS* 31 (1985), 336–56

Doyle, M., *Empires* (Ithaca, NY: Cornell University Press, 1987)

Drexler, H., 'Untersuchungen zu Josephus und zur Geschichte des jüdischen Aufstandes', *Klio* 19 (1925), 277–312

Duling, D.C., 'The Promises to David and their Entrance into Christianity – Nailing Down a Likely Hypothesis', *NTS* 19 (1973), 55–77

Duling, D.C., 'Solomon, Exorcism, and the Son of David', *HTR* 68 (1975), 235–52

Duling, D.C.,'The Therapeutic Son of David: An Element of Matthew's Christological Apologetic', *NTS* 24 (1978), 392–410

Duling, D.C., 'Kingdom of God/Heaven (OT, Early Judaism, and Hellenistic Usage)' in D.N. Freedman (ed.), *Anchor Bible Dictionary. Volume 4* (New York: Doubleday, 1992), 49–56

Duling, D.C., 'Matthew's Plurisignificant "Son of David" in Social Science Perspective: Kinship, Kingship, Magic, and Miracle', *BTB* 22 (1992), 102–3

Duling, D.C., '*BTB* Readers' Guide: Millennialism', *BTB* 24 (1993), 132–42

Duling, D.C., 'Matthew and Marginality', *HTS* 51 (1995), 1–30

Duling, D.C., 'Millennialism' in R.L. Rohrbaugh (ed.), *The Social Sciences and New Testament Interpretation* (Peabody: Hendrickson, 1996), 183–205

Duling, D.C., 'Matthew 18.15–17: Conflict, Confrontation, and Conflict Resolution in a "Fictive Kin" Association', *BTB* 29 (1999), 4–22

Duling, D.C., 'Matthew as Marginal Scribe in an Advanced Agrarian Society', *HTS* 58 (2002), 520–75

Duling, D.C., '"Whatever Gain I Had ...": Ethnicity and Paul's Self–Identification in Phil. 3.5–6' in D.B. Gowler, L.G. Bloomquist and D.F. Watson (eds), *Fabrics of Discourse: Essays in Honor of Vernon K. Robbins* (Harrisburg, IL: Trinity Press International, 2003), 222–41

Duling, D.C., *The New Testament: History, Literature, and Social Context* (Belmont: Thomson/Wadsworth, 4th edn 2003)

Dunn, J.D.G., *Christology in the Making: A New Testament Inquiry into the Origins of the Doctrine of the Incarnation* (Grand Rapids, MI: Eerdmans, 1989)

Dyson, S.L., 'Native Revolt Patterns in the Roman Empire' in H. Temporini (ed.), *Aufstieg und Niedergang der römischen Welt. II.3* (Berlin: de Gruyter, 1975), 138–75

Dyson, S.L. 'Native Revolts in the Roman Empire', *Historia* 20 (1971), 239–74

Ehrenberg, V., and A.H.M. Jones, *Documents Illustrating the Reigns of Augustus and Tiberius*, 2nd edn (Oxford: Clarendon Press, 1955)

Eisenstadt, S.N., *The Political Systems of Empires: The Rise and Fall of the Historical Bureaucratic Societies* (Glencoe: Free Press, 1963)

Eisenstadt, S.N., 'Processes of Change and Institutionalization of the Political Systems of Centralized Empires' in G. Zollschan and W. Hirsch (eds), *Exploration in Social Change* (Boston, MA: Houghton Mifflin, 1964), 432–51

Eisenstadt, S.N., 'Introduction' in S.N. Eisenstadt, *Decline of Empires* (Englewood Cliffs, NJ: Prentice Hall, 1967)

Elliott, J.H., 'Social-Scientific Criticism of the New Testament: More on Methods and Models' in J.H. Elliott (ed.), *Semeia 35. Social-Scientific Criticism of the New Testament and its Social World* (Decatur: Scholars Press, 1986), 1–33

Esler, P.F., 'Political Oppression in Jewish Apocalyptic Literature: A Social-Scientific Approach', *Listening: Journal of Religion and Culture* 28 (1993), 181–99

Esler, P.F., 'The Social Function of 4 Ezra' in P.F. Esler, *The First Christians in their Social Worlds: Social-Scientific Approaches to New Testament Intepretation* (London: Routledge, 1994), 110–30

Esler, P.F., 'Sorcery Accusations and the Apocalypse' in P.F. Esler, *The First Christians in their Social Worlds: Social-Scientific Approaches to New Testament Intepretation* (London: Routledge, 1994), 131–46

Esler, P.F., 'God's Honour and Rome's Triumph: Responses to the Fall of Jerusalem in 70 CE in Three Jewish Apocalypses' in P.F. Esler (ed.), *Modelling Early Christianity: Social-Scientific Studies of the New Testament in its Context* (London: Routledge, 1995), 239–58

Esler, P.F., 'Palestinian Judaism' in D. Cohn–Sherbok and J.M. Court (eds), *Religious Diversity in the Greco-Roman World* (Sheffield: Sheffield Academic Press, 2001), 21–46

Esler, P.F., *Conflict and Identity in Romans: The Social Setting of Paul's Letter* (Minneapolis, MN: Fortress, 2003)

Fearnley, H., 'Reading the Imperial Revolution: Martial *Epigrams* 10' in A.J. Boyle and W.J. Dominik (eds), *Flavian Rome* (Leiden: Brill, 2003), 613–35

Feldman, L.H., 'Rabbinic Insights on the Decline and Forthcoming Fall of the Roman Empire', *JSJ* 31 (2000), 275–97

Ferguson, J., *Utopias in the Classical World* (Ithaca, NY: Cornell University Press, 1975)

Fiensy, D.A., *The Social History of Palestine in the Herodian Period: The Land is Mine* (SBEC 20; Lewiston: Edwin Mellen Press, 1991)

Finley, M.I., *Ancient History: Evidence and Models* (London: Pimlico, 2000)

Fish, S., *Is there a Text in This Class? The Authority of Interpretive Communities* (Cambridge, MA: Harvard University Press, 1980)

Foley, J.M., *Immanent Art: From Structure to Meaning in Traditional Oral Epic* (Bloomington, IN: Indiana University Press, 1991)

Foster, P., *Community, Law and Mission in Matthew's Gospel* (WUNT 2/177; Tübingen: Mohr Siebeck, 2004)

France, R.T., *The Gospel of Mark* (NIGTC; Grand Rapids, MI: Eerdmans, 2002)

Frankemölle, H., *Jahwebund und Kirche Christi* (NTAbh 10; Münster: Aschendorff, 1974)

Friedrich, J., W. Pöhlmann and P. Stuhlmacher, 'Zur historischen Situation und Intention von Röm 13.1–7', *ZTK* 73 (1976), 131–66

Fuller, R.H., 'Christology in Matthew and Luke' in R.H. Fuller and P. Perkins (eds), *Who Is this Christ? Gospel Christology and Contemporary Faith* (Philadelphia, PA: Fortress, 1983), 81–95

Galtung, J., 'A Structural Theory of Imperialism', *Journal of Peace Research* 8 (1971), 81–117

Garland, R., *The Eye of the Beholder: Deformity and Disability in the Graeco-Roman World* (Ithaca, NY: Cornell University Press, 1995)

Garlinsky, K., *Augustan Culture: An Interpretive Introduction* (Princeton, NJ: Princeton University Press, 1996)

Garnsey, P.D.A., and C.R. Whittaker (eds), *Imperialism in the Roman World* (Cambridge: Cambridge University Press, 1978)

Garnsey, P.D.A., 'Introduction' in P.D.A. Garnsey and C.R. Whittaker (eds), *Imperialism in the Roman World* (Cambridge: Cambridge University Press, 1978), 1–6

Garnsey, P.D.A., *Famine and Food Supply in the Graeco-Roman World* (Cambridge: Cambridge University Press, 1988)

Geertz, C., 'Thick Description: Toward a Theory of Culture' in C. Geertz, *The Interpretation of Cultures* (New York: Basic Books, 1973), 3–30

Geertz, C., *The Interpretation of Cultures* (London: Collins/Fontana, 1993)

Gench, F.T., *Wisdom in the Christology of Matthew* (Lanham: University Press of America, 1997)

Gerhardsson, B., 'The Christology of Matthew' in M.A. Powell and D.R. Bauer (eds), *Who Do You Say That I Am? Essays on Christology* (Louisville, KY: Westminster John Knox, 1999), 14–32

Goldsworthy, A., *The Roman Army at War, 100 BC–AD 200* (Oxford: Oxford University Press, 1996)

Goodman, M.D., *The Ruling Class of Judaea. The Origins of the Jewish Revolt against Rome AD 66–70* (Cambridge: Cambridge University Press, 1987)

Grabbe, L.L., *Judaism from Cyrus to Hadrian* (London: SCM, 1992)

Gradel, I., *Emperor Worship and Roman Religion* (Oxford: Clarendon Press, 2002)

Gramsci, A., *Selections from the Prison Notebooks* ed. and trans. Q. Hoare and G.N. Smith, (London: Lawrence & Wishart, 1971)

Gundry, R.H., *Matthew: A Commentary on his Handbook for a Mixed Church under Persecution* (Grand Rapids, MI: Eerdmans, 2nd edn 1994)

Hadas-Lebel, M., *Flavius Josephus: Eyewitness to Rome's First Century Conquest of Judea* (New York: Macmillan, 1993)

Hagner, D.A., 'Matthew: Apostate, Reformer, Revolutionary?', *NTS* 49 (2003), 193–208

Hahn, F., *Christologische Hoheitstitel: Ihre Geschichte im Frühen Christentum* (FRLANT 83; Göttingen: Vandenhoeck & Ruprecht, 1963)

Hanson, K.C., and D. Oakman, *Palestine in the Time of Jesus. Social Structures and Social Conflicts* (Minneapolis, MN: Fortress, 1998)

Hare, D.R.A., 'How Jewish is the Gospel of Matthew?', *CBQ* 62 (2000), 264–77

Harris, D.R. (ed.), *The Archaeology of V. Gordon Childe: Contemporary Perspectives* (Chicago, IL: University of Chicago Press, 1994)

Harris, W.V., *War and Imperialism in Republican Rome* (Oxford: Clarendon Press, 1979)

Hart, H.St.J., 'Judaea and Rome: The Official Commentary', *JTS* 3 (1952), 172–98

Heil, J.P., *The Death and Resurrection of Jesus: A Narrative-Critical Reading of Matthew 26–28* (Minneapolis, MN: Augsburg Fortress, 1991)

Hendrix, H.L., 'Archaeology and Eschatology at Thessalonica' in B.A. Pearson (ed.), *The Future of Early Christianity: Essays in Honor of Helmut Koester* (Minneapolis, MN: Fortress, 1991), 107–18

Hengel, M., *Judaism and Hellenism* (London: SCM, 1974)

Hengel, M., *Between Jesus and Paul* (Philadelphia, PA: Fortress, 1983)

Herzog, I., 'Rome in the Talmud and in the Midrash' in I. Herzog, *Judaism: Law and Ethics: Essays by the Late Chief Rabbi Dr Isaac Herzog* (London: Soncino Press, 1974), 83–91

Hill, D., 'Son and Servant: An Essay on Matthean Christology', *JSNT* 6 (1980), 2–16

Horsley, R.A., *Sociology and the Jesus Movement* (New York: Crossroad, 1990)

Horsley, R.A., *Paul and Empire: Religion and Power in Roman Imperial Society* (Harrisburg, IL: Trinity Press International, 1997)

Horsley, R.A., *Jesus and Empire: The Kingdom of God and the New World Disorder* (Minneapolis, MN: Fortress, 2003)

Horsley, R.A., *Religion and Empire: People, Power, and the Life of the Spirit* (Minneapolis, MN: Fortress, 2003)

Horsley, R.A. and J. Hanson, *Bandits, Prophets, and Messiahs: Popular Movements at the Time of Jesus* (Minneapolis, MN: Winston, 1985)

Horsley, R.A. and N.A. Silberman, *The Message and the Kingdom: How Jesus and Paul Ignited a Revolution and Transformed the Ancient World* (Minneapolis, MN: Fortress, 1997)

Hurtado, L.W., *One God One Lord: Early Christian Devotion and Ancient Jewish Monotheism* (Philadelphia, PA: Fortress, 1988)

Huskinson, J., *Experiencing Rome: Culture, Identity and Power in the Roman Empire.* (London: Routledge, 2000)

Iggers, G.G., *Historiography in the Twentieth Century: From Scientific Objectivity to the Postmodern Challenge* (London: Wesleyan University Press, 1997)

Jones, B.W., 'The Reckless Titus' in C. Deroux (ed.), *Studies in Latin Literature and Roman History VI* (Brussels: Latomus, 1992), 408–20

Jonge, M. de, 'Josephus und die Zukunftserwartungen seines Volkes' in O. Betz, K. Haacker and M. Hengel (eds), *Josephus-Studien: Untersuchungen zu Josephus, dem antiken Judentum und dem Neuen Testament. Otto Michel zum 70. Geburtstag gewidmet* (Göttingen: Vandenhoeck & Ruprecht, 1974), 205–19

Jonge, M. de, 'Messiah' in D.N. Freedman (ed.), *Anchor Bible Dictionary. Volume 4* (New York: Doubleday, 1992), 777–88

Käsemann, E., *New Testament Questions of Today* (Philadelphia, PA: Fortress, 1969)

Kautsky, J.H., *The Politics of Aristocratic Empires* (Chapel Hill, NC: University of North Carolina Press, 1982)

Keck, L., 'Toward the Renewal of New Testament Christology', *NTS* 32 (1986), 362–77

Keener, C.S., *A Commentary on the Gospel of Matthew* (Grand Rapids, MI: Eerdmans, 1999)

Kheng, C.B., *Social Banditry and Rural Crime in Kedah, 1910–1929* (Oxford: Oxford University Press, 1988)

Kieval, P., 'The Talmudic View of the Hasmonean and Early Herodian Periods in Jewish History' (Brandis University dissertation, 1970)

Kingsbury, J.D., *Matthew: Structure, Christology, Kingdom* (Philadelphia, PA: Fortress, 1975)

Kingsbury, J.D., *Matthew as Story* (Philadelphia, PA: Fortress, 1986)

Klauck, H.-J., *The Religious Context of Early Christianity: A Guide to Graeco-Roman Religions* (SNTW; Edinburgh: T&T Clark, 2000)

Klijn, A.F.J., '2 (Syriac Apocalypse of) Baruch (early Second Century AD)' in J.H. Charlesworth (ed.), *The Old Testament Pseudepigrapha. Volume 1. Apocalyptic Literature and Testaments* (London: Darton, Longman & Todd, 1983), 615–52

Kottaridis, D., 'Empires: A Comparative Study in a World Context' (*http://www.whc.neu.edu/whc/gradstudy/bibliograd/themes/KottaridisD.html*)

Kristeva, J., 'The Bounded Text' in L.S. Roudiez (ed.), *Desire in Language: A Semiotic Approach to Literature and Art* (New York: Columbia University Press, 1980), 36–63

Kuschel, K.-J., *Abraham: Sign of Hope for Jews, Christians and Muslims* (New York: Continuum, 1995)

Ladouceur, D.J., 'Josephus and Masada' in L.H. Feldman and G. Hata (eds), *Josephus, Judaism, and Christianity* (Detroit, MI: Wayne State University, 1987), 95–113

Lange, N.R.M. de, 'Jewish Attitudes to the Roman Empire' in P.D.A. Garnsey and C.R. Whittaker (eds), *Imperialism in the Roman World* (Cambridge: Cambridge University Press, 1978), 255–81

Laqueur, R., *Der jüdische Historiker Flavius Josephus: ein biographischer Versuch auf neuer quellenkritischer Grundlage* (Darmstadt: Wissenschaftliche Buchgesellschaft, 1920)

Lendesta, G., *The American'Empire'* (Oslo: Norwegian University Press, 1990)

Lenski, G., *Power and Privilege: A Theory of Social Stratification* (New York: McGraw-Hill, 1966)

Lenski, G., 'Rethinking Macrosociological Theory', *American Sociological Review* 53 (1988), 163–71

Lenski, G., 'Societal Taxonomies: Mapping the Social Universe', *Annual Review of Sociology* 20 (1994), 1–26

Lévi–Strauss, C., 'The Structural Study of Myth', *Journal of American Folklore* 68 (1955), 428–43

Lichtheim, G., *Imperialism* (New York: Praeger, 1971)

Lindner, H., *Die Geschichtsauffassung des Flavius Josephus im Bellum Judaicum* (Leiden: Brill, 1972)

Linton, R., 'Nativistic Movements', *American Anthropologist* 45 (1943), 230–40; repr. in W.A. Lessa and E.Z. Vogt (eds), *Reader in Comparative Religion: An Anthropological Approach* (San Francisco, CA: HarperCollins, 4th edn 1979)

Little, D., 'Local Politics and Class Conflict: Theories of Peasant Rebellion in Nineteenth-Century China' (paper of the Bellagio Conference on Peasant Culture and Consciousness, January 1990. *http://www–personal.umd.umich.edu/˜delittle/ BELLAGI2.PDF*)

Loewe, R., *'Render unto Caesar': Religious and Political Loyalty in Palestine* (Cambridge: Cambridge University Press, 1940)

L'Orange, H.P., 'The Floral Zone of the Ara Pacis' in H.P. L'Orange (ed.), *Art Forms and Civic Life* (New York: Rizzoli, 1985), 211–30

Luomanen, P., 'The "Sociology of Sectarianism" in Matthew: Modelling the Genesis of Early Jewish and Christian Communities' in I. Dunderberg, C. Tuckett and K. Syreeni (eds), *Fair Play, Diversity and Conflicts in Early Christianity. Essays in Honour of Heikki Räisänen* (Leiden: Brill, 2002), 107–30

Luz, U., *Matthew 8–20: A Commentary* (Minneapolis, MN: Augsburg Fortress, 2001)

M'Neile, A.H., *The Gospel According to St Matthew* (New York: St Martin's Press, 1965)

McLaren, J.S., *Power and Politics in Palestine. The Jews and the Governing of their Land, 100 BC–AD 70* (Sheffield: Sheffield Academic Press, 1991)

McLaren, J.S., 'Christians and the Jewish Revolt: AD 66–70' in A.M. Nobbs, C.E.V. Nixon, R.A. Kearsley and T.W. Hillard (eds), *Ancient History in a Modern University. Volume 2* (Grand Rapids, MI: Eerdmans, 1997), 53–60

McLaren, J.S., 'The Coinage of the First Year as a Point of Reference for the Jewish Revolt (66–70 CE)', *SCI* 22 (2003), 135–52

McLaren, J.S., 'Josephus on Titus: The Vanquished Writing about the Victor' (forthcoming)

MacMullen, R., *Roman Social Relations. 50 BC to AD 284* (New Haven, CT: Yale University Press, 1974)

Malherbe, A.J., *The Letters to the Thessalonians* (AB 32B; New York: Doubleday, 2000)

Malina, B.J., *The New Testament World: Insights from Cultural Anthropology* (Atlanta, GA: John Knox, 3rd edn 2001)

Mann, M., *The Sources of Power, Volume 1: A History of Power from the Beginning to AD 1760* (Cambridge: Cambridge University Press, 1986)

Martínez, F.G., *The Dead Sea Scrolls Translated: The Dead Sea Scrolls in English* (Leiden: Brill, 1994)

Mason, S., *Flavius Josephus. Translation and Commentary. Volume 9. Life of Josephus* (Leiden: Brill, 2001)

Mason, S., 'Flavius Josephus in Flavian Rome: Reading On and Between the Lines', in A.J. Boyle and W.J. Dominik (eds), *Flavian Rome* (Leiden: Brill, 2003), 559–89

Mason, S., 'Josephus, Daniel, and the Flavian House' in F. Parente and J. Sievers (eds), *Josephus and the History of the Greco-Roman Period. Essays in Memory of Morton Smith* (Leiden: Brill, 1994), 161–91

Matera, F.J., *Passion Narratives and Gospel Theologies: Interpreting the Synoptics through their Passion Stories* (New York: Paulist Press, 1986)

Matera, F.J., *New Testament Christology* (Louisville, KY: Westminster John Knox, 1999)

Mattern, S., *Rome and the Enemy: Imperial Strategy in the Principate* (Berkeley, CA: University of California Press, 1999)

Mattingly, H.C., *Coins of the Roman Empire in the British Museum Volume 2: Vespasian to Domitian* (London: British Museum Press, 1966)

Meeks, W., 'A Hermeneutics of Social Embodiment' in G. Nickelsburg and G. McRae (eds), *Christians among Jews and Gentiles* (Philadelphia, PA: Fortress, 1986), 176–86

Meggitt, J.J., *Paul, Poverty and Survival* (SNTW; Edinburgh: T&T Clark, 1998)

Meier, J.P., *The Vision of Matthew: Christ, Church, and Morality in the First Gospel* (Mahwah, NJ: Paulist Press, 1979)

Metzger, B.M., 'Methodology on the Study of the Mystery Religions and Early Christianity' in R. Berkey and S. Edwards (eds), *Historical and Literary Studies: Pagan, Jewish, and Christian* (Grand Rapids, MI: Eerdmans, 1968), 1–24

Metzger, B.M., 'The Fourth Book of Ezra (Late First Century AD)' in J.H. Charlesworth (ed.), *The Old Testament Pseudepigrapha. Volume 1. Apocalyptic Literature and Testaments* (London: Darton, Longman & Todd, 1983), 517–59

Millar, F., *The Roman Empire and its Neighbours* (London: Duckworth, 2nd edn, 1981)

Moles, J., 'The Date and Purpose of the Fourth Kingship Oration of Dio Chrysostom', *Classical Antiquity* 2 (1983), 251–78

Montesquieu, Charles de Secondat, Baron de, *Spirit of the Laws* VI (1748)

Moore, S., *Literary Criticism and the Gospels: The Theoretical Challenge* (New Haven, CT: Yale University Press, 1989)

Morris, L., *The Gospel According to Matthew* (Grand Rapids, MI: Eerdmans, 1992)

Motyl, A.J., *Imperial Ends. The Decay, Collapse, and Revival of Empires* (New York: Columbia University Press, 2001)

Moule, C.F.D., *The Origin of Christology* (Cambridge: Cambridge University Press, 1977)

Mowery, R.L., 'Son of God in Roman Imperial Titles and Matthew', *Biblica* 83 (2002), 100–10

Muecke, D.C., *The Compass of Irony* (London: Methuen, 1969)

Müller, M., 'The Theological Interpretation of the Figure of Jesus in the Gospel of Matthew: Some Principal Features in Matthean Christology', *NTS* 45 (1999), 157–73

Murphy, F.J., '2 Baruch and the Romans', *JBL* 104 (1985), 663–9

Myers, C., *Binding the Strong Man: A Political Reading of Mark's Story of Jesus* (Maryknoll, NY: Orbis, 1988)

Naquin, S., *Millenarian Rebellion in China: The Eight Trigrams Uprising of 1813* (New Haven, CT: Yale University Press, 1976)

Neusner, J., W. Green, and E. Frerichs (eds), *Judaisms and their Messiahs at the Turn of the Christian Era* (Cambridge: Cambridge University Press, 1987)

Nolan, P. and G. Lenski, *Human Societies: An Introduction to Macrosociology* (Boston, MA: McGraw Hill, 8th edn 1998)

Oakes, P., *Philippians: From People to Letter* (SNTSMS 110; Cambridge: Cambridge University Press, 2001)

Oakes, P., 'God's Sovereignty over Roman Authorities: A Theme in Philippians' in P. Oakes (ed.), *Rome in the Bible and the Early Church* (Carlisle/Grand Rapids, MI: Paternoster/Baker, 2002), 126–41

Oakes, P. (ed.), *Rome in the Bible and the Early Church* (Carlisle: Paternoster, 2002)

Oakes, P., 'Christian Attitudes to Rome at the Time of Paul's Letter', *Review and Expositor* 100 (2003), 103–11

Overman, J.A., 'The First Revolt and Flavian Politics' in A. Berlin and J.A. Overman (eds), *The First Jewish Revolt* (London: Routledge, 2001), 213–21

Oxford English Dictionary (Oxford: Clarendon Press, 2nd edn 1969)

Pearson, B.A., '1 Thessalonians 2.13–16: A Deutero-Pauline Interpolation', *HTR* 64 (1971), 79–94

Perry, M., 'Literary Dynamics: How the Order of a Text Creates its Meaning', *Poetics Today* 1 (1979–80), 35–64

Powell, M.A., *What is Narrative Criticism?* (Minneapolis, MN: Fortress, 1990)

Price, J.J., *Jerusalem under Siege: The Collapse of the Jewish State, 66–70 CE* (Leiden: Brill, 1992)

Price, S., 'Gods and Emperors: The Greek Language of the Roman Imperial Cult', *JHS* 104 (1984), 79–95

Price, S., *Rituals and Power: The Roman Imperial Cult in Asia Minor* (Cambridge: Cambridge University Press, 1984)

Rabinow, P. (ed), *The Foucault Reader: An Introduction to his Thought* (London: Penguin, 1986)

Rabinowitz, P.J., 'Whirl without End: Audience-Oriented Criticism' in G.D. Atkins and L. Morrow (eds), *Contemporary Literary Theory* (Amherst, MA: University of Massachusetts Press, 1989), 81–100

Rajak, T., *Josephus: The Historian and his Society* (London: Duckworth, 1983)

Rajak, T., 'The *Against Apion* and the Continuities in Josephus's Political Thought' in S. Mason (ed.), *Understanding Josephus: Seven Perspectives* (Sheffield: Sheffield Academic Press, 1998), 222–46

Rajak, T., 'Friends, Romans, Subjects: Agrippa II's Speech in Josephus' *Jewish War*', in T. Rajak, *The Jewish Dialogue with Greece and Rome. Studies in Cultural and Social Interaction* (Leiden: Brill, 2001), 147–59

Rajak, T., 'Dying for the Law: The Martyr's Portrait in Jewish–Greek Literature' in T. Rajak, *The Jewish Dialogue with Greece and Rome. Studies in Cultural and Social Interaction* (Leiden: Brill, 2001), 99–133

Redfield, R., *Peasant Society and Culture* (Chicago, IL: University of Chicago Press, 1956)

Rich, J., and G. Shipley (eds), *War and Society in the Roman World* (London: Routledge, 1993)

Rich, J., 'Fear, Greed and Glory: The Causes of Roman War-Making in the Middle Republic' in J. Rich and G. Shipley (eds), *War and Society in the Roman World* (London: Routledge, 1993), 38–68

Rich, J., and A. Wallace-Hadrill (eds), *City and Country in the Ancient World* (New York: Routledge, 1991)

Richard, E., *Jesus. One and Many: The Christological Concept of New Testament Authors* (Wilmington, DE: Glazier, 1988)

Riches, J., *Conflicting Mythologies: Identity Formation in the Gospels of Mark and Matthew* (SNTW; Edinburgh: T&T Clark, 2000)

Riches, J., 'Introduction' in K.L. Schmidt, *The Place of the Gospels in the General History of Literature* (Columbia, SC: University of South Carolina Press, 2002), vii–xxviii

Rickman, G., *The Corn Supply of Ancient Rome* (Oxford: Clarendon Press, 1980)

Rohrbaugh, R.L., *The Biblical Interpreter: An Agrarian Bible in an Industrial Age* (Philadelphia, PA: Fortress, 1978)

Rohrbaugh, R.L., 'Methodological Considerations in the Debate over the Social Class Status of Early Christians', *JAAR* 52 (1984), 519–46

Rohrbaugh, R.L., 'The Preindustrial City in Luke–Acts' in J.H. Neyrey (ed.), *The Social World of Luke–Acts: Models in Interpretation* (Peabody: Hendrickson, 1991)

Rohrbaugh, R.L., 'The Social Location of the Markan Audience', *Interpretation* 47 (1993), 380–95

Rubinkiewicz, R., 'Apocalypse of Abraham (First to Second Century AD)' in J.H Charlesworth (ed.), *The Old Testament Pseudepigrapha. Volume 1. Apocalyptic Literature and Testaments* (London: Darton, Longman & Todd, 1983), 681–705

Saldarini, A.J., 'The Gospel of Matthew and Jewish–Christian Conflict' in D.L. Balch (ed.), *Social History of the Matthean Community* (Minneapolis, MN: Fortress Press, 1991), 38–61

Saldarini, A.J., 'The Gospel of Matthew and Jewish–Christian Conflict in the Galilee' in L.I. Levine (ed.), *The Galilee in Late Antiquity* (Cambridge, MA.: Harvard University Press, 1992), 23–38

Saldarini, A.J., *Matthew's Christian–Jewish Community* (Chicago, IL: University of Chicago Press,1994)

Schmeller, T., 'The Greco-Roman Background of New Testament Christology' in R. Berkey and S. Edwards (eds), *Christology in Dialogue* (Cleveland, OH: Pilgrim Press, 1993), 54–65

Schnackenburg, R., *Jesus in the Gospels* (Louisville, KY: Westminster John Knox, 1995)

Schwartz, D.R., 'Rome and the Jews: Josephus on "Freedom" and "Autonomy"' in A.K. Bowman, H.M. Cotton, M. Goodman and S. Price (eds), *Representations of Empire. Rome and the Mediterranean World* (Oxford: Oxford University Press, 2002), 65–81

Schwertheim, E., *Arastirma Sonuclari Toplantisi* 7, 230

Scott, J.C., *Moral Economy of the Peasant: Rebellion and Subsistence in Southeast Asia* (New Haven, CT: Yale University Press, 1977

Scott, J.C., *Weapons of the Weak: Everyday Forms of Peasant Resistance* (New Haven, CT: Yale University Press, 1985)

Scott, J.C., *Domination and the Arts of Resistance: Hidden Transcripts* (New Haven, CT: Yale University Press, 1992)

Scott, K., 'Statius' Adulation of Domitian', *AJP* 54 (1933), 247–59

Scott, K., *The Imperial Cult under the Flavians* (Stuttgart: Kohlhammer, 1936)

Scroggs, R., 'The Sociological Interpretation of the New Testament: The Present State of Research', *NTS* 26 (1980), 164–79

Senior, D., *The Passion of Jesus in the Gospel of Matthew* (Wilmington, DE: Glazier, 1985)

Senior, D., 'Between Two Worlds: Gentiles and Jewish Christians in Matthew's Gospel', *CBQ* 61 (1999), 1–23

Shaw, B.D., 'Josephus: Roman Power and Responses to it', *Athenaeum* 83 (1995), 357–90

Siker, J., *Disinheriting the Jews: Abraham in Early Christian Controversy* (Louisville, KY: Westminster John Knox, 1991)

Sim, D.C., 'The "Confession" of the Soldiers in Matthew 27.54', *HeyJ* 34 (1993), 401–24

Sim, D.C., 'The Gospel of Matthew and the Gentiles', *JSNT* 57 (1995), 19–48

Sim, D.C., *Apocalyptic Eschatology in the Gospel of Matthew* (SNTSMS 88; Cambridge: Cambridge University Press, 1996)

Sim, D.C., *The Gospel of Matthew and Christian Judaism: The History and Social Setting of the Matthean Community* (SNTW; Edinburgh: T&T Clark, 1998)

Sim, D.C., 'Matthew's Anti-Paulinism: A Neglected Feature of Matthean Studies', *HTS* 58 (2002), 767–83

Sim, D.C., 'Matthew and the Gentiles: A Response to Brendan Byrne', *ABR* 50 (2002), 74– 9

Sjoberg, G., 'The Preindustrial City', *American Journal of Sociology* (1955), 438–45; repr. in G. Gmelch and W.P. Zenner (eds), *Urban Life: Readings in the Anthropology of the City* (Long Grove: Waveland Press, 3rd edn 2001), 20–31

Sjoberg, G., *The Preindustrial City: Past and Present* (New York: Free Press, 1960)

Sjoberg, G., and A. Sjoberg, 'The Preindustrial City: Reflections Four Decades Later' in G. Gmelch and W.P. Zenner (eds), *Urban Life: Readings in the Anthropology of the City* (Long Grove: Waveland Press, 3rd edn 2001), 94–103

Slemon, S., 'Modernism's Last Post' in I. Adam and H. Tiffin (eds), *Past the Last Post: Theorizing Post-Colonialism and Post-Modernism* (Hemel Hempstead: Harvester Wheatsheaf, 1991), 1–11

Smallwood, E.M., *The Jews under Roman Rule: From Pompey to Diocletian* (Leiden: Brill, 1976)

Spilsbury, P., 'Flavius Josephus on the Rise and Fall of the Roman Empire', *JTS* 54 (2003), 1–24

Stanton, G.N., *A Gospel for a New People* (Edinburgh: T&T Clark, 1992)

Stark, R., *The Rise of Christianity* (Princeton, NJ: Princeton University Press, 1996)

Stegemann, E.W. and W. Stegemann, *The Jesus Movement: A Social History of its First Century* (St Paul: Fortress, 1999)

Stemberger, G., 'Die Beurteilung Roms in der rabbinischen Literatur' in H. Temporini (ed.), *Aufstieg und Niedergang der römischen Welt II.19.2* (Berlin: de Gruyter, 1979), 338–96

Stern, M., 'Josephus and the Roman Empire as Reflected in *The Jewish War*' in L.H. Feldman and G. Hata (eds), *Josephus, Judaism, and Christianity* (Detroit, MI: Wayne State University Press, 1987), 71–80

Stone, M.E., 'Reactions to the Destruction of the Second Temple: Theology, Perception and Conversion', *JSJ* 12 (1981), 195–204

Stone, M.E., *Fourth Ezra: A Commentary on the Book of Fourth Ezra* (Hermeneia; Minneapolis, MN: Fortress, 1990)

Strack, H.L., and G. Stemberger, *Introduction to the Talmud and the Midrash* (Edinburgh: T&T Clark, 1991)

Strecker, G., *Der Weg Der Gerechtigkeit* (FRLANT 82; Göttingen: Vandenhoeck & Ruprecht, 1962)

Sullivan, J.P., *Martial: The Unexpected Classic. A Literary and Historical Study* (Cambridge: Cambridge University Press, 1991)

Suny, R.G., 'The Empire Strikes Out: Russia, the Soviet Union, and Theories of Empire' (academic paper discussed at the conference 'Empires and Nations: The Soviet Union and the Non-Russian Peoples', University of Chicago, IL, 24–26 October 1997)

Sweet, J., *Revelation* (TPINTC; London: SCM, 1979)

Taagepera, R., 'Size and Duration of Empires: Growth–Decline Curves, 600 BC to 600 AD ', *Social Science History* 3 (1979), 115–38

Taylor, G., 'Karl A. Wittfogel' *International Encyclopedia of the Social Sciences, Volume 18* (London: Collier, 1979), 812

Thackeray, H. St. J., *Josephus: The Man and the Historian* (New York: Ktav, 1929)

Thackeray, H. St. J., *et al.* (eds), *Josephus* (9 vols, LCL; Cambridge, MA: Heinemann, 1926–69)

Theissen, G., *The Miracle Stories of the Early Christian Tradition* (SNTW; Edinburgh: T&T Clark, 1983)

Theissen, G., 'Jesusbewegung als charismatische Wertrevolution', *NTS* 35 (1989), 343–60

Theissen, G., *A Theory of Primitive Christian Religion* (London: SCM, 1999)

Thompson, E.P., *The Poverty of Theory and Other Essays* (New York: Monthly Review Press, 1978)

Thompson, L., *The Book of Revelation: Apocalypse and Empire* (Oxford: Oxford University Press, 1990)

Thrupp, S. (ed.), *Millennial Dreams in Action: Essays in Comparative Study* (The Hague: Mouton, 1972)

Toynbee, P., 'The Last Emperor' *Guardian Unlimited* (13 September 2002)

Trilling, W., *Das wahre Israel* (Munich: Kösel, 1964)

Tuckett, C., *Christology and the New Testament: Jesus and his Earliest Followers* (Louisville, KY: Westminster John Knox, 2001)

Turner, J., *Societal Stratification: A Theoretical Analysis* (New York: Columbia University Press, 1984)

Vermes, G., 'Ancient Rome in Post-Biblical Jewish Literature' in G. Vermes, *Post-Biblical Jewish Studies* (Leiden: Brill, 1975), 215–24

Vledder, E.-J., *Conflict in the Miracle Stories: A Socio-Exegetical Study of Matthew 8 and 9* (JSNTSS 152; Sheffield: Sheffield Academic Press, 1997)

Waetjen, H., *A Reordering of Power. A Socio-Political Reading of Mark's Gospel* (Minneapolis, MN: Fortress, 1989)

Walbank, F.W., 'Monarchies and Monarchic Ideas' in *The Cambridge Ancient History, Volume 7.1* (Cambridge: Cambridge University Press, 1982), 62–100

Walbank, F.W., ' "Treason" and Roman domination: two case–studies, Polybius and Josephus' in F.W. Walbank, *Polybius, Rome and the Hellenistic World: Essays and Reflections* (Cambridge: Cambridge University Press, 2002), 258–76

Wallace-Hadrill, A., 'The Golden Age and Sin in Augustan Ideology', *Past and Present* 95 (1982), 19–36

Walton, S., 'The State they Were in: Luke's View of the Roman Empire' in P. Oakes (ed.), *Rome in the Bible and the Early Church* (Carlisle: Paternoster, 2002), 1–41

Weaver, D.J., 'Power and Powerlessness: Matthew's Use of Irony in the Portrayal of Political Leaders' in D.R. Bauer and M.A. Powell (eds), *Treasures New and Old: Contributions to Matthean Studies* (Atlanta, GA: Scholars Press, 1996), 179–96

Wengst, K., *Pax Romana and the Peace of Jesus Christ* (Philadelphia, PA: Fortress, 1987)

Williams, P., 'Colonial Discourse and Post-Colonial Theory: An Introduction' in P. Williams and L. Chrisman (eds), *Colonial Discourse and Post-Colonial Theory: A Reader* (New York: Harvester Wheatsheaf, 1993), 1–20

Williams, P., and L. Chrisman (eds), *Colonial Discourse and Post-Colonial Theory: A Reader* (New York: Harvester Wheatsheaf, 1993)

Wittfogel, K., *Oriental Despotism: A Comparative Study of Total Power* (New Haven, CT: Yale University Press, 1957)

Wolf, E., *Peasants* (Englewood Cliffs, NJ: Prentice Hall, 1966)

Woodman, T., and D. West, *Poetry and Politics in the Age of Augustus* (Cambridge: Cambridge University Press, 1984)

Woolf, G., 'Inventing Empire in Ancient Rome' in S.E. Alcock, T.N.D. Altroy, K.D. Morrison and C.M. Sinopoli (eds), *Empires: Perspectives from Archaeology and History* (Cambridge: Cambridge University Press, 2001), 311–22

Worsley, P., *The Trumpet Shall Sound: A Study of 'Cargo' Cults in Melanesia* (London: Paladin, 1970)

Wright, R.B., 'Psalms of Solomon (First Century BC)' in J.H. Charlesworth (ed.), *The Old Testament Pseudepigrapha. Volume 2. Expansions of the 'Old Testament' and Legends, Wisdom and Philosophical Literature, Prayers, Psalms and Odes, Fragments of Lost Judeo-Hellenistic Works* (London: Darton, Longman & Todd, 1985), 639–70

Yavetz, Z., 'Reflections on Titus and Josephus', *Greek, Roman and Byzantine Studies* 16 (1975), 411–32

Ziolkowski, A., '*Urbs direpta*, or How the Romans Sacked Cities' in J. Rich and G. Shipley (eds), *War and Society in the Roman World* (London: Routledge, 1993), 69–91

INDEXES

INDEX OF REFERENCES

BIBLE

Index of Authors